Force a Miracle

to the Donovan
family

keep ED

Daryl Green

Force a Miracle

Darryl C. Didier
Forward by Mike Ditka

Writer's Showcase
San Jose New York Lincoln Shanghai

Force a Miracle

Writer's Showcase
an imprint of iUniverse, Inc.

For information address:
iUniverse, Inc.
5220 S. 16th St., Suite 200
Lincoln, NE 68512
www.iuniverse.com

ISBN: 0-595-22688-4

Printed in the United States of America

Contents

Forward vii

CHAPTER 1   Everything Was Coming Up Roses 1

CHAPTER 2   The Best-Laid Plans...Go Astray! 7

CHAPTER 3   Let's Get It Done and Good Luck! 15

CHAPTER 4   No Sympathy; I Will Be Back! 27

CHAPTER 5   A Burden of Love 45

CHAPTER 6   Take Two and Hit to the Right. 63

CHAPTER 7   Laugh at Life and What It Brings 79

CHAPTER 8   The Power of Commitment 95

CHAPTER 9   Don't Be a "Wimp." Get Up and Adapt!. 109

CHAPTER 10   Do the Best with the Hand You Are Dealt 125

CHAPTER 11   Keep Up the Intensity! 141

CHAPTER 12   Keep Up the Pace!. 155

CHAPTER 13   Shoot for the Moon. 165

CHAPTER 14   No Guts, No Glory. 175

CHAPTER 15   Do the Best You Can or Don't Do It at
All! 187

CHAPTER 16   There Is Never Too Much Spirit! 209

Forward

by Mike Ditka

I read a book recently that states two facts. First, life is hard. Second, life isn't always fair, but it sure beats the heck out of the alternative.

I'm always amazed and amused by how people handle adversity, setbacks, losses and disasters. I believe that to persevere above all is to have great love for life (which is a Gift from God), a respect for health and all those around us, to really live by the Golden Rule.

Winston Churchill spoke about the importance of never, never, never giving up. I believe you never lose life until you quite trying. Success is not permanent, and failure is not fatal.

A few years ago I started corresponding with a young man named Darryl Didier. To me Darryl Didier is one of the truly great heroes in our society. Darryl doesn't play baseball, basketball or football and really is not famous, outside of a few of us who have been blessed to know him.

To put it plain and simple, Darryl is a warrior, a fighter, a winner and a helper to those more fortunate than him.

Who is Darryl Didier? Let me explain the best I can. Darryl is the epitome of effort, dedication and perseverance. He doesn't know the meaning of quit, give up, you're beaten or the party's over. Darryl had a wonderful life. He was intelligent, good looking and had a great job. His life was so promising and full of opportunity.

Whammo. Here comes the curve ball. He was diagnosed with a malignant brain tumor. After emerging from surgery, Darryl had lost most or all of his speech, memory, movement, and mental ability. He was diagnosed to live as a semi-invalid in a nursing home for the rest of his life.

Stop the press, because lo and behold, this man defied all odds. Darryl is a functioning, intelligent young man doing service and helping his fellow man in every way possible.

Darryl's story is documented in his book, "Force a Miracle". In the Bible, the book of Jeremiah in the Old Testament, chapter 29, verses 11-13, God spoke to Jeremiah. "I know the plans I have for you, plans for peace, not disaster; plans to give you hope and a future. Then you will seek me with all of your heart". I believe God has a plan for all of us. Sometimes we may not understand, but he does.

Darryl is an inspiration and a hero to me because I'm an old fashioned guy. I like winners and achievers; those who face problems and find solutions.

This book is a must read, especially if you have a tendency to think that life has dealt you a bad hand.

Mike Ditka

Hall of Fame football player

Former Head Coach
Super Bowl Chicago Bears
and New Orleans Saints

1

Everything Was Coming Up Roses

Two years out of college, at age 23, I tried to develop a solid career with Merrill Lynch. I'd always wanted to work for a large corporation and be part of a team. My goals were high and I believed that this company would give me unlimited opportunities to achieve.

In August 1989, I started as a "cold-caller" at Merrill Lynch in Northbrook, Illinois, a suburb of Chicago. I was not an employee of the company, but, rather, of two partners who were VPs. They paid the check. I did not have medical coverage, but I wasn't concerned as I considered myself healthy. I was "in the game," surrounded by important and influential people. I had a chance to really succeed. *There is no excuse. Go out there and get it done!* Make the contacts, get the appointments, do what it takes to earn respect.

My bosses were the top producers at the Northbrook branch. They were my mentors in the business, providing me with the chance to show them what I could do. The respect which they and other employees gave me fostered commitment on my part. My goal was to go through the side door rather than the front (the human resources department). I did not want to be lost in the shuffle.

The partners gave me the ultimatum of landing two hot leads that would turn into functional accounts in one year. If I met the goal, Merrill Lynch might hire me. *No problem! I will do it!*

I often consulted with my dad, who had played in the minors for the California Angels baseball organization. His philosophy was: "The more times you step up to the plate, the more hits you will get!" Then he followed with: "Darryl, great things are accomplished with enthusiasm." Those statements really put things into perspective for me. I jumped at the chance and, as they say in the industry, I "smiled and dialed." I called and called, an average of 50 calls a day. I worked five days a week, eight hours a day, with no security. I knew what I wanted, and this was one hurdle to overcome. When I called prospective companies, I went through a large amount of screening by the receptionist, and experienced many rejections. I had to refine my script with the right formula of phraseology to attract interest. A good attitude was a must, even if the rejections were overwhelming. For every 80 calls, about 15 actually got through to somebody who could make a decision. If I was effective, I might acquire one scheduled appointment.

No leads were generated in two months. I talked with my boss about what to say and how to sell the program. I implemented a new version of my sales call. It finally clicked: Be informative and be yourself. Enthusiasm, hard work and dedication can overcome many rejections. Keep in mind that the usual success rate is three percent.

I visited with my boss again and again, wanting to pick his brain. I needed to understand the point of view of a top producer. We discussed various economic and social issues. John told me that he was impressed with my attitude: "Keep it up," he said. That was really a boost! I felt that I was handling myself in the right manner. *That's it. I must do something!* Practice, practice, practice. In the car, on the way to work: "Hello, my name is Darryl Didier, Didier, Didier…" Didier Farm. "Didier Farm" is a fresh vegetable farm in Illinois owned by a possible distant relative. I had to warm-up or stretch before the game began.

I arrived in my cubicle at work. Before the first sales call, I phoned my friend, Paul, and practiced the sales-pitch on him. He was like a brother, a guy who had red hair like me and we were often believed to be brothers by strangers. He owned his own fresh fish store called "Paul's Fish House" in Glencoe, an upper-crust North Shore suburb. Paul offered suggestions on my delivery and tone. I wanted a critical comment from the other side of the phone so I could make adjustments and be influential. "How did I sound?" He advised on my delivery: "More excitement, more conviction. Wake up and get going!"

"Good morning, Mr. / Ms. Smith. I know you are busy, but may I take a moment of your time?" If you want to sell it, you have to be forceful and say it. Do not mumble. Have confidence in your abilities. Don't be a little person.

April, 1990. I met the ultimatum. I established three new institutional accounts, $1.5 million dollars of new billings. I went to dinner and to a Chicago Black Hawks play-off game, treated by the partners. I was becoming one of them. I was comfortable, so comfortable; I was able to joke with Joe, one of the partners, outside the Chicago Stadium. Amidst the crowd, people were selling T-shirts with gusto. "Hey, Joe, you can find a cold-caller down here!"

One afternoon, the partners wanted to have a conference call set up between three parties located in three different states. Their financial assistant did not set up the call correctly. Tension built between them. "Mr. Smith, good afternoon..." (I was making cold-calls.) I looked up and there was Joe. He really fit the part of a top executive: a tall, handsome individual with a booming, confident voice. He put me on the spot as he asked in a deep, authoritative voice, "Can you set up a conference call between three companies and an executive from a money-management firm?" I answered, "Yes, I can!" Very calmly, I called the Operations Department to ask how a conference call could be set up. Once I understood the directions, it was successfully established. Two days later, the partners summoned me into their office to have a chat; it was about 4:00 p.m. As all three of us stood around a large, dark-oak desk, they asked if I would like to be their administrative assistant and be hired by Merrill Lynch. *What?* I was elated. I had a huge lump in my throat. *Oh my gosh, my dream is unfolding!* My memory went on a happy rampage! I recalled the time when my high school counselor told me that I had limited ability to go on to college. Not only did I now have my degree, but I was employed by the top financial company in the world. I was in an environment that radiated success. What a situation to be in for a 24-year-old trying to build a career. However, there was an obstacle in the way. The Administrative Manager had to interview me to find out if I qualified to be a Merrill Lynch employee. I was a nervous wreck all day, all night, and most of the day, before the interview the next evening. *This is my career! I have to make a leap! At least I have my Series-7 License! That's an advantage!* It was an advantage because many first-year assistants were not licensed.

The Series-7 License legally allows an individual to be a certified broker, registered with the National Association of Security Dealers. It gives one the authority to legally advise and trade financial products. *I've landed three top accounts, plus I have my Bachelor of Science degree. I was recommended! So what's the problem?*

An hour after the interview, I was hired; I met my goal. The Administrative Manager treated me with a great deal of respect. For example, I did not have to have any formal training for the new position of Financial Assistant, although training was the norm.

I was in a "sink or swim" situation. I had to step up to the plate without a warm-up, facing a 90-mile-an-hour closer. An enormous amount of responsibility was on my shoulders. I had to: 1) Effectively administrate and govern the institutional accounts; 2) Initiate the buy-and-sell orders instructed by a money-manager for the institutional accounts according to their allotment; 3) "Cold-call" and attract new accounts. I came in early every day and on Saturday mornings to keep things afloat. I didn't want to blow the opportunity, so I kept up a high pace.

July 10, 1990. I smoked a cigar with my two bosses after the market closed, 3:00 p.m., Central Standard Time. It was a sign of a very profitable day. To me, that was a symbol of acceptance into "The Club," meaning that you have gained the confidence of your superiors when they treat you as a colleague, not as an employee.

At 5:00 p.m., the hectic but enjoyable workday ended. I swung through the exit doorway to the parking lot, eyeing my new investment, bright red *Acura Integra*. Then I smiled broadly as I thought about a new friend for whom I really had strong feelings. Vicki, a junior at the University of Illinois in Champaign, was a highly motivated, highly driven individual. She had big brown, caring eyes with long thick twirls of golden-blonde hair, lots of it. She was tall and loved to run. We enjoyed discussing social and business issues. We often agreed, but other times debated on a professional level.

I continued through the parking lot as the astonishing sunset enveloped my thoughts: This was a dream coming true; I had started to establish myself. I looked forward to being with the company for 20 years. I loved the everyday challenge of handling changes every minute with such a prestigious company. Everything was going according to plan. I stopped and sighed with pleasure, feeling at peace with myself. Hey, I am doing the right thing! I felt wanted, needed, and useful.

2

The Best-Laid Plans…Go Astray!

July 15, 1990, was a very pleasant day; No worries, no emergencies came up at work. Things went very smoothly, which was unusual because there was always something going on: a last-minute letter, late-fill order, a client who wanted a statement from four years before, etc. I went to meet Vicki at 5:30 p.m. in Barrington, where she was employed during her summer school break. Barrington is an upscale community, 20 miles west of Northbrook. We drove east to the Chicago Botanic Gardens in Glencoe. The gardens, which occupy approximately 280 acres, have walking paths that intermingle among 16 different types of gardens; for example: waterfall garden, vegetable garden, wild prairie grasses, etc. Since it is located near Lake Michigan, there are many natural lagoons on the property. There is also a central convention hall and two greenhouses; one that typifies southwestern flora, and the other, a tropical environment.

It was dusk, a beautiful evening. The setting sun filled the sky with streaks of orange and red. Vicki and I sat on a wooden bench at the "Waterfall Garden" that was surrounded by pines and maples. The bench was on a 50-foot ridge where the waterfall began. It was so peaceful. We listened to the sound of water gushing into a small pond, 50-feet below, sharing our thoughts about the beauty of the scene as we overlooked the pristine Japanese garden—a 10-acre island scattered with mature bonsai trees. It was so perfect! After an hour elapsed, Vicki and I walked from the "Waterfall Garden" down the prairie grass slope. Then something very strange happened! On the way down the 40-degree incline, my equilibrium became a little shaky. As we all do, I denied any problem and hoped that it would go away. I was floating on air anyway, without a care in the world.

Once at the bottom of the slope, I was fine. We left the gardens, and as we drove a few miles to the west, I followed my impulse to treat Vicki to the best-tasting, smoothest homemade ice cream at "Deerfield Bakery" in downtown Deerfield. We sat at an outdoor table as dusk closed. Vicki looked at me with those beautiful, brown eyes and asked me why I took her to all of these nice places. I shrugged my shoulders and smiled. Soon after, I drove her back to Barrington, and I felt terrific on the way home.

July 16, 1990. I was living at home in Lincolnshire, a suburb located 40 miles north of Chicago, and I had the house all to myself because my parents were on vacation. Four days before, they had driven to Maine to visit close family friends, my adopted Aunt Betty and Uncle Richard Finney. The following morning, they planned to take an excursion boat to Nova Scotia, an area where Mom's roots are. Brenda, my sister, two years older than I, a strawberry-blonde whirlwind, also lived at home. Brenda was the head choreographer at Pheasant Run, one of the largest resorts in the Midwest, and she was conducting a rehearsal that night for the musical, "Best Little Whorehouse in Texas." Opening night was just around the corner. Since the rehearsals often ran late into the night, Brenda usually took advantage of one of her perks, a resort room to avoid the late-night 40-minute drive home.

Since I had the house to myself, I planned to take advantage of the opportunity and had invited Vicki for dinner. It was an unusually slow day at work; I made out the shopping list of the ingredients needed to prepare "Eggplant Parmesan." I wanted to impress my friend and follow through on my claim, "Oh, I can cook a great Eggplant Parmesan!" In reality, I had never even tried to prepare a meal, let alone

Eggplant Parmesan. I'd had some experience behind the stove making bacon and eggs, but to take on that task! *Am I nuts?*

At 4:30 p.m., I hurried to the local grocery store and bought the necessary ingredients, but had a hard time finding the right kind of lettuce for the salad. I hastily made the choice. When I returned home, I pulled out Mom's recipe box and found the card for Eggplant Parmesan. It was complicated, but I put it together. While the gourmet cuisine was baking in the oven, I frantically set up the dining room table. I used my mother's best china set on a beautiful handmade white tablecloth; dim lighting, along with candlelight. Everything was ready; the eggplant had finished baking. I mixed a side salad with plump red tomatoes cut into quarters. Perfect! It was ready to go! I was really nervous because Vicki was very special to me, and I was trying to make a lasting impression on her. Wow! She liked the setting, the conversation, the main course, even the salad. *Oh my gosh!* Since I was so concerned about it, I asked if the salad was good. I had no idea what kind of lettuce I had bought. It was thicker than regular lettuce and light green in color. *It's not the right kind!* After the meal, we enjoyed a very stimulating conversation, as we always did. At 10:00 p.m., she said goodnight and thanked me for the wonderful dinner. As she walked out the door, she turned back and said with a smile, "The cabbage salad was excellent."

I started to clean up the kitchen, but felt tired from all the excitement, so I turned in thinking, *I'll do the dishes tomorrow!*

At 11:30 p.m., I awoke from a deep sleep with a severe headache, due to what I now know was hydrocephalus (blocked intracranial spinal fluid) that increased pressure on my skull as it damaged parts of the brain. I ran downstairs to the kitchen and swallowed two *Bufferin,* thinking that was all I needed. I went down to the basement to rest on our cot, where I often sprawled when I was under the weather, hoping the headache would dissipate. It persisted. I went back upstairs to the kitchen and picked up the receiver on the old-fashioned telephone to call my friend, Paul, who lived a few blocks away. I was hoping not to disturb his parents. Suddenly, the headache became so severe that I curled up on the kitchen floor. The next thing I knew, I could hear my sister. With a quivering voice, I told her of the problem. She called the emergency room at Lake Forest Hospital, and I heard her frantically asking someone: "Should I bring him to the emergency room?" Brenda did not dial 911. She thought she could drive me there quicker at that time of the night, since there were few cars on the road. She ordered me, at the top of her lungs, to "Get in the car!" As I had a hard time maintaining my balance, she grabbed my right arm and assisted me to the garage door. There I sat on the outside step, frantically trying to put on a pair of shoes, any shoes! They turned out to be my mother's, which were four sizes too small. Brenda, 5'2", 113 pounds, assisted my 5'10", 185-pound frame to her car in the driveway. She drove rapidly to the hospital with the passenger window down as I hung my head out and dry-heaved. I still had hopeful thoughts that this emergency would be minor, like a virus. I just wanted to find out what was happening and return home, get some rest and go to work.

We arrived at the emergency entrance in a quick 10 minutes, unlike the 20 it usually takes to get there. As Brenda lugged me out of the car, I heard the screeching of another car. I squinted and took notice over my right shoulder as a squad car slammed on the brakes directly behind us. I was sure the policeman wanted to know why we had driven so rapidly, but no questions were asked and no help was offered. The pain increased so much that my eyes shut. Immediately, without checking me in, the doctor administered a CT (computed tomography) scan. (A CT scan records tissue at changing angles, therefore the results are more precise than an x-ray.) A nurse enabled me into a hospital bed and placed me in a private emergency room as she pulled the pale-yellow curtains closed. The attending nurse administered pain medication for my throbbing head. It worked! When the pain eased, I opened my eyes as she said, "Oh my, they are blue." *She likes me!* Under the crisis, I was still the same, still intrigued by the opposite sex. I began to feel better and became impatient. I asked Brenda what was taking the CT results so long, as an hour passed. The nurse replied that it must be something they had detected. *Uh-oh! What??* Worried as I was, I asked Brenda, who stood at the side of the emergency bed, what she thought it might be. She said she didn't know, but to focus on the bright side. So I sat up in the bed and talked with Brenda about how rehearsals went.

The CT scan results came through the following morning at 2:16. The Radiology Association (SC Department of Radiology), Lake Forest Hospital report said:

> *The scan revealed a moderately severe diffuse ventricular dilatation. There was an enlargement of the frontal horns, lateral ventricle, third ventricle and prominence of the cerebral aqueduct and apparent enlargement of the fourth ventricle. There was evidence consistent with a large midline cerebella. A follow-up MRI was recommended for further study.*

In other words, there was a mass in the fourth ventricle of the cerebellum, the center of all motor functions in the back of the brain. .

I looked up from my bed and saw a tall, older, doctor who appeared to be the head honcho. Dr. Pawl was a neurologist. It was the emergency room's practice to call in a neurologist if there was a head injury trauma. Dr. Pawl told me that I had water on the brain. He explained that there are four ventricles in the brain that regulate the flow of spinal fluid along with the subarachnoid space that encircles the brain. The mass was disrupting the flow. I needed to have an operation to drain the fluid as soon as possible, to save my life! "It could be a brain tumor." *What? That damn accident!*

While attending Indiana State University in 1988, during my senior year, second semester, I was involved in a serious automobile accident. It was 11:00 p.m. I took a left turn on a green light that changed to yellow as I entered the intersection. A car sped through the intersection from the left. It was later estimated that the car was traveling 55 mph in a 30-mph zone. It slammed into the door of my '73 Chevelle on the driver's side. My forehead bashed into the metal strip that separates the windshield from the side window. Two friends were in the car and, thank God, they weren't hurt. The emergency crew had to cut me out of the car with the "jaws of life." The driver of the other car was drunk, .25 blood alcohol content, and she was not injured. I was in a coma for three days. The hospital called Mom and Dad in the early-morning hours to tell them the grim news. They drove four hours in the cold of February and stayed in a room at the hospital for five days. I dropped out of school that semester because I was hospitalized for two weeks and my balance was clearly affected; I hobbled when I walked, for the next two months, due to damage to my cerebellum. The accident left a one-inch "character" scar above my left eyebrow. I had numerous psychological tests performed that concluded I had lost some memory. The doctor in charge of my case questioned the probability that I could return to school and graduate, let alone with a decent GPA. But, I went to summer school and made up my last semester with a full load, while working 30 hours a week at a local hardware store. I graduated with a B+ average. I was conditioned to the challenge that lay ahead of me now.

They have to operate as soon as possible! "Let's get it over with." *I like challenges!* I combated the horrible situation and was preparing myself to be a warrior on a mission to overcome. *Let's go!*

Ronald P. Pawl, MD, wrote a consultation report:

> *At the time of admission, patient was alert, oriented. When I initially saw him at the emergency service, he was alert and oriented. He was quite cognitive as far as his whereabouts and his condition. After discussion with the patient, I recommended transfer to the University of Illinois at Chicago Hospital. I discussed his case with Dr. Stone and with resident Dr. Paul Arnold, who are accepting him in transfer for placement of an extraventricular drainage or shunt system. The patient was agreeable to this and he was deemed safe in my opinion to be transferred to the University of Illinois at Chicago Hospital for further care.*

UIC was the only hospital available at that time to handle my case. The other two options, Illinois Masonic and St. Francis Hospital, were full.

I called Vicki from the emergency room to let her know what had happened. I wanted to reach out for comfort to someone who was very close to my heart. I needed someone to talk to, a mental hug for support. At the outset, she thought I was kidding as I always joked around; then she realized that I was serious. Caring as she was, she rushed to the hospital. A short while later, I was transferred by emergency bed to an ambulance to be transported to the hospital on the south side of Chicago. Brenda wanted to call Mom and Dad in Maine, but didn't know the number off the top of her head. She then faintly recalled the name of the remote town in Maine—Belgrade Lakes. She dialed information for Aunt Betty's number and made contact with our parents in Maine at 3:50 a.m., Eastern Standard Time. They were just getting ready to leave for Nova Scotia. If the call had been only a few minutes later, they could not have been contacted—they wouldn't have known. Mom and Dad were in shock! According to Aunt Betty, Dad was shaking with disbelief. Dr. Pawl called Dad in Maine, soon after Brenda's call. Dad asked the doctor if they should fly back. Dr. Pawl told Dad that it wasn't necessary; they could drive back. Mom and Dad drove without saying a word as they faced hours of uncertainty and worry.

Meanwhile, everything seemed to have moved so fast, even though four hours had elapsed. I didn't know the severity of the situation and how close to death I really was. I was naive during the emergency procedure, treating it like a game, a competition. But this was a competition of life or death.

I began to notice my surroundings as the ambulance traveled southbound on the Dan Ryan Expressway that links the north and south suburbs to the city. I turned my head to the left and glanced out the side window. I noticed that it became a little lighter as the early-morning fog lifted. Observing the heavy traffic as the ambulance swiftly drove on, I was disgusted as people rushed to work, their goals continuing; mine, suddenly halted. *Life goes on!*

I arrived at UIC. The paramedics quickly rolled me down the hall of the emergency department. The first person I saw was a petite Cambodian nurse: "Hey, Mai Tai!" The medical staff was perplexed by my cheerfulness in a life-threatening situation.

The first step was to drain the backed-up brain fluid that cleanses and protects the brain and spinal cord. It was a life-saving but simple procedure. The entire process fascinated me. A surgeon administered local anesthesia. He made a horseshoe-like incision in the right frontal area of my skull, where my scalp began above my right eye. As the doctor drilled a small burr hole into my skull, I heard the crackling sounds. He asked from time to time how I was doing: "Great! Great!" Enthusiasm was the only way I could cope.

The horseshoe-shaped ventricular catheter, an inch above my right eye, was tapped and out poured a rapid gush of clear fluid. My extra fluid drained down a five-foot clear tube and dripped, like coffee percolating, into a surgical bag hooked up to an IV pole. When the doctor completed the process, I gave him a high-five, saying: "Good job! Way to go!" I was not going to give in, no way. *I am not going to be complacent and caught off-guard.* By now, I assumed that Dr. Pawl was right—I had a brain tumor. *The facts are there. There has to be brain surgery. So why be upset? It's hard to face a negative situation with a negative attitude. Try to make the best out of it. This is your life, your chance to win!*

Two years later, Brenda recollected that on July 16, 1990, she was tired after conducting rehearsals for "The Best Little Whorehouse in Texas" and was thinking about staying at the resort that night. Something in her mind told her to go home; that something was wrong. If Brenda had not heard that message, I would have gone into a coma and died. I wouldn't be here to bug her today!

3

Let's Get It Done and Good Luck!

BRAIN TUMOR! The words sounded like bullets piercing my heart. Nevertheless, I asked myself two questions: Should I be down and, as a result, drag down my family and friends? Or should I be up and keep my family and friends up? I decided on the latter. At that time, the immediate surgical team and medical staff were perplexed that I did not recognize the severity of my condition. I couldn't understand that. Many health care professionals today recognize that the power of a positive outlook plays a critical role in medicine. I didn't want to recognize the life-threatening, changing situation. Hey, I was happy I was still around!

The telephone rang that night. When I stretched out my right arm to pick up the receiver on the night stand, the IV almost pulled out. I took a deep breath in anticipation. "Hello!" The hospital operator told me it was my father. "Darryl, how are you?" With a large amount of bravado, I said, "Hey, Dad, what's going on? Nothing to worry about. I feel great; this is no big deal." I was myself, enthusiastic, even though a tube protruded out of my head to drain the excess brain fluid. "Hey, where are you guys?" He said they had stopped off at a hotel in Ohio. I sighed with relief. I worried more about Dad and Mom than about myself. I wanted them to feel at ease. I was sure they were in shock, while under a great deal of stress to return as quickly as possible.

The next day, Dr. Stone administered an MRI (Magnetic Resonance Imaging) to scan my brain to detect the exact location of the tumor. I was heavily sedated so I wouldn't feel claustrophobic when mechanically fitted into the tube. An MRI is a large, oval-shaped diagnostic device that uses a combination of magnetic fields and radio waves that change the direction of atoms in the brain. It records the detailed three-dimensional results via computer. The MRI confirmed that the mass was on the floor of the fourth and pons (back of the head and neck), and Dr. Stone concluded from the location that it was a medulloblastoma—**malignant: cancer.**

I felt lucky. Before the onset of the MRI in the late '80s, neurosurgeons often performed exploratory surgery on medulloblastomas, and survival rates were a dismal 10 percent. Survival now is 60 percent after 5 years and 48 percent after 10 years.

That afternoon in the SICU room, Vicki discussed the results with me in a factual way. She had an added interest in the case since she was studying to be a psychologist and understood the medical terminology. I sat up and listened intently, as if I understood what she was telling me. In reality, I had no idea of the location of the tumor or what benign or malignant meant. *Oh, good! It's malignant!* I was so focused on the positive that I blanked out the negative.

On the second morning, after everything calmed down, a nurse helped me with my early-morning hygiene. She placed an S-shaped blue tub on the table. I used a blue toothbrush that was like a bristle pad, and washcloth with soap. *I love these dang sponge baths!* After a few minutes, the morning meal was served. After I gobbled up the stupendous (ha!) breakfast, I immediately turned on the TV as a remote control was built into my bed on the left railing, perpendicular to my pillow. *This is state of the art.* The TV became a real hit. I watched it, in the upper left corner of my room, every morning, turning on "Stock Watch." It was a real savior, keeping my mind busy as I thought about the markets and the economy, instead of focusing on the medical urgency that was present. I developed a real interest in the program and had fun. For example, nurses asked me questions about the market, investing, and their current holdings. They prodded me for financial suggestions. It felt great—like I was still at work! *Wow! They respect me for the knowledge I'm providing. Knowledge?* Well, I did communicate very emphatically about *Euro Disney* when it opened its doors just outside of Paris, France. The stock was a really hot buy at the time. I was convinced about its future gain, even though it later tanked. I even called constituents who had an active interest in the market. We conversed about the micro-and macro-economic issues of the times. I then debated with them about the movement of the overall market with the use of economic indicators, provided by the financial program, to back my claims.

Dr. Arnold entered my room on the second afternoon. A 9th-year resident (out of 10 years to become a neurosurgeon), he was one of the four doctors who were going to perform my surgery. Dr. Arnold overheard the financial discussions I was having with two nurses and eagerly wanted to know what kind of work I did. With a great deal of confidence, I sounded off: "I'm a pension consultant assistant!" I went on to babble in the financial jargon of my profession. I wanted to be *fired up!* I wanted to relate 'positivism'. The doctor and I sprang into a conversation about his financial holdings. He then asked if I had read *Liar's Poker*, about the high-flying commercial debt market of the '80s, and I said no. He suggested that I read it since I was in the investment field. I immediately asked for the book that night when Mom and Dad visited. My mother delivered it the next day. That book started my small hospital library of reading material and mind-boggling crossword puzzles. But I couldn't stay focused on anything or scroll to the right or left. *It must be something that's degenerating!* I glared at a particular word or phrase, mentally inspiring my eye muscles to keep my eyes focused. I thought that maybe they would get stronger and improve.

Later that day, a nurse entered my room to test my neurological functions. I slid the heel of my right foot down my left leg, from my knee to my ankle. I didn't stay on a steady course; my right leg jiggled.

I then repeated the maneuver with the heel of my left foot down my right leg, from my knee to my ankle. I concentrated hard not to make a mistake and I passed that test. *See? No problem!* The nurse then held up her forefinger about three inches from my nose and asked me to focus on her index finger. My eyes followed her finger to the right, then to the left. It was a difficult task. "Nystagmus," the nurse called it. *Hey, I am not that crazy! I learned something today! I can still retain new information. That was exciting!* N-Y-S-T-A-G-M-U-S. My eyes oscillated involuntarily when scanning to the right or left, then would tremor. Irritation to the vestibulocochlear nerve (VIII) regularly brings about nystagmus. That was the reason I couldn't scan a page and remain in focus: my right eyeball jiggled. *Wow! I had experienced this same sensation a few days ago while going to work.* I was pulling out of our neighborhood onto the main two-lane road. As I scanned perpendicularly to the right, I couldn't focus in on the traffic flow. I had to twist my neck to the right and then peer, but I ignored the symptom. And guess what? I rationalized—I thought it was due to the aging process. I was getting older. If I would have gone to an ophthalmologist, he would have noticed that my optic nerve had swelled, due to the built-up brain fluid caused by the tumor.

That evening, my parents arrived safe and sound. They had driven directly to the hospital in three days; under normal circumstances, it takes four. They entered the SICU room not knowing what to expect: "Hey, Mom and Dad, how ya doing?" *What a relief!* They bent down and gave me a half-hug and I enthusiastically shared the good news with them: "It's malignant." They didn't say anything about it as they wanted to keep my spirits up. Even when friends of the family stopped by for a visit, I enthusiastically shared the news.

Support was abundant from my immediate family and friends, to my co-workers, friends from the health club, and the hospital employees. On my second day in the hospital, there were nine supporters present, which relieved my mental anguish: Mom and Dad; Paula Ryan, who is my ex-college girlfriend's mother, and her kids: Heather,

16, Meagan, 6 and Dan, 13. They drove from Goodland, Indiana, to the hospital; a two-hour drive. Soon after came Chris Larson, a jolly fellow with whom I played baseball and worked out at a local gym; Heidi Hoffman, my sister's good friend, and her mother Barbara who wore a colorful spring bonnet to brighten up the drab hospital room. According to visitation rules, I was only allowed two visitors at a time in the SICU room.

During the SICU party, everyone was at ease; in fact, we were all so comfortable that Chris even joked about my head bonnet. Suddenly, Chris noticed that the readings from the heart monitor above me were beeping rapidly, the result of my merry laughter. A few minutes later, a frantic nurse ran into the room, thinking something was drastically wrong. "Hey, what's going on?" Understandably, the nurse asked us to tone things down as we were disturbing other patients. Heidi nicknamed us "The Loud Family."

For the next five days, I continued to radiate energy to family and friends. I wanted them to feel positive, so, in turn, they replenished me with more positive feedback. There was a great deal of positive energy all around me, which made things much easier—like a circle of support. The patient feeds positive feedback to the support staff. In turn, the support staff feeds the patient more positive feedback: hospital psychology at work, using the "Darryl Didier Model." Hmm, that could be an idea!

Doctors can seem quite negative at times. "Be realistic!" Be realistic that you might die. So then, why do we live? Why do we have goals to achieve? Why do we go to school? Why do we do anything? Being too realistic may limit one's ability to succeed. In the winter of 1991, a paraplegic's goal was to climb the highest mountain in North America. If he was realistic, he never would have entertained the thought of attempting the climb. But he actually did it!

I'd been in the hospital five days; it was mid-July! *What am I doing here? Let's go and operate now so I can enjoy the last part of summer!* I wanted to spend time with Vicki before she had to return to school in a

few weeks. Time dragged; it was very frustrating having to sit in the
hospital bed. I'm the kind of guy who can't sit still in one place for five
minutes, let alone five whole days. *Geesh!*

That evening, *Ah! Vicki is here. Oh great!* Whenever I saw her, it was
like seeing the sun. She radiated with the sun's warmth and energy.
When she was present, everything was wonderful. My heart thumped
when I saw that smile and those shining eyes. I began to feel the love I
had for her. I felt the electricity between us. At that moment, I realized
the negative predicament I was in. I broke down and cried in her arms
as we both held each other. A nurse entered to take my blood pressure,
but she witnessed the embrace of two souls. She turned, quietly left the
room, and closed the door. We remained with each other for the following hour and spoke about the bright side of things. We planned
activities for after I was released, in a couple of weeks, and before she
returned to school, August 29. When the visitation hour ended at 8:30
p.m., Vicki stopped at the door, turned back and smiled, with tears in
her eyes. That was so hard to deal with; I wanted to leave with her.

The meals? What can I say? They were good. But then again, I like
any kind of prepared food, if it's not liver and onions. Dinner was a
challenge and I looked forward to the activity. A nurse entered my
room and placed the tray on the yellowish table that hung over the
bed. I reached out with my right hand and dragged the table over my
lap. When I began the process of dining, I became elated: Cut with
your left hand; coordinate the fork in your right hand, and lift vertically, 50 degrees. Now, angle your forearm 30 degrees and deliver the
grub into your mouth. Begin with a controlled motion. Chew with
your jaw then swallow with your throat. That's how excited I was!
After the meal, I tried to read again, but since my eyes would not let
me, I watched television. The programs were boring so I tried to fall
asleep. It was difficult to enter dreamland as I remained straight up at a
70-degree angle in order for the brain fluid to drain properly. I
couldn't simply turn over and doze.

Many calls about my condition began to flood into the nurses' station. The nurses acted as if they were my secretaries, as they were seriously inconvenienced. One afternoon, I was watching a financial program on TV. I had often viewed that program when I studied for the Series-7 License a couple of years before. The nurse I'd named Mai-Tai entered and said: "That's it—you answer your own phone!" She hooked up my own communication line so I could dial out or people could call in directly. I was thrilled that I could reach the outside world.

The holding period started to irritate me. My backside became uncomfortably sweaty. I felt like a stale potato chip. *I hate sitting! Why is this wait so long?* But I had to be stabilized; the excess fluid needed to be drained and the swelling in my brain reduced. I was annoyed at having sponge baths every morning. I couldn't wait until I could take a normal shower. Every time I needed to go to the bathroom, I had to use a urinal or a bedpan. I had the hardest time with those tasks. *How can somebody go "number one" lying in bed? There is no gravitational force.* I pleaded with the nurse to allow me to go to the washroom. She agreed, and I was really pleased about that. The nurse stood by my bed. I tried to sit up, but couldn't do it. I was too weak, and my poor equilibrium made me dizzy. I had no independence; I had to rely on somebody else. I tried again to sit up—this time with the nurse's assistance—and was able to sit, and then stand. I walked very gingerly while sliding along the IV pole with the aid of the nurse, about eight feet to the washroom. Afterwards, I had to push a call button for assistance back to bed. I was disgusted with myself for being so weak, physically, and believed it was from inactivity, lying around in the hospital. I couldn't wait to get out of there and start to rebuild my strength. I even began doing sit-ups in bed until the attending nurse ran in because my heart monitor was going crazy. What could I do?

Meanwhile, telephone calls kept pouring in, which was a savior. The phone provided me with a sense of normalcy and control. I called my friends as often as possible to assure them that I was okay, which in turn reassured me. Was it a lie? I didn't know, but it sure helped. They were shocked, not only by the events that had occurred, but also because of my optimism and cheerful disposition. When a friend called, I'd always respond, "Hey, how are you doing?" "What's going on?"

I called a close friend I'd gone to high school with, Bill Seitz, who had been the class clown. We often pulled silly pranks during high school and had many funny memories of our crazy behavior. When I contacted him, he responded in a joking manner, which meant so much to me. There was no worry as he exuded confidence.

On the sixth night, Paul and Bill showed up, both having driven separately from the North Shore—Glencoe and Lake Forest. Bill worked as a mechanic at Standard of Lake Forest, a family business, and, as I mentioned before, Paul owned a fish market. The drive for both of them took an hour and a half in heavy traffic on the expressway. *What support?* That was so soothing to me because we were having fun under such stressful circumstances. Bill noticed that I had my *WalkMan* and said, "Hey, I have some tapes in my truck; I'll get them." He came back with some classic tapes from the '70s: the "Who," "Stones," "Led Zeppelin." The tapes reminded me of the fun times we all had together, fishing, playing softball and football, or lounging around having a beer. The atmosphere was so relaxed that Paul even opened up a beer in the hospital room. He later told me he needed a drink to feel jolly, his best friend was laid-up. We enjoyed the get-together so much that Paul and Bill stayed until 11:30 p.m., well beyond the visiting hours of 11:00 a.m. to 8:30 p.m.

The eighth afternoon, 20 hours before surgery: Mom, Dad, and Brenda dropped in and brought me a hot dog, fully loaded with everything but sauerkraut, and a large ice-cold soda from the cafeteria. Since I wasn't allowed to eat anything for 12 hours before the surgery, I jokingly said, "This is my last supper!" I wanted a positive reaction from my parents and sister. They said I would be fine. Thank God for them! That was the most enjoyable hot dog I ever ate. I get hungry today just thinking about it! After an hour of small talk and hugs, they left the room. Brenda then turned and said, "See ya tomorrow morning at 5:30 before you go into surgery." I responded, "You don't have to." But my sister wanted to get one last glimpse of her normal brother.

That night, I tried to focus on a book while I was listening to Hip-Hop tunes on my *WalkMan. How motivational!* I practically bounced around to the rhythm of the beat. Three of the team of four doctors entered the fray. The primary neurosurgeon, Dr. Stone, was busy with another case. They lined up in front of me, their arms crossed over their white coats. Dr. Arnold smiled and said: "He looks like he is going to have brain surgery tomorrow." They all chuckled. "Yep," I said. *I guess they like the attitude!* Then, as I took off the headphones, Dr. Arnold asked, "Do you realize what you are going to go through?" "Yes," I responded again. I placed the headphones back on and cranked up the volume. I had no idea what was going to happen to me; I did not want to know. The team left. The following is what I think would have been said to me—if I would have listened to them.

Hey, Darryl, there is something we want to tell you. Did you know that the tumor is a cerebella medulloblastoma with hydrocephalus? Did you know that the tumor is a differentiated malignant neoplasm, composed of tightly packed cells of spongioblastic lineage? Did you know that the cranial nerves V, VI, VII, VIII, originate there and they control facial movement, facial sensation, tongue movement, taste, salivation, eye movement, hearing and balance? Did you know that the cerebellum coordinates all voluntary muscular activity? Did you know that the pons maintains operations between the cerebrum and the cerebellum by relaying impulses between them? Did you know that the medulla oblongata makes up part of the floor of the fourth ventricle and controls heart rate, blood pressure and breathing? A lesion to this part of the brain often proves fatal. Did you know that 30 percent of these tumors occur between the ages of 20 and 24? Did you know that medulloblastoma in adults is a rare disease—five-tenths of one percent incident rate per 100,000? Did you know the survival rate between 5 and 10 years is 60 percent, then dwindles down to 48 percent thereafter?

If you do survive the operation, there will be a year of rehabilitation to relearn motor coordination? There will be droopiness on one side of the face, one-sided smile and drooping eyelid, speech and swallowing difficulties? There will be abnormalities with your eyes, cross-eyed, vision impairment? You might have personality changes; that you may not be able to drive a car or be employed? You might be a quadriplegic. You will be a changed individual. Try not to worry, though—we will do our best.

As the nurse turned off the lights, thoughts were running through my head to put myself in a positive mood and get psyched up, like the day before a football game. The room was pitch black. I heard the rumblings of the El tracks outside my window. I sat back and tried to visualize the Ryerson Forest Preserve near my house, which Paul and I often explored during our childhood. Ring ring ring…the telephone? Wow, whom could it be at this crazy hour, disturbing my peace? What peace? In a monotone voice, I answered the phone. "Hello, Chris?" Besides being good friends, Chris and I had been rivals in football at two different high schools in the area, Stevenson and Carmel. Chris asked, "How do you feel, Darryl?" "Good," I said, "despite the fact I'm going to have brain surgery tomorrow." Chris asked, "Darryl, remember that football game when you were the starting nose guard?" "Yeah," I said. He went on, "The game is tied, the ball is on the one-yard line, and there are three seconds left in the game. What are you going to do about it?" I said, "Kick its ass! I am going to go crazy!" Chris responded, "You will not lose! I will talk to you tomorrow."

The morning of the ninth day, July 24: I had been fired-up all night. It was a double-edged sword. This was the first step toward getting out of the hospital, but on the other side, who could know what effect the surgery would have on my mental capacity and physical ability? I must admit that I placed a higher concern on the mental aspect—the power of the mind, which provides you with the ability to think on your own, make sound judgments and communicate with others effectively. This was a large concern of mine.

Brenda and Heidi entered the SICU room at 5:30 a.m., and we talked about how I felt. "I feel great! Let's go get 'em!" The surgical team entered and gave me the ride of my life, as they rolled me, in bed, to the surgery room. Yeah, I was nervous, but the only way for me to deal with the situation was to be determined to meet the challenge face-to-face. I told the doctor, "Let's go and get it done and good luck!" As a nurse rolled me out of the room, I looked back and saw Brenda and Heidi wave and smile.

4

No Sympathy; I Will Be Back!

On the stretcher, I was given general anesthesia through an IV and oxygen was provided through an endotracheal tube that passed through my throat, windpipe, and larynx. It was part of the ventilator that mechanically sustained the correct blood, oxygen and carbon dioxide mixture in and out of my lungs, the same as a paralyzed patient is given. I was then transferred to the operating table. Since the tumor was in the back of my head and neck, a scrub-nurse placed me face down in a 3/4 prone position with the Mayfield device that held my head suspended.

Dr. Stone made a straight-line incision at the back of my head and neck. It started four centimeters above my first cervical vertebrae, the axis that supports my skull. The incision then continued down three centimeters below my third cervical vertebrae, encompassing about six inches. When the surgeon made the incision, he was careful not to perforate my foramen magnum, which would have damaged my sense of taste, my ability to chew, swallow and articulate. He then used a hot knife, bipolar cautery, to clear my wound of tissue and muscle. Another doctor then drilled four holes, two laterally on either side of my skull. The bone of my foramen magnum was removed, along with the arch of my first cervical vertebrae. Dr. Stone then spread apart the dura in a "Y" fashion, eight centimeters on either side for maximum exposure. Then, under microscopic guidance, he identified my purplish vascular tumor and found that it extended into the floor of my fourth ventricle and pons. My tumor compressed my left cranial nerves that controlled sensation and movement in my head and body. The team of doctors had to decide what could be accomplished in terms of tumor removal. They did not want to harm my quality of life if I did survive the operation by destroying any of the 12 cranial nerves adjacent to the tumor that control: smell; eye movement (inward/upward);-eye movement (downward/upward); -chewing, sensation of face, scalp and teeth; -eye movement (lateral); -facial expression, taste, salivation and tearing; -hearing and equilibrium; -salivation, swallowing, sensations in throat and tonsils; -swallowing, breathing, talking, heart rate and throat sensations; XI-shoulder movement and head rotation; -tongue movement.

With the continuation of microscopic guidance, Dr. Stone removed the tumor by careful suction. The tumor had a large amount of blood supply so they reverted to bipolar cautery to minimize bleeding. The doctors then recorded, from my scalp, brain stem auditory responses that elicited a click in the doctor's earplugs. The results showed no abnormalities.

About six hours passed. Dr. Stone had sent a frozen sample of my tumor to Pathology for diagnosis. The report came in as expected: medulloblastaoma, cancer. As the operation continued, Dr. Stone found that the remaining 15 percent of my tumor was gritty, hard and stuck to the floor of the fourth ventricle. He quickly decided to stop the operation and ended up settling for partial removal, 85 percent. A portion of the medulla oblongata is in the floor of the fourth ventricle. Stopping the operation short was another instance in which the doctors were careful not to harm my quality of life. Dr. Stone closed the wound as the surgery ended 14 hours later. A nurse transported me back to the SICU room in stable condition.

I heard Dad say in a loud voice: "The surgery went great! Everything went well!" I bounded with happiness in my mind even though I was in no state to outwardly respond. Then I heard Vicki's energetic voice: "Darryl, you are all yellow. You are going to look great going back to

Merrill Lynch in your suit all yellow." I was mentally aware and jok-ingly envisioned giving her the finger!

Not again! Dang it! A few minutes later, I sensed the breathing tube drooping in the left corner of my mouth. I knew something was wrong! The left side of my face was paralyzed since the left facial nerve was highly compressed and had been unavoidably injured with tumor decompression. All my life I have been extra sensitive about my speech. In grade school, I never talked because of a speech impediment caused by a severe case of buck-teeth and three bouts with braces. During my high school and college years, my speech was adequate. No one asked me to repeat myself. I had a strong voice, but muddled through the words. I talked a lot, but I needed to concentrate. During college, vari-ous people said I talked too fast and assumed I was from New York City. So when I had just begun cold-calling at Merrill Lynch, I tried the laid-back approach. That didn't work. For instance, when I called a potential client, the woman said, "What? I don't understand you. What are you trying to say? Speak up!" *Dang it! All right then! Hey!* All those thoughts invaded my mind as the tube dangled from my mouth.

The nurse with the low voice won the coin-flip over the other nurse. A day before surgery, two of the nurses who checked on me thought it was cute of me to be so confident: "I will be out of here in two weeks!" I said. So they bet by a coin-flip on who would be my day nurse after surgery. As the day progressed, I became lethargic. I opened my eyes only to voice commands. It was an early sign of a blood clot by the wound site, an epidermal hematoma which can cause coma by con-stricting the brain. This is a common occurrence after a head trauma. The nurse was aware of this as she wheeled me through the hall for a CT scan of my whole skull. Being moved from the emergency cart to the CT-scan room was very painful. My head was extra sensitive, with a deep grinding pain. The nurse pulled me over with the help of an orderly, who handled me in an uncaring, haphazard fashion. I halluci-nated during the scan. The walls were changing sizes and angles. It seemed as though I was in Apollo 13. The scan was completed a half-hour later and I was unaware of the results. However, as I was carted back to the SICU room, I sensed that something was wrong. As I was approaching my room, I saw the image of two doctors face-to-face as their heads bobbed and hands flared. *Now what?* I was terrified! The results of the scan had, in fact, detected a complication: a blood clot in the wound-site.

That damn nurse! I wanted privacy and time to heal. I was angry that she took me in for surveillance. The team of doctors had to re-open the wound. *Gosh! I thought it was over!* Vicki's brother, Andy, was present in the hallway along with my family. He gave the "thumbs up" sign three times.

The nurse quickly rolled the emergency cart down to the operation suite. I became even more terrified once I was in the operating room. Once again, I was placed in a 3/4 prone position with the Mayfield frame. I had been given a general anesthetic through the endotracheal tube, but it had not taken effect yet. As I looked to the left, I faintly saw the silver surgical tools pile up as they clanged together. *Those are going to be used on me!* Soon I heard the pleasant sound of good rock music. *Hey, the Rolling Stones!* Just as they accused me, I accused them. *They are taking this too lightly! Or, maybe this is a way to keep them energized!* I then zonked out.

Dr. Stone re-opened the wound-site where he found 50 cc's of clotted blood. He drained and cleaned the wound thoroughly. A nurse transferred me back to the SICU room in stable condition. The following day, Dr. Desalvo entered my room and changed the bandages. I overheard him express his sympathy as he chatted with a nurse: "Poor guy, I really feel sorry for him." I wished I could have said something to let him know: *Hey! Don't feel sorry for me! I will be back! I do not want sympathy!*

Later that day, my mom, dad, and Vicki visited, and my two college buddies, Mike Ekan and Craig Kelm, drove up from the Merriville, Indiana area. Craig said the news had devastated him, but he felt confident that I would win the battle. Later, he told me he could not believe what he saw when he entered my room: Everything was white—the walls, the bed sheets and the large bandage around my head. He saw the tubes strewn everywhere, even out of my mouth. He said Vicki was there and that she told me she couldn't wait to go on a run with me. Craig then jokingly responded that it would take me years. He said I immediately kicked him and the nurse threw him out of the room. He didn't know I could hear him, but after that, he said he knew I would be fine. "You were your old self."

That tube felt as if it was a Bratwurst lodged in my throat; it seemed to be projecting five feet out of my mouth! I didn't like it, it didn't like me. I made a hasty decision. I was hallucinating because of all the sedation drugs. On the second morning, I believed that Dr. Arnold and two nurses stood over me. He gave me the green light, so I thought, "Ready, Darryl, on the count of three, pull it out! 1-2-3!" I pulled and tugged on that thing (ventilator tube), then yanked it out of my mouth. According to the medical records, I pulled it out on my own: "self-extubated." *I removed it prematurely!* I have always been very impatient, as the medical staff soon learned. Nevertheless, they allowed me to try on my own.

I coughed and coughed and coughed! A nurse entered the room like a drill sergeant. "Come on, cough it up and spit it out!" I spit up mucus into a paper cup. The nurse then instructed me to take deep breaths with an oxygen mask. What coordination it took to take a deep breath with the oxygen mask, then lift the mask, cough, cough, cough. "On three, lift your head and spit out the mucus." There was no time for rest as I coughed and spit every second and every minute of the day. I felt as if I was going to choke. Every half-hour, a nurse entered the room to gauge my breathing rate. The respiratory therapist asked me to lean forward. With the stethoscope positioned on my back, between the shoulder blades, she asked me to take deep breaths. She wanted to make sure that my lungs were clear. I didn't pass the first couple of tests; the tickle in my lungs was too great.

Two hours elapsed. I became worn-out by the effort, feeling as though I was running the last lap of a timed mile for football tryouts back in college. You are ready to collapse from exhaustion, but you have to keep going. The fourth time the nurse conducted the test, my coughing had finally diminished. *All right!* I desperately wanted to end this exhaustive activity and be successfully weaned off the ventilator. I took the deepest breath I could to impress the nurse and slowly let it out. I concentrated hard on exhaling slowly. I was not going to give in, as I felt tickles in my lungs. I had one last exhale to go until the lungs emptied. The tickle was too great, so I coughed. I was still forced to keep up the rendition of coughing, spitting, and breathing with an oxygen mask. My mouth became severely dry from the oxygen and my lips cracked. I couldn't swallow or even talk to a nurse to express my frustration. It may have been only minutes, but it seemed like hours.

Finally! The nurse had a heart! She provided a paper cup filled with small ice crystals that soothed the dryness sensation. Well, the satisfaction lasted for only a short while until the cup emptied and my mouth became scorched again. *Hey, nurse!* There was no way I could communicate. *Hey, nurse!* It felt as though I was alone in the middle of the desert, with no relief in sight. *Aah!* The nurse came through, finally. She listened to my lungs; not a sound was emitted. The respiratory therapist tested my level of oxygenation. I performed in the 96th range out of 100, so he deemed that I could breathe independently, without the assistance of a ventilator.

That evening, Dr. Arnold came into the SICU room. He told me excitedly that he and his wife were going away for the weekend to celebrate their anniversary in San Francisco and that when he returned on Monday he would see to it that I was moved to a more peaceful environment, the step-down floor. *Great!* The doctor believed in me; he had confidence that I would improve. That night, as my mom, dad and Vicki visited I wrote on the clipboard and asked Mom if she could bring a huge bowl of mixed fruit the next day. I love fruit, especially Michigan red cherries. *Uhm!* All I dreamed about that night was eating fruit and feeling the cool sensation soothe my throat. I had to write the request over many times because it was scribble as my right hand was jittery. Intentional muscle movement can occur without the cerebellum, but often results in sporadic motions.

The next morning, a dietitian, along with a speech therapist, tested liquid purees that I could swallow without difficulty since the tube was down my throat for 48 hours. *It's about time! Real food!* The therapist fed me with a spoon: canned pears, apricots and peaches, as I remained sprawled out in bed. *Hey! My taste buds still work!* I couldn't see what they fed me, but I sure could taste it. The two therapists debated with each other over whether I could effectively chew and swallow a piece of sliced banana. The outcome: Yes, my throat worked! They repeated the tests and I was thrilled. The banana slice tasted so good, along with the sensation of something cool sliding down my throat. *I am actually eating something!* "Now, Darryl, slow down and take smaller bites and chew thoroughly."

All right! I passed the eating test. That morning for breakfast, the dietitian allowed me to eat a soft puree diet. With a plastic spoon, I began to slurp the strawberry milkshake. A nurse then bellowed, "Swallow slowly, Darryl, and take small bites." I wanted to impress the nurse so she would leave me alone. After a few cooperative renditions, the nurse felt safe and allowed me to continue on my own. *All right!* I gulped the shake, and part of it seeped into my lungs. My breathing pattern became abnormal. On an emergency basis, I was back on the ventilator, with that tube jammed down my throat, and chest X-rays were taken.

I was extremely angry with myself. *Why did I do that?* A nurse soon entered the SICU room and very abruptly told me that I had pneumonia and my right lung had collapsed. *Dang it!*

The Chest Surgery Service brought me to the operating theater. Through a technique which visualized the primary respiratory tract, the respiratory surgeon inserted a special needle into my chest to remove the extra fluid. The right lung was brought back, but the pneumonia still posed a problem.

That evening, my mom called to find out how things were going before she and Dad drove down for a visit. The nurse on duty advised them not to bother then cried over the phone when she shared the disheartening news of the emergency procedure. Since Dr. Arnold was away, his assistant, a petite Korean female doctor, induced large doses of antibodies through my IV, and suctioned out built-up fluid from my lungs late into the night. Mom said the nurse saved my life. "We almost lost him," the doctor told Mom. Pneumonia usually occurs in patients who have been in the SICU room longer than 48 hours, and frequently in those who are on a ventilator and any type of catheter. I was back on the ventilator again with the tube.

My lungs were clear by the next morning. The nurse guided my bed through the corridors to the Chest Services Department. I had an X-ray to see if my lungs remained clear. As I lay on the X-ray table, I heard the enthusiastic voice of a young medical student. UIC is a teaching hospital where medical students often view procedures. He then shouted in amazement about how clear and strong my lungs looked. *It's from all the exercise I did.* I was soon transported back to the SICU room.

After all my time in the hospital, I was becoming acquainted with my surroundings. I heard the regular high-pitched beeping of the heart monitors, the voices of nurses and doctors discussing medical charts, the sounds of papers being rustled, the usual yelps, the low-toned groans, the humming sounds. Then suddenly a car drove over my chest. Well, that's what it felt like when I was caught off-guard. A male X-ray technician, middle-aged and stout, with a keg of beer for a belly, plopped a 5-pound lead apron over my chest, which was used to ward off minimal radiation exposure. X-rays were prescribed to monitor my lungs for any liquid build-up, after the fiasco. The machine made a constant, low-toned humming sound whenever maneuvered. *Now I know what that sound is!* The apparatus was like a portable crane. The base was 5' by 5' with four large yellow wheels, like an oversized Tonka toy. A 6-foot-high pendulum swung the large light-green scanner over my chest. I looked up and saw a milky white screen. "Don't move!" The technician reached up and a high-pitched sound emitted. He changed the film, which was the size of poster board paper. He photographed again, made a change, and photographed again three times. For the first two mornings, he took the pictures with the protective flap. A few mornings later, the technician became lazy and took readings without the protective sheath. At first I didn't think anything of it until the nurse took notice and ordered the technician to: "Put it on! He is only twenty-four years old." *What? That guy stopped using the flap two days ago! Great, radiation poisoning from the x-ray? Who is that guy?* The lead apron was used to protect the gonads so my sperm production would remain intact.

A few days later, the nurse transferred me to the operating room so that the external shunt or drain could be changed, thus preventing infection from occurring again. I had a local anesthetic, as it was a simple procedure. Dr. Arnold re-opened the previous horseshoe incision and removed the old drain. He then inserted the new drain that soaked in an anti-infective agent. After the procedure, a nurse rolled me back to my domain.

That evening, Dr. Arnold's young assistant entered the room and told me she was going to insert a tube, a nasogastric tube, through my left nostril, down the throat to the small intestine. As she began the process, I glanced towards my nose. The leader was silver, the size of a small fishing weight, and pointed like an arrow. As she slithered it through the transnasal route, I wanted to cough up but couldn't. It felt as though I had swallowed a cashew nut whole and I could not get it out. She inserted the tube so that I could receive large amounts of nutrients, way beyond the norm. The doctors wanted to aid the healing process since I had not eaten for eight days.

The tube worked as prescribed. That night, I had to go to the bathroom very badly, but I could not orally communicate. I became desperate. I tried to shout my need mentally, but the plea was not heard. Thank God Brenda appeared right then! I raised my right hand as though I wanted to write something. She gave me the clipboard and pen. I couldn't see, but felt the clipboard. I wrote the request, my right arm shaking. It was like playing Charades. "What, birds?" *Come on!* By the third desperate scribble, she finally recognized the word—"bed pan!" Brenda told the attending nurse and he quickly brought one to me. My digestive system still worked. The nurse was elated with the bowel movement that showed everything was working properly.

The following morning, my mind was really playing games with me. I thought that I was in a courtyard filled with patients dressed in white who were playing Cricket. I saw my hospital room door from the out-field. The outside wall, covered with vines, was very similar to the out-field wall at Chicago's Wrigley Field. I imagined that I was in the hospital garage, secretly plotting a way to get the breathing tube out of my mouth. I lay face-down in a rolled-up rug in the overhead storage space. The garage door was ajar, the cold wind and rain blowing in from the outside. *This nurse is crazy! I can't believe I am exposed to these conditions!* I told the nurse how stupid she was for having such a silly idea, and I hurt her feelings. What was I thinking? Boy, did I halluci-nate. I was so focused on removing that tube.

Late that afternoon, I was having a difficult time breathing regu-larly. I kept hiccupping and taking in too much air through the tube. I had pain in my chest. I tried to alter my breathing pattern by taking deep breaths and slowly exhaling, thinking that would put a halt to the hiccupping, but it didn't. The bothersome breathing continued. It felt like I'd stuffed down a hot dog too quickly, only there was no soda to wash it down; it just kept persisting. There was no relief in sight. *Come on! Dang it!*

Through my blurry vision, I saw a Catholic priest enter the room. He was short, with round-rimmed spectacles that had a greenish tint. *Hey, father! What's he doing here? I will be all right! I don't need to be given my last rights!* I felt his presence next to me. He whispered in a soothing Spanish accent: "God is with you." He kept on repeating and repeating it while massaging my arm. I was overjoyed. He said that I was a fighter and he made me feel confident that I would make it. Suddenly, the hiccupping stopped. I knew I wasn't hallucinating then, because the priest visited daily until I was transferred out of the SICU room—a period of two weeks.

My IV was changed often. The vein that had been used for the IV had bruised after a day's use. As a nurse searched my arms for a new victim, she continuously remarked, "Mmm, you have really good veins." *Hey, thanks, I exercise often.* I was proud. The nurse then zoned in on the chosen vein, and attacked.

On August 1st, I was in the middle of being weaned from the ventilator for the second time. I went through the normal routine of coughing and spitting up mucus and then breathing with the added oxygen mask. During the process, the medical staff that had performed the surgery ordered an MRI scan, so a nurse transferred me to the basement. Having an MRI is like being packed into a tube like a sardine. You lie on a cot, head-first, while the technician inserts ear plugs to combat the outlandish rattling. Mechanically, it slowly squeezes you through a skinny tube with no space to expand. Then bam, bam, bam, like a machine gun firing! It sounded like a WWII documentary about the invasion of Normandy, with the volume on the TV all the way up. Fifteen minutes went by. "Don't move; we will be finished soon," the MRI technician communicated to me through the intercom. *Good, I want to get the heck out of here!* Minutes later, the coughing began. The technician kept telling me to hold still, but there was no way that I could. My throat tickled so much. The respiratory therapist had just taken me off the ventilator, so what could I do? Cough, cough, cough. I actually coughed up the mucus into the oxygen mask. I started to drown. I had no way to breathe. *I have to get out of here!* There was no way to orally communicate with the technician operating the MRI. She kept insisting that I hold still. Frustration and desperation resulted; I felt as if I was looking up while underwater. You see your friends above. They wave, thinking what a great swimmer you are, but in reality, you are drowning. You need help quickly! The technician said I was moving so much because I was crazy: "He is hallucinating because of all the drugs." *Hey, wake up!* The nurse had the common sense to know that something was wrong. She ordered that the MRI be stopped and I was mechanically removed, just in time. The nurse ripped off the oxygen mask. She immediately offered me a towel to spit and cough into, spit and cough, and then she replaced the oxygen mask. That was the end of the MRI, and the nurse brought me back to the SICU room.

A few hours passed and I was still coughing and spitting. The nurse entered and I felt her finger on my wrist. She raised her voice to announce the news that my vitals were being taken. "Hey, Darryl!" I heard the energetic voice of Brenda as she entered the room. The nurse took my blood pressure. Brenda was on the right side of the bed, telling me how much she wanted to see me walking freely along the beach. "Darryl, I can't wait to get you home." The nurse overheard the conversation and told Brenda that I was incoherent and unaware of her presence. *What?* I made the sign for the clipboard. *I am going to tell her off!* I wrote in retaliation. **I AM VERY COHERENT!** I held up the clipboard as high as I could so the nurse could see it. Brenda grabbed it and laughed. "Look at this; he even spelled it right. HA! HA!" The nurse didn't say a word. *I taught her something!*

The seventh day following surgery, I went through another external shunt drainage change, but this time at bedside. I was having further respiratory problems, and Dr. Stone came to share some news. In a somber voice, he said that a tracheotomy was imminent. Since I'd had a hard time being weaned from the ventilator the first two times, he was not going to take a chance with that tube down my throat for the third time. "There is no other alternative. The only way for you to eventually breathe on your own is to perform a tracheotomy." *What is going on? I should not be having all these setbacks! I can't believe this!* I was angry and upset about having my throat slit open, and possibly ending up with a scar, like a long-term smoker. I had the nurse call Vicki right away to share the news and hear her voice for consolation.

The Ear, Nose, and Throat specialist performed the tracheotomy the next day, making a 2-cm slit at the base of the neck in the middle. He then fitted the tracheotomy tube into place. The circular tube penetrated 11 cm down the trachea (the windpipe that transmits air to the lungs). A nurse brought me back to the SICU room and the wrestling matches concluded.

The ENT intern disturbed my peace three times each day. An Asian man in his mid-thirties, he stood over me like a giant. He cleaned the trachea with saline to deter infection and to make sure the wound would not heal shut. Tracheotomy care is critical. The ventilated air must be humidified so the patient can be easily suctioned in order to sustain a free flow of air. The amount of air pressure also has to be monitored at a low level or else hemorrhage to the trachea can occur.

While I began to improve after the tracheotomy, my ventricles developed an infection. I was stabilized with an antibiotic, Vancomcyin, developed from an isolated culture of an Oriental strain. The infection cleared up the following day, and I finally started to become stabilized.

Seventeen days following surgery, I had another operation, but this was a no-brainer. Dr. Arnold was to change my external shunt, which drained the extra brain fluid, to a VP shunt—an internal shunt. The new shunt would drain my brain fluid to my stomach and I would not be rigged up to the IV pole. I could be more mobile and take part in an intense rehab program. I was transferred, again, to the operating suite. As I was positioned on the surgical bed, Dr. Arnold made an incision to the right of the belly button, horizontally. The tube, three-eighths of an inch, was fed up to the shoulder through the fourth layer of skin. Dr. Arnold then removed the previous shunt and a rush of clear fluid was drained into an IV bag. The doctor placed the new external shunt into the old horseshoe-shaped wound. The tube was then passed through my neck, under the skin, and connected to the abdominal tube. The excess fluid would drain, if necessary, into my stomach, where it would dissolve on its own. With the little range of motion I had, I could finally move independently without dragging along an IV pole. In a sense, I was back to normal. *How pleasurable! Now I can sleep at a flat level, facedown in the pillow instead of face-up at a 70 degree angle.* I had slept at that angle since day one, July 17.

The 20th day following surgery, I finally was able to get off the ventilator and change to a tracheotomy collar, Kistmer Tube. This allowed for oral communication. When I covered the air hole with my forefinger, a weird sound came out. I talked out loud to myself for hours, like "Kermit The Frog"; this was entertaining. I was able, for the first time since surgery, to orally communicate with my family and friends. I talked and talked. "Listen to this…" I enjoyed sharing the strange sound.

On the same day, my eyes were examined in the Neuro-Ophthalmology Department. The findings were as expected because of the location of my surgery. My vision was intact when I looked straight ahead, but when my eyes were examined separately, my left eyeball could not gaze to the left past the middle; instead, it remained focused inward towards my nose because of a weakness to the left abducens nerve—the VI cranial nerve. The eyeball could not move up or down independently. My left eyelid could not blink, constrict or converge, nor could it produce natural tears as a result of the left nerve being cut (the VII cranial nerve). My face was so strange, they gave it a name: "Bell's Phenomenon," which, by definition, is peripheral facial paralysis. *Huh!* Now the right eye was tested. It still had nystagmus—jerky movements—when the eyeball drifted to the right, then returned rapidly.

To combat the negative effects left by the surgery that removed 85 percent of my tumor, the nurse now administered eye drops as she made her rounds every couple of hours. The drops were soothing. As my left eye dried, it felt like a bee was stinging the left corner. When the nurse made her rounds at night to give out medication, she squeezed some gooey oil-based liquid into my left eye for long-lasting lubrication. It was also prescribed that I wear a plastic cream-colored eye patch that was riddled with pinprick holes, for air circulation, over the left eye. The purpose was to protect the retina from being scratched by the pillow or bed sheets because the left eyelid would not close. Well, the patch didn't stay on very long. When I awoke the next morning, it was off, probably on the floor.

On the 23rd day following surgery, I was moved to the step-down room. I was free of everything—no more IV, ventilator, tracheotomy tube, or monitor.

Oh, no. That redheaded nurse is back! She looked like "Annie" from the musical; however, she was 30 years older and not as pleasant. And she told me, face to face, she was excited about being transferred with me to the step-down floor. *Geesh!* She drove me nuts! She always talked about her boyfriend and how she was going to corner him into marriage. Oh, no! I heard that story every morning when she helped Ed, my 89-year-old roommate, eat his breakfast. I silently admonished her: *Keep quiet! I am sick of hearing about it!*

I was very fortunate that my roommate was a great person, very special. Ed had 24 grandchildren. He always had something encouraging to say when I said something pessimistic. I was angry that the improvement process was taking so long—longer than the two weeks I had anticipated. "You are still young; be patient," Ed would say.

My dad enjoyed visiting with Ed. The elderly gentleman had played baseball in the Negro baseball leagues for the famed Kansas City Monarchs in the 1930's: the top team in the league at that time. Because my dad had been a baseball player, he was fascinated. Dad was a starting catcher for Pepperdine in California then continued to play in the minors for the Angels organization for a few years. (He was even summoned to be the pitching coach for a Cub farm club in Wichita, Kansas.) Dad loved to talk baseball. I overheard their conversations. Dad would drop a name and Ed would respond in his deep, resonant tone, "Oh, yeah! Well, ya know..." The conversation then progressed as they talked about the old leagues for hours, and I would doze off. Ed was so friendly. According to my father, he paid the night guard to sneak candy to me every evening. (The hospital had night guards to ensure that the corridors and the parking lot remained safe, since the hospital was in a gang-infested area, on the southwest side of Chicago.) Ed was moved to a Veterans hospital a few weeks later and had his leg amputated. He had a severe case of diabetes. That was the last I heard about him. God rest his soul (if he's no longer in this world). As I see it today, he was an angel.

On the 27th day following surgery, the nurses encouraged me to sit up straight in a lounge chair—cardiac chair. I was very comfortable in bed so I was displeased with this idea. "All right," I whimpered. With the help of a nurse, I twisted to the left side of the bed, facing the lounge chair that was two feet away. I was transferred as the nurse held on tightly to the front of my body. We took two slow steps then she turned my body so that my backside was aimed at the seat, and gracefully placed me down. It was a real chore just to sit up straight to control my body from slipping down to the right or to the left. "I'm going back to bed," I said. "This is too hard." The nurse then explained to me the overall benefit: "It will help your lungs drain the excess fluid." After that, I sat in that lounge chair as often as I could. Even when the food tray came, I ate the meal in the chair as the nurse moved the bed tray over. *I like this!* I wanted to take self-responsibility and do whatever I could to assist in the healing process. I even told the nurse I wanted to sleep in the chair. *I am never getting pneumonia again!*

The following afternoon, I thought I was dreaming. I was strategically munching, chewing slowly on my lunch, while five staff members walked by at a very fast pace. Suddenly, I realized that the feisty red-headed nurse had me out by the main nurses' station, in the middle of the hallway! At first I thought I was in a fog, hallucinating again. Later that day, I found out from one of the nurses that the sole purpose was to put me in contact with people. What? I just wanted to eat and be a slob in private.

Thirty days post-surgery, my eyes started to improve; I began to watch television, and that was exciting! I recalled the time in early August when I was in the ICU room. I couldn't even focus on the TV screen or read a book. According to my friend, Chris, my right eye swam like a crazed goldfish racing around. I had told myself that I would read Braille and become a success. How grateful I was now to be able to do something as simple as watch TV.

Thirty-nine days post-surgery, I was still having a hard time urinating. I had the sensation, but nothing was eliminated into the urine bottle. I still had urine retention and was catheterized again. I took a deep breath as the nurse slid a skinny tube through my penis to the bladder. Seconds later, I was relieved. *Aahh.* It had the same soothing feeling as the time I drank cold lemonade after hours of digging a trench in the hot summer sun, back in high school. I was brought to the operating room to detect the nature of the problem. My bladder was examined with the flow of dye. The results showed that my bladder was filled beyond capacity—900 cc's of fluid; the bladder can only hold 700 cc's. The urologist found that my bladder would not open when I strained. Muscles in the bladder are stimulated by impulses of the III, VII, IX and XI cranial nerves, which were in the area of the tumor. It was concluded that I would remain catheterized on an as-needed basis.

I continuously watched TV and especially enjoyed the advertisements for "hot wings" by Kentucky Fried Chicken. Boy, did that tantalize my taste buds for some real food—for chicken wings! Well, a nurse on night duty, who was very attractive, with long, thick brown hair, visited with me. We talked about various things—friends, family and music. Sally noticed that I listened to my WalkMan often. She told me that her father had a medical problem and needed care 24 hours a day. She said she grew up in Florida, attended Florida State, and now resided with her sister in Chicago's Wrigleyville area. We had very enjoyable conversations. She said I was the only one she could relate to because of my age, then 24; she was 23.

The next night, she entered the room and asked what I was thinking. That's when the monster awoke. Chicken wings! All I kept seeing on TV were advertisements for hot, spicy chicken wings! *Yummy!* I was frustrated because I couldn't satisfy my craving. Sally listened to my complaining, then left the room to tend to another patient-or so I thought. Ten minutes passed; it was about 11:00 p.m. I looked at the bed-table and there they were. Divine intervention had just occurred. Hot spicy chicken wings! I thought I was hallucinating again. Sally had ordered them from a local pizza joint and had them delivered. I was astounded. *These are real chicken wings! They even have the traditional celery!* I devoured them in no time, leaving a mess of dark-red hot sauce all over my hospital gown and bed.

The reason I said this woke up the monster was because it made me realize that eating cuisine from the outside world was so much more delicious than the bland hospital food. When friends and relatives called, I immediately ordered snacks as a prerequisite for a visit. The healing aspect: At that point, I could consume solid food and I told myself that the way to successfully heal was to eat as much as possible to provide my body with energy to make it better.

Three days elapsed. In the afternoon, Sally, the friendly nurse, stopped by my room to share a musical tape she had recorded for me. Later, I found out that was her day off. I thank god for her care, attention, and kindness.

5

A Burden of Love

Forty-eight days post-surgery, I was transferred to the rehabilitation floor for intensive rehab. I was upgraded to the normal menu schedule and became more aware of my surroundings. I was able to eat and able to rest. A nurse did not barrage me every other hour to fill my mouth with pills, check my blood pressure or my temperature. A nurse actually shut the door and turned off the lights. The most important happening, though, was the establishment of "Da Pantry": a wide variety of snacks always accessible to me.

Forty-nine days post-surgery, I awoke very early and attempted to look at the small digital clock to my right. I tried hard but I could not do it. The shapes gleamed in orange and bounced in different directions. *Where is breakfast? I do not hear anything. Here it comes!* When I began to eat, the telephone rang and I was disrupted. I had to drop all the utensils. I had to L-E-A-N back and R-E-A-C-H with my right hand to grab it. "Good morning, Darryl. How ya doing today?" "Hey, Pop!" Dad had begun to call me every morning to lift my spirits and to find out how I was. "I'm feeling great, no problems!" I had obstacles, but I did feel great! Why should I be down and make the situation worse? This was my attitude.

After breakfast, a talkative, jolly caregiver named Claire arrived and grabbed my attention with her personal touch: "Hi, sweets!" Her purpose was to make sure that each patient received the menu so they could order for the next day's meals.

At that moment, Brenda arrived, too. She had the honors to read aloud the menu selections to me. I made my choice and responded: "Times two, times two." This meant that I ordered double portions of everything, for each meal. The nurses knew that I liked to eat. *I am still hungry!* I had what was medically termed Hyperphagia, meaning that even though I ate and ate and ate, I did not feel the sensation of being full. According to the medical staff, I had a fascination for food. *Baloney! The more someone eats, the more they heal!* I had lost 40 pounds; my body was weak—it needed food to heal.

Sue, occupational therapist, soon entered. With a soft voice, she said she was going to help me take a shower, brush my teeth, shave and dress for the workday. *Oh no, I want to stay in bed and sleep!* Cautiously, the strong therapist strategically guided my inert body into a wheelchair and took me into the washroom. I took one look in the mirror and was in total shock! I couldn't believe my eyes. *Oh my gosh!* All of my muscle mass was gone. I had crazy hair; one side of my face drooped; I was broken-out and swollen. *Man, I have a long way to go!* I didn't think about the reality of the horrible situation. All I cared about was that all the exercise and lifting I had performed the past summer went for naught. I was skinny! Fragile!

I was assisted by Sue to the shower seat and I took what seemed like an everlasting shower. I enjoyed every minute of it. *No more sponge baths!* Dressed by Sue, I wore bright green shorts with a blue and green striped mock-turtleneck shirt. I looked stylish. The patients on the floor were encouraged to dress in their own garb to retain a sense of normalcy. Mom had brought me sweatpants, sweatshirts and shorts. I felt good. I was getting closer to escaping that place. The particular ensemble I wore that day was a gift from a very special friend, Gabriela Zilinski, another whirlwind in her early twenties, who had danced with my sister. Gabriela had a wide, gentle smile, though she, too, had a difficult challenge. She had been seriously injured in a head-on car collision with a drunk driver. Gabriela missed her senior prom and graduation from high school, and was told she would never dance again, which was her true love. She went through multiple surgeries and overcame them with great strides. Today, she lives in California and has recently graduated from UCLA. (By the way, she is taking ballet lessons again. How motivating!)

After Sue finished her duty, a transporter entered and wheeled me to the sixth-floor elevator bank. It was such a smooth transition, like a choreographed ballet. We descended seven flights to the rehabilitation department in the basement, where every type of rehabilitation imaginable awaited: physical therapy, occupational therapy, speech therapy, vocational therapy, cognitive testing, and radiation therapy. You name it, I had it. Here we go!

I was perturbed because of the constant waits I had to endure in the rehab reception room. It was like a typical wait at a doctor's office! I arrived at the scheduled time, but I had to wait at least 30 to 40 minutes. That's when I first knew that I was getting back to my old self. One of my pet peeves is tardiness. If you are scheduled to be somewhere at a certain time, you should be there and ready to go. If you are late, that means you are not interested in the planned event or person. *Come on, let's go!* I became impatient as I watched people who seemed to be involved with the outpatient program wander in and out of the waiting room. *I bet they were in my situation not too long ago!* Watching those people encouraged me.

Finally, I was taken to the rehab gym. I had to wait again! *Come on!* I noticed eight patients, in wheelchairs, lined up ahead of me, waiting for their chance to "perform." I peered out in front of me and hazily saw parallel bars. On the other side of the gym, there was an older patient on a wooden structure that resembled a staircase with three steps. I became envious as he stepped up and down with no problem. *I cannot wait to get to that stage.* I turned to my left and noticed a large, navy-blue wrestling mat on a one-foot-high wooden table. On the mat, two patients sat rolling two beach balls from side to side with their feet.

Hey, it is my turn! A physical therapist stopped by with a walker and put a gait belt, similar to a kidney belt that a weight lifter wears, around my waist so she would have a better grasp for control. I was slowly hoisted out of the wheelchair to a walker, a three-sided aluminum walking aid. In the rehab environment, the walker is the first step after the wheelchair. I stood unsteadily, clutching the walker as the therapist instructed me to do. She said I was so bad off that I didn't even know when I was off-balance and could not compensate.

Unsteadily, I attempted to walk. I slumped down and attempted to move my right leg forward; it shook. I did the same with the left leg, and took frequent rest breaks as I tried to maneuver to the middle of the gym, 15 feet. *Hey, Brenda!* Brenda came to watch from the sidelines. Her presence made me "Goofy," as she called me. *I am under the gun! I hope I do well!* I was sure that it was hard for Brenda to see her once-standing-taller-and-stronger brother so damaged by an out-of-control disease. I had the urge to make light of the situation, to reassure her that this was no big deal. *I will not be kept down. I can handle it!* I looked at Brenda, who observed me from the entrance 10 feet away. Out of sheer goofiness, I let go of the two bars on the walker. I raised both of my hands in the air, signaling a touchdown. *Hey, look! No hands! I am okay. See, I am still goofy!* The physical therapist panicked and quickly clasped my hands to the walker. When I reached the middle of the gym, I slowly turned step by step and I unsteadily crossed my feet back to the wheelchair, 30 feet. *Man!* It felt as though I had played a rough-and-tumble football game. I was exhausted.

Isn't it time to go back to my room? Nope. *I was wheeled by the PT* to a three-classroom-sized occupational, vocational, and cognitive therapy area. The PT transferred me onto a large mat. I tried so hard to stay upright, leaning on my arms from behind as a brace, but they would tremor and it took too much effort. I fell back and went to sleep. Sue arrived and woke me up with her kind voice. I struggled to sit upright while she placed a large red, blue and yellow beach ball on the floor in front of me. She instructed me to position my feet on the ball and roll it from side to side. I concentrated with full force. My legs shook and had little control. I tried to stay upright, but flopped to one side. *I hate this game. It's way too dangerous.* (The purpose was to re-teach balance coordination.)

All right, we are finished—or so I thought! Sue transferred me to a maroon picnic table in the middle of the room. She placed a board in front of me with eight circular chips, in slots across the board. Sue scattered the chips, which were the size of my palm—red on one side and black on the other. She instructed me to place all the chips, red side facing up, on the left side of the board, and the black sides facing up on the right side while she timed me. "Ready, go!" I did terrible, three times! *What a waste of time! Why are we sitting here doing this?* The game was to benefit my motor skills and my decision-making process.

Back on the rehab floor, I ate lunch with other patients: a mix of people in wheelchairs, walkers and canes, and others independent of any medical device. Not a word was spoken. Everybody's head was down, focused on the meal. I was confused. When my father arrived on the scene during his lunch break from his downtown office, I said, "I am in the psycho ward." I asked the nurse if we were all going to sing songs after the meal. Dad laughed. I was relieved when he assured me that this was the rehabilitation floor, not the psycho ward. He added, "That's across the street."

When the lunch hour culminated, the transporters arrived in their navy-blue jumpsuits as if they were a rescue squad or a S.W.A.T. team.

◆   ◆   ◆

Nancy, the speech therapist, maneuvered me to a round table. There I worked on speaking clearly, without the full use of my left lip. (I had 50 percent lip closure.) I was having a hard time pronouncing "F" and "B" words, and Nancy, who was deliberate and caring, instructed me to over-enunciate all the letters of the alphabet then read a paragraph from Time Magazine. "Aaah, Bee, Wee, Dee." *This is driving me nuts! Hey, I am thirsty.* I was always thirsty because my severed left facial nerve decreased my salivation. By the way, whenever I drank liquids, I had to pinch my left lips together around a straw so I wouldn't dribble.

Physical therapy again? I repeated the same exercise as the first time, but was not goofy; Brenda wasn't present.

"Darryl, wake up!" said the physical therapist, Mary, in a commanding voice! *Already?* I saw the golden gate—my wheelchair. *Ah, we made it!* Like a Robot, I turned with the guidance of the therapist then uncontrollably flopped into the wheelchair. Mary transported me to the OT, VT, PT department. *No way, not again! This is way too boring!* Sue tested me again with those round chips, then onto the mat for the crazy beach ball routine. What a pain in the butt!

A few minutes later, I was at the picnic table again, but this time I had vocational therapy, which addressed my reasoning skills with a crossword puzzle. *Mmm! I have no idea, etc....* (This was the scheduled occurrence of rehab events until my release.)

◆   ◆   ◆

All right, food! "Darryl, slow down and take smaller bites," Nancy continuously said. *Darn it! How can I eat slowly and be finished in time when I have double portions?* Mom agreed with Nancy and said that eating slowly was for my own good as Dad, Mom and Iris, my mother's friend and garden consultant, huddled around me in the day room, watching with a detective's eye. Why was I so stubborn? I followed the instructions and began to chew slowly.

Later that day, Dad told me that the Notre Dame Football team was going to play Miami, Florida, on national TV that night. *Great! I have something to look forward to!* Like my father, I was a Notre Dame fan. The nurses encouraged the patients to get together in the day room and watch TV or play cards. I prepared myself to clash with other patients who might want to view a different program. I manually wheeled off towards the day room with a three-pound can of popcorn provided by Mom's friend. To my surprise, the day room was all mine!

I scanned the various channels on the TV set. *What in the world is going on?* I simply could not scan and select the "on" switch, like I had done just one week before. I had to stoop down to get a microscopic view then scan the multi-variety of buttons. It was very difficult. *Come on! There it is!* By the way, I watched the entire game and devoured most of the popcorn. (Notre Dame won by a touchdown.)

Fifty-two days post-surgery, my mental grogginess started to lift. I actually realized that I had been administered intense radiation therapy three times a week for the past 33 days, first thing in the morning. The treatments were designed to destroy and prevent the spread of the 15 percent of my remaining tumor by decreasing the rate of division of the DNA that had created the cancer cells. Medulloblastoma in adults responds well to radiation, but can stunt development in children.

The radiation unit was in the basement, just opposite the rehab gym. The transporter parallel-parked me next to a white wall where I faced the corner entrance of the room, 20 feet away. There I sat and waited again.

It's about time! The technician finally wheeled me into the dark room. He carefully loaded me onto the table. With his baritone voice, he instructed me to lie face-down into a pillow. I felt the technician's hands as he marked targets on the back of my head with what, from the smooth texture, felt like chalk. When everything was set, the technician left to operate the linear accelerator. Five minutes later, I heard a zap—the stream of gamma rays composed of electrons, protons, and neutrons. Then complete silence; then zap; then silence; then zap again and again. No pain. After some time went by, I became excited; *maybe I will be late for physical rehab and even speech therapy. I will get some more sleep!*

Already finished? Darn! The technician arrived at the table and transferred me to the hallway to wait and wait and wait.

Each day was about the same for the following 55 days post-surgery. My right hand still shook all over the place. *Dang it! Oh well, I will get it down one day!* I tried to sit upright on an elevated mat. Simply holding my upper torso took a great deal of effort. *No control!* My body still trembled. A lesion in the cerebellum can cause uncontrollable movement. Plop! I still had to wait for what seemed like hours between each therapy session and I grew impatient. I wanted to get out of there and get going. *Why is everything taking so long?*

Throughout this ordeal, my stash of food was important to me. "Da Pantry" provided me with a sense of control—I could eat whenever I pleased, but the nurses became concerned about my voracious appetite. They confiscated my snacks and hid them in the closet. Little did they know that I paid careful attention. After I slowly gobbled up my lunch, I coaxed Dad to wheel me back to my room so I could snack some more, but I was caught and "Da Pantry" was hidden again. The battle continued. I called my parents and desperately pleaded that I needed something besides hospital food. Aunt Betty and Mom lovingly prepared a lasagna dinner and homemade cheesecake; boy, was I spoiled! The next night when the family visited, they brought the fine meal, thinking they were performing a good deed. Immediately, the nurses intercepted them. They said that I had already eaten double portions at dinner.

This is a funny, but necessary, side note. I have always loved food with a passion, especially snacks. When I was a youngster in grade school, I had the best lunches in my homeroom class. My lunch always included Hostess treats: a "Twinkie," "Ding Dong," "Suzie Q," etc. On Wednesdays, Mom went to the Wonder Bread outlet store to stock up on all the Hostess goodies at wholesale prices. One day, when I was in the sixth grade, the light came on in my head. Mom placed all the goodies under lock and key in the basement freezer. There was a glitch. Where was the key to unlock the safe? On nice spring days I rode my bike to school; it took only 20 minutes. I would be home at 3:00 and Mom would not be home until 4:00. I had an hour to search. I invited my neighborhood friends, Paul and Peter, over to help search for the "Holy Grail." The search went on for days! Finally, we found the key. With awe, we slowly opened the large vertical freezer door and out came this dense cloud. The treasure twinkled in its glorious radiance. Our eyes were wild and wide as we took notice of the names on the stack of boxes: "Ding Dongs," "Cup Cakes," "Twinkies" and "Suzy Q's." We were in ecstasy! We ate and ate—they were very tasty, even though they were frozen. When 4: 00 rolled around, we closed the freezer door and returned the key to its original secret hiding place. We came back for more the following day, but the key was gone. My mother had the smarts and knew with whom she was dealing. Again we searched and searched. The key was found again. It was promptly hidden again! This cat-and-mouse game went on periodically for two years until I absolutely couldn't find the key again. To this day, Mom will never tell me where she hid it!

◆   ◆   ◆

Sixty-one days post-surgery: I rose early, before anybody was around. *Hey, come on! Get going!* With Sue, I went through the morning routine of getting ready for the rehabilitation day. At the time, I was in the final phase of taking the cognitive IQ tests that began three days post-surgery. Frustrated as I was, I tried to entertain myself along with the cognitive therapist. "For a multiple-choice question you do not know, bang your fingertips on the desk. The index finger represents A, the middle B, the ring C and the pinky Dthe one that hurts the longest is the answer."

The head cognitive therapist who directed the program shared my results with the family in early October. I did terribly; the therapist concluded that I had cognitive deficits. I wasn't surprised. When the tests were administered in early September, I wasn't in the mood to take them. I learned that damage to the cerebellum is a hindrance to knowledge and social language.

Sixty-two days post-surgery, Todd Pruesker, a very good friend from high school who resembled a young John Candy, came for a visit. *How on earth did he know I was down here?* Todd, being sensitive to my pleas to contribute to "Da Pantry," brought a bag of potato chips. He was with me in the vocational therapy room while I performed the checkerboard game. *Poor Todd! He is probably bored stiff.*

As I was being wheeled back to my room, Todd following behind, I was caught by surprise. Wheelchair aerobics had started in the day room. Six other patients, three in wheelchairs and three in regular chairs, imitated the instructor by flaring their arms out and over their heads. It was like a revival concert, but trite music played via an out-moded cassette deck. *Here I am doing wheelchair aerobics! Is that manly?* I was embarrassed because Todd and I had often gone head-to-head on the high school football field and tempers flared. To relieve the tension, I joked. I commanded Todd to participate, thinking there was no way he would. To my pleasant surprise, he grabbed a chair and joined the group. I laughed and Todd laughed along with me.

Sixty-six days post-surgery. With the therapist holding on, I walked with the walker the entire length of the gym and back in 45 minutes. *Yeah!* I made some progress, but was drained.

Sixty-nine days post-surgery. During cognitive therapy that afternoon, Sue said I would soon be able to prepare a "snack" or some kind of cuisine and asked what I wanted to make. Well, I was still stuck on Eggplant Parmesan and remembered Mom's recipe. *Ha, I surprised her. She did not know I was this sophisticated. She probably thought that I wanted to boil a hot dog or make grilled cheese.* Sue said she would buy the necessary ingredients so we could make the delicious meal.

Seventy days post-surgery. My great friend, Paul, arrived as always for a visit around 9:00 p.m. He did the majority of the talking, and he often made me laugh with his fish stories. I loved the contact. We were having fun, or so I thought, but this time I noticed pain in his eyes. It was very difficult for him to see me in bad shape, just as it would have been for me if he were in my shoes. Before the surgery, I was always the motivator to Paul, the "get-up-and-go" guy. *Now I was down.*

Seventy-eight days post-surgery, the radiation treatments officially ended. The protocol was sectioned off into four areas: Whole brain, 21 treatments in 29 days; neck and spine—down to the middle of the back, 24 treatments for 34 days; lower back, 24 treatments for 34 days; back of the brain, posterior fossa, 31 treatments for 46 days. The total exposure was 5500 RADs (Radiation Absorbed Dose of ionizing radiation). The human body can only take 6500 RADs to one area.

As I was wheeled from the room, I heard the technician's loud voice telling me that the treatments had gone well! *All right!* However, there were side effects: dysfunction to the hypothalamus, thyroid and pituitary glands, which regulate all hormonal activity in the body. Radiation also caused fatigue and dysphagia (trouble with swallowing) as an ulcer developed on my epiglottis, the upper part of my larynx (voice box). The epiglottis prevented food and liquid from seeping into my lungs when I swallowed and created hoarseness in my voice. I developed a severe case of acne and facial discoloration that was treated with a special cream. An infection erupted in my urinary tract which eventually cleared up with antibiotics. Radiation to the whole brain can also cause long-term cognitive and memory problems which, fortunately, did not affect me. Well, eight years later, I have to read on a regular basis to stimulate my mind. *Hey! Where are my keys? Carelessness!*

After dinner that night, I relaxed in the hospital bed, but then my scalp began to itch. I looked at my hand! *Wow! My hair is falling out by the handful and it just grew back after it was shaved for surgery!* Later that evening, a good friend and high school sweetheart, Holly Steffens, stopped in for a visit. "Do you want to see something crazy?" I rubbed my hand in my hair. "Look, my hair is falling out." She replied in a shrill manner: "Well, then, don't keep rubbing it out." But I was fascinated; I kept on rubbing and rubbing, until I was bald.

I thought I would look good bald, but that night I had a nightmare about baldness. I was in a futuristic health club run and owned by the hospital. It was like a space capsule with no gravity as I floated horizontally on the stationary bike, I looked at the reflection from the mirrors around the club. *I look terrible bald, especially with all those bumps on my head!* I sapped out of the dream. *So much for thinking I would look good bald!*

I was still concerned the next morning, and when the floor nurse entered the room, I asked, "Do I look stupid bald?" She didn't say a word. "How long will it take for my hair to grow back?" The nurse replied that it would probably take six months. "What, six months? That is way too long."

During all this tension, my parents remained very calm and positive. Mom said that an outside influence helped her sleep through the night. This was the whistle and the smooth hum of a distant freight train that clanged along the "Soo" line tracks 15 miles west of our house. Mom said it had a soothing effect on her, reminding her of her young, care-free life in California.

Eighty days post-surgery. Saturday morning, Linda, the nurse, entered with the walker and gait belt. *No way! This is Saturday!* We strolled down the hallway with her close assistance, a grand total of 100 feet along the corridor and back in an hour's time. When we made it back into the room, I immediately went to bed and fell asleep.

A couple of hours passed and Linda re-entered. I refused to get up and go. She said that sitting around feeling sorry for myself would not help my recovery. "You will probably never walk again!" That did it! *First of all, I am not feeling sorry for myself! Second, you do not know me! Let's go!* I angrily agreed and swiftly turned to the left side of the bed. Linda transferred my determined yet frail body into the walker. She buckled the gait belt and we were slowly walked up and down the corridor twice, 200 feet. Motivation by the patient plays a critical role in rehabilitation when there is head trauma or head injury. The second day after surgery, Dad had asked Dr. Stone what the prognosis would be. The doctor said he did not know; it depended on how hard the patient worked.

Eighty-three days post-surgery. I woke up, rubbed my eyes, then glared at the yellow poster board calendar straight in front of my view which Lisa, a former girlfriend, had made. *Wow! It is October 14th. Where did the time go?*

One hundred days post-surgery: a Halloween that I will always remember. It was a huge production and well advertised, so Brenda, Vicki and my parents attended. My sister brought a costume for me to wear—a gold-metallic wig with a bright orange shirt. My mother said I looked like a pumpkin as I was swollen from the side effects of steroids used to decrease swelling of the brain during radiation. The holiday was celebrated during the lunch hour in the day room, and the entire staff—therapists, nurses, and doctors—dressed in costume. The head rehabilitation doctor came through as a ballerina and wore a pink tutu.

My room was like a thick jungle with orange and black streamers dangling from the ceiling. Among the streamers was an array of scary Halloween cut-outs. *What a sign of support!* Vicki and Brenda, together, had decorated the room while I was absent. The decorations remained for a few days longer. Every time I was brought back to the room via a wheelchair, or if a nurse entered, I glowed with pride. *See, somebody loves me!* Support was so important!

One hundred and two days post-surgery. I was in the cognitive therapy room that afternoon finishing up a writing exercise. I glanced up. *Hey! Mr. O'Donnell!* He was a senior VP at Merrill Lynch, whom I had talked to periodically about economic trends. He looked at me with a tentative smile and said: "Hello." He dropped off a small square gift and dashed out. When I see Mr. O'Donnell today, he can't believe how much progress I have made. He says he thought I had no chance to go on—yet live. *Yeah, I made it!!!*

One hundred and four days post-surgery. The physical therapy session was outdoors. *What a beautiful fall day.* The PT provided a light jacket and we traipsed into a courtyard laid with red bricks. I walked very slowly with a walker, 100 feet. *Damn, it's still a struggle!* I was resting under a large maple tree that gleamed in orange. "Will I ever walk again independently?" I asked. I was feeling low at this point, even questioning my spirit! "Will I always be bald? Will I be able to walk?" I asked the therapist over and over until she finally said, "You might not improve; it's all up to you." I made no comment—I just soaked it in. *Let's go!* Then we really began to walk. "Come on, let's do it again!"

One hundred and five days post-surgery. The attending nurse shocked me that Friday morning with the news that I would go home for the weekend. I was apprehensive. I sighed and told myself that it was too bad things had to change. By now, I liked the hospital, attention, activity and safety. I didn't want to leave. The experience of leaving the safety net and going out into the real world was scary!

My parents arrived that evening and signed the weekend release form. With the help of a hospital aide, Dad guided the wheelchair down a one-foot step backwards, with me in it, at a 40-degree decline grade. I was squeezed into the front seat of the maroon four-door '89 Oldsmobile. Was that an experience! We took the Kennedy, a six-lane expressway that links the city to the western suburbs. The drive was comparable to a video game being played with space ships flying at you. The headlights from cars traveling in the opposite direction glared, and red back lights gleamed from cars in front. All I could see were the lights, not the shapes. *Everything is so bright; even the billboards! Everything is going by so quickly. Why am I in the front seat while my mother is in the back?*

When we approached the first toll booth near O'Hare Field, Dad asked me to gather up the 40 cents change to pay the toll. He handed over his coin pouch and I fumbled through it for the correct combination of coins. A dime, nickel and a quarter! *That was easy!* He was delighted that I was able to do it. *What is the big deal? He was highly influenced by the negative results of the cognitive testing, but I knew it would be no problem!*

My family cautiously handled my stay. My loving mother prepared a very special dinner that evening. The entire family had rib steak with an herb salad, a specialty of my mother's, plus a steamy baked potato. *Boy, what a treat! This sure beats the hospital food!* What was really a pleasant surprise was the African lobster tail. *For me only! Unbelievable!*

I actually ate the meal slowly and chewed and chewed and chewed before I swallowed. The dinner was superb (especially because it was made with so much love).

That night I went to bed in my own room. With the walker and the gait belt, Dad guided me through the kitchen to the hallway. I rubbed up against a dried-flower arrangement and petals descended all over the floor. *Sorry, Dad!* Dad folded up the walker to carry it with him. Sitting on my rump, backwards, I went up the 14-step staircase. Dad followed to the top of the stairs, then unfolded the walker, and I was ready to motor. We turned to the left and made it to my room. I flipped the switch. My room looked the same, only cleaner: twin beds with red, white and blue spreads, on a red shag rug. A bookshelf with three drawers separated the beds. The side walls were blue, while the north wall was papered white and decorated with a story-line of a pirate and his treasure, with matching window shades. A slightly slanted ship captain's desk stood in the left corner. My room hadn't changed since I was in grade school.

Dad told me to hold still as he pulled back the covers. A few moments later, he assisted me from behind to the bed, two feet. He helped me turn 180-degrees with the walker, and I sat on the bed, then moved over perpendicularly. On my back, with my legs in the air, I changed into sweatpants. Before the long sleep, Dad squeezed the oil-based lubricant in my left eye. "Thanks, Dad." He tuned off the lights and reminded me that the urinal was just to the right of the bed.

Twice, in the middle of the night, I awoke with incredible heartburn. I rang a cowbell that took the place of the nurses' call-button to signal for help. Mom had been creative. Unlike the hospital, which would take 30 minutes or longer, there was an instant response. Mom flicked on the light switch, and I described the fire that was raging through my chest. She quickly went downstairs to the kitchen to get the light-blue bottle of Mylanta. She dripped the creamy pink liquid into a tablespoon and fed me. *What a relief!* The fire was out moments later.

Saturday morning I felt hesitant, not sure what to do. I was confused in my own room and felt lost as I got myself ready for a sponge bath with Mom providing the necessary tools. I still don't recall the early-morning events, but I distinctly remember that it was a beautiful fall day. We live in a heavily wooded suburb with a variety of wild game that roam the area: deer, opossum, raccoon, squirrels, etc. To the left of our neighborhood is 20 acres of flood plain: the Des Plaines River Valley. Across the river is the Lincolnshire Marriott Resort, situated on 200 acres of land with an 18-hole golf course.

That Saturday morning, Dad opened the sliding glass door. He managed to tilt the wheelchair at a 40-degree angle, backwards, with me in it, down one step to a large cement block that was ready to collapse, due to the neighborhood chipmunks having turned the block into public housing. Beyond the patio is a small lawn with an abundance of trees that limit the sunlight filtering through during the summer and fall. *Wow! This is so beautiful!* The sky was clear blue and the sun shone brightly. The temperature was perfect. *What a day! This sure does beat the hospital!* The sun permeated my back with its warmth, seeming to say, "Welcome back! Where have you been?" I sat back in wonderment, taking a deep breath and sighing. I gazed at the sky through streaks of fall-colored leaves and turned to peek through the back woods and absorb nature's greatness. *God, thanks for allowing me to witness this.* I had seen that view many times before, but never with so much appreciation. I remained in that position for half the day.

During the mid-afternoon, my parents took me for an excursion around the neighborhood. I was embarrassed that the neighbors could see me in my current condition. I wanted to hide.

Sunday morning, on the trip back to the hospital, I felt very ambivalent. I'd had a tremendous experience, but a large part of me looked forward to going back to the safe haven of the hospital.

That night, back in my hospital bed, I looked at the large yellow calendar and noticed that I would be officially released in seven days—114 days post-surgery

In early November, 1990, Carol, my case coordinator, told my parents that my rehabilitation therapy should be continued at an inpatient rehabilitation center after I was released from the hospital. She said I would be a burden on the family if I went home, because I would probably stay in my present situation for good: relying on a wheelchair; unable to prepare a meal on my own so that I could feed myself; needing assistance to go to the bathroom to wash or bathe, needing help getting off the toilet; requiring assistance to my bed and lubricating my left eye; needing my clothes to be picked out for the next day so I could dress myself; needing to be driven everywhere since I was unable to drive on my own. She highly recommended that I enter the Rehabilitation Institute of Chicago (RIC) at Northwestern University Medical Center. Mom did not like the idea, because I would be away from home and would feel abandoned. She stood firm and told the coordinator that I was coming home! Yes, I might be a burden, but it would be a burden of love. My family was happy to have me come back home. I was their son and Brenda's brother. My parents then embarked on a search for an outpatient rehabilitation center closer to home.

As Mom and Dad made decisions, Barbara, the hospital social worker, told them that the only outpatient rehabilitation center in the area was in Kenosha, Wisconsin, 40 miles away. Luckily, a nurse on the floor overheard their discussion and gave them a pamphlet about an outpatient rehabilitation center only 20 minutes away—practically in our back yard: the Rehabilitation Achievement Center in Wheeling. In the meantime, my Aunt Betty and Uncle Dick worked overtime to offer love and support. For example, they visited the Center with my parents for the sole purpose of meeting the therapists to learn what their rehabilitation program included. Their first investigation was favorably influenced by the fact that the rehabilitation center had a transportation unit to offer patients rides to and from home. The personable feeling they received from the Case Coordinator, Beth Fazio, reinforced the decision. I could be as close to a normal life as possible. *I can live at home!* However, a major concern of the immediate family remained: "How can Darryl be assisted getting dressed and fed in the morning?" My parents both worked full-time. They left early in the morning, usually 6:30 a.m. At the outset, my parents actively contemplated hiring a nurse from an in-home healthcare agency. We were blessed again as Beth came to the rescue. She said that RAC could make adjustments: They could provide an on-staff nurse to assist with dressing, grooming, and breakfast preparation then furnish a ride to the Center, through December, until my strength increased. My sister would then take over the duties in the morning. According to Ms. Fazio, I would be semi-independent. So, the decision was made by me and my parents, along with the wisdom of Aunt Betty and Uncle Dick, that I would rehabilitate at RAC.

Back at the hospital, Dad talked excitedly about this wonderful center. His tone became most animated when he mentioned that they challenged their patients with the use of computers in therapy. Dad liked the idea because I would be re-familiarized with the technology I had worked with at Merrill Lynch. He also related that there was a young man about my age who lived in Lincolnshire and received rehabilitation at the Center. The decision was made. *Hold on!* I still had to be interviewed by Beth Fazio. As I sat waiting after lunch in the day room at the hospital, I heard my name being called. I turned my head to the right. A bright-eyed, attractive woman in her mid-thirties greeted me with a big smile. *Life and vigor! Now I will pay attention!*

6

Take Two and Hit to the Right

November 13, 1990. The hospital finally released me. *It is time to beat this cancer thing!* I started to become more acclimated to my surroundings—I was actually re-hatching.

During a very strenuous time, I remained calm and collected. Why? My mother and father were my coaches to focus on the bright side and help me exude confidence. My family and I were not concerned about the medical facts or jargon. We focused more on the recovery aspect: getting back on my feet and returning to work. Also, we, as a family, were going to try to put things back into working order and learn to deal with the challenges that faced us in a very normal and constructive manner. In other words, we worked to live every day to the best of our ability and most of all, have fun with it.

November 14, 1990: The Rehabilitation Achievement Center wanted to evaluate me that morning, so my father did not go to work. He wanted to be sure I made it off to the Center safely while my mother and sister each went off to their place of work.

It was interesting to wake up in the morning and greet the day in my own room. *I made it! What a relief!* (I made it back home; I was out of the hospital). I turned my head to the right to see the time on the large green and black digital clock. The clock was on a three-level, book-shelved dresser that separated the two beds. The images of the time display still bounded out of control. *How strange!* I performed the same maneuver as in the hospital. I closed my right eye to block out the images of my swimming eye then focused with my left eye.

It was 6:00 a.m. I yawned, staring at the ceiling. *Hey, where are the tiles to count?* I was apprehensive about being home again. *Will I be safe in this new environment?* As I lay there, I decided that I needed assistance into the bathroom so I jiggled the cowbell.

I shakily lifted my hand from the pillow and greeted my father. "Good morning." *Aaahrrrrr* We had always greeted each other in the morning with a growl, so why change now? Dad brought the walker with the gait belt and fastened it around my waist (the gait belt quickly became part of my wardrobe, as common as underwear). I slowly turned and made sure that I had a firm grip on the walker then rose as Dad pulled up on the gait belt. When I became stable, Dad guided me like a puppeteer across the room to the doorway. There I turned to the left. I meticulously ambulated four feet into the yellow bathroom. I cautiously turned and sat down in a regular wooden chair that didn't have any armrests, directly facing the sink. *Hey, Dad, you were thinking!* Dad scooted the chair until I was at the edge of the white basin. I glanced into the mirror and saw the reflection of my "Jekyll and Hyde" fat face riddled with acne. *Mmm! I better not stare too long; the mirror might crack!* I opened my brown drawer at the left, grabbed the toothbrush and tube of toothpaste and prepared for the activity. As I leaned into the sink and brushed, Dad reminded me not to splatter toothpaste all over the mirror. *Great! A real toothbrush, not those bristle-pad toothbrushes I had to use in the hospital. Yea!* Brushing my teeth was difficult because my left lip drooped. *Oh, well.* I pulled up the cheek with my left hand and brushed. *Why should I brush there anyway? I can't smile all the way across! Well, I might be able to someday!*

I also shaved, *on my own with a blade!* Shaving was a really difficult task because my vision had been altered. It was very difficult to judge the angles of my face, especially the left side. My left eye would not move; I couldn't simply glance. I had to guess by feeling the angles around the left side of my face. *I think that's the jaw!*

When I finished with the shaving, I arose from the chair with the aid of a walker and my father. I was amazed that I was even able to take a shower. That was a concern of mine about returning home: *will I be able to take a shower and not fall and hurt myself?* That problem was resolved. Two weeks prior to my official release from the hospital, Dad had a plumber install a grab-bar in the bathtub, a shower seat and a flexible shower head with a long flexible hose.

We turned to face the tub, three feet away. I scaled over the edge of the tub, four feet high, and braced my left hand on the tiled wall to assist with stabilization. Once in the tub, I grabbed the bar and slowly sat on the shower seat. I wanted to wake up, so I purposely kept the water on the cool side.

"Hey, Dad, I am done!" I was shivering from the cold water as cool air circulated. Dad hurried into the washroom and provided a towel. After I dried off, I slowly rose and repeated the process it had taken to enter the tub, only opposite. With the walker and the assistance of my dad, I sat on the toilet seat at the left and put on my undergarments, sweats and a stylish sweatshirt.

When I was ready, the next task was to get downstairs, a grand total of 14 steps. Dad was perplexed about what to do. "Don't worry, Dad, it will be easy. Remember what I used to do when I was a little guy?" I was so sure and confident that I had the right idea. *No problem. I will sit on my behind and slide down, step by step, instead of sliding head-first like I did when I was a toddler. Aah, that reminds me.*

When I was five years old, I had surgery for a double hernia. The day after the surgery, in the summer of 1971, Mom was given instructions by the doctor that I should keep quiet for 24 hours and avoid going up the stairs. She cautiously drove home from the hospital, trying very hard to avoid the bumps in the road. Afterwards, I was resting in the rocking chair in the family room next to the sliding glass door. My mother went upstairs since I had fallen asleep. I soon awoke and seized the opportunity: I immediately went outside to play. When I came back inside the house, I walked up the stairs, then slid down head first, and then ran outside to play some more until Mom found me. I was hauled in to find out if there was any harm done, but luckily, the stitches stayed in place. I had to sit in the corner in the family room until Dad got home from work—all day! *I could not be kept down then and I will not be kept down now!* The early signs? *Mmm!*

Well, the time came. It was just like getting ready to go off to day-care. I was downstairs in the kitchen eating my cereal when the doorbell rang. My father, in his strong, friendly voice, said: "Good morning!" It was the van driver, named Jan. I was placed in the wheelchair and wheeled to the front door. Dad was faced with another dilemma: He had to figure out a way to transport the wheelchair, with me in it, from the front doorway to the front porch, a one-foot drop. The matter was discussed between Dad and the van driver as I waited again impatiently. Dad recalled what the medical assistant had taught him about how to transport a wheelchair down a step, with me in it. *Oh, man, no way! This is dangerous!* I was turned backwards and tilted up 40 degrees, then tugged down a step. After the thrill ride, we had to do it again, this time a three-foot drop from the porch to the sidewalk. AH! Now Dad tilted me at an angle and wheeled me down the sidewalk, 48 feet, to the blue van parked in the driveway. I was transferred, very professionally, by Jan, via the gait belt, to the front passenger seat. Since it was a van, there was a very steep rise from the wheelchair to the front seat—four feet. *No problem! I have strong arms and a good grip! 1, 2, 3, aah,* plop. I could tell that Jan knew what she was doing, especially rapidly folding and packing the wheelchair into the back of the van. Then Jan jumped into the van and backed out of the driveway.

I was nervous about going to a new place so I posed a pressing question to Jan: "Are the therapists at AAC going to help me walk again?" Jan assured me that the personnel at the Center would definitely get me back on my feet again. I was put at ease and became positive that I would make it back; there was no doubt in my mind. I hadn't had any psychological setbacks, and I looked at rehabilitation as a challenge—a means to really accomplish something.

As we drove through the early morning traffic, Jan turned on the radio to an FM rhythm and blues station. The music was very enjoyable and further decreased my apprehension. Jan was down-to-earth and friendly, seeming to really care. As we conversed, I found out that Jan loved catfish, broiled or fried. My theoretical mind clicked on. *I am so dependent on my family to provide for me. I am back to the basics of a child's needs and wants. I have a long way to go, but I will do it! Go with the Mike Ditka mind-set!* I had a vision that when I left RAC, I would be my same previous physical self. *Hey, I am not helpless!*

We arrived at RAC at around 10 minutes to eight. *Boy, this feels weird, going somewhere new.* I was nervous about being exposed to a group of strangers. Would I be accepted? The Center was in a medium-sized one-story office complex, which was like a strip mall, with many other tenants. The driver came around and opened the door, eased me into the wheelchair, then pushed me up the slight incline in the sidewalk, 20 feet to the front door. Jan then opened the door, squeezed me into the vestibule, and opened another door to the Center. *Here I am! Hi, I am Darryl Didier!* I had a chance to see the other patients as they waited in the homey seating area by the front entrance. There were three medium-sized brown couches in the waiting area, one next to the north wall, one on the east side, next to the office windows, and one just opposite, to square off the room. Directly in the right-hand corner was a large jug of water and just to the left of that, a closet for coats. Although five people were present, not one word was spoken, and I surely was not ready to speak to anyone or do anything entertaining.

As I waited, I noticed that the other patients were all very different in terms of their physical ability. One middle-aged, heavyset woman sat in a wheelchair. A middle-aged gentleman was sitting on the couch with a four-pronged cane (a quad-cane) placed next to him, while another male, in his early twenties, who sat in a wheelchair, had a computerized speaking device. He couldn't talk. *A good looking kid; life can be so unfair!* Another male, in his mid-twenties, walked in through the front door unaided. He was free as a bird! I wanted to be like him, because he was getting wonderful praise for his accomplishments. I was jealous. *Just wait and see what I am going to do!* I wanted to emulate that guy. What a sense of recovery. *This place must help. Let's go!*

Here I was in an unfamiliar place and I was supposed to mingle with strangers. How could I make a good impression on them when I was slumped in a wheelchair, bald, and one side of my face drooped? Obviously, I had a very poor self-image at that time.

The therapists all rushed out of a meeting room, which was behind closed doors, and spread out in all directions. Small slips of paper on the counter-top of the administration credenza were custom-tailored schedules for every client. I had my slip taped to the left armrest of my wheelchair by Karen, head nurse on staff, who would be assisting me in the morning for two months. Of average height, with lots of curly brown hair, Karen was very warm, with a soft, gentle voice. We became friends instantly because she treated me like a normal human being; she spoke to me with respect. Karen laughed with me at my little comments, or when she tried to put my shoes on over my very swollen feet—a result of the steroids.

My day was filled with every conceivable kind of therapy: 1) Physical—rehabilitation was needed to increase my control of the overall muscular system, to walk independently; 2) Vocational to increase my mental concentration, and improve my handwriting skills; 3) Occupational, to increase my employability; 4) Psychological, to cope with the situation, but there wasn't a problem to cope with in my case; 5) Speech, to increase my oral communication structure with enunciation. Well, that was to be expected. I needed therapy—except for one, I thought: the psychologist. I was perplexed. *I'm fine. What is the big deal? There are no problems; just challenges.* For example, I was not angry at life or at God. *I loved life before and I love life now. I will not be denied!* That way of thinking had been the source of my strength and drive. Yes, there was a large amount of work to be done, but I had faith in my ability and in God. I knew I would make it back and take advantage of what life really had to offer. I want to mention that in my high school and early college days, I took life for granted. I was blessed with many talents, athletically, but I didn't develop my full potential because I didn't work hard enough; I lacked dedication. For example, I had great natural ability to perform well in football and baseball, but it all ended during my early college years when I didn't make the cut for the teams. I walked away dejected and gave up on my dream of playing ball. Instead of working harder and harder, I stopped practicing. "I should have..." That's the worst phrase ever conjured up in a person's mind. One should work as hard as possible for what he/she wants to attain. I shouldn't have given up so easily. That thought still made me very angry with myself. I did not work hard enough! *Get out there and do it! Unbelievable. Now I have a second chance and I had better work hard with dedication and determination!*

Rehabilitation was truly a full-time job, eight hours a day, five days a week. It was real LIFE. As my adopted uncle and neighbor Uncle Keith always said: "You do not have anything if you do not have your health." That statement really hit home. He also believed: "Your body is a temple from God. Treat it that way."

Before the events began that morning, I was greeted very warmly by my case coordinator, Beth Fazio, as she scrunched down to my left and gazed up at me. She welcomed me and explained that I was in good hands, providing assurance that they would see to it that progress would be made. A double dose of hope was furnished, unlike what most of the medical staff offered in the hospital.

During the first morning, I was under the care of Karen. She wheeled me to the first therapy session on my schedule. After each hourly session, Karen would enter the office and scoot me along the corridors in my black and red sporty wheelchair to the next scheduled event. The goal that morning was to introduce me to the new system, and to the location of each therapist. It was mind-boggling. *How am I going to remember all these names?*

Finally a break and I was hungry! I'd brought my own lunch, brown-bagging the feast made by Mom in the morning. Gosh, here I was, 24 years old and my mom was making my lunch. I was a dependent kid again. It was very hard to go from dependence to independence and then back to dependence again. I'd had a very promising future while striving for financial independence. With one unexpected curve ball, I'd become dependent, like a small child learning to walk again. Fortunately, though, I kept the 24-year-old mental capacity, and since our family is very close, it was not a difficult situation. *Have fun with it!*

My supportive sister came to RAC for a visit to see how I was adjusting to the new environment. It was great seeing a familiar face among total strangers. RAC encouraged visits by family and friends.

Lunch was eaten in the kitchen, which resembled a regular kitchen with all the appliances—even a microwave and counter tops, in order to introduce the patients to the challenges of preparing a meal. I sat at one of the two folding tables, each of which was set for six clients, and again, I was not in the mood to meet anyone. I was seated across from an exceedingly frail, wispy-haired young woman, about 21 years old. Her name was Maureen Mulkrone—a good Irish name. Maureen was admitted to the Center a day before I was. In the summer of her junior year in college, Norberts, in Depeere, Wisconsin, she was diagnosed with viral meningo-encephalitis, a virus that causes the brain to swell. Since the virus had concentrated in the cerebellum, it damaged her motor nerves. (In Maureen's case, her doctors don't know the long-term outcome, since she has beaten the odds. Eight years later, she is not supposed to be able to walk as she does, aided by a walker; she is not supposed to be taking swimming classes or even to be working at a college library as a researcher for professors.)

Brenda and I were arguing over the gender of Jan, the van driver, who had driven me to rehab that morning. I thought for certain that the driver was a he, and my sister said the person was a she. After 20 minutes of bickering, my sister convinced me that the driver was a woman. *Oh!* Maureen got a kick out of the light-hearted bantering between brother and sister. *Hey, somebody accepts me. I can't believe it! A friend!* At that very moment, I noticed Maureen's doting smile and her enjoyment sitting with me. I was accepted and that felt so good. Once accepted, who couldn't tell what I would do—but in a respectful manner.

Maureen, who craved chocolate, had a very high-pitched voice and spoke haltingly. She was a godsend, an angel. We sat across from each other during lunch and constantly made jokes during the year we were at the Center. I loved to make her laugh; I would do anything. For example, I would try to mimic a Scottish brogue and recite that I was from "Scotland Yard, in Scotland." Maureen would always correct me, saying, "Scotland Yard is in England." She was very knowledgeable about geography and told me emphatically that I was wrong. Since I wanted to give her a hard time, I kept on debating her knowledge. Both of us got a big kick out of our lunchtime escapades. This reinforced to me the importance of laughter and self-directed humor. Take things lightly. (By the way, Maureen achieved her goal of receiving her Masters degree in Library Science in the summer of '95.)

Again, I loved to make Maureen laugh and that, in turn, made me laugh, which was very therapeutic (the Darryl Didier method!). Laughter made us forget our problems and enjoy the time. Lunch ended, my sister left, and I returned to work. Three more therapy sessions awaited me.

After the rehabilitation day was finished (4:00 p.m.), I was driven home in the RAC van with two other clients who lived in the same 30-mile radius. (The transportation department consisted of five vans that were organized regionally.) I was in the worst condition, so I had the pleasure of being assisted into the front seat; the other two sat in the back, one independent, and the other transferred from her wheelchair. During the tour of southern Lake County, the other two clients and the driver, Jan, carried on a conversation. *Mmmm! They seem to be long-time friends!* Thirty minutes later, the first client, a man in his mid-forties, was dropped off at a beautiful home with a lot of trees in suburban Buffalo Grove. He simply slid the van door open and scooted out without an aide. *Mmmm!* Moments later, as we backed out, I glared with

envy at the client through my passenger window. He walked effort-
lessly to his mailbox, then up the driveway. I poked my nose against
the window until the van turned the corner to the right, and he was
out of view. *I am going to be like that one day!* We drove 30 minutes to
drop off the next client, a woman, also in her mid-forties. We pulled
into her short driveway to a quaint one-story, bluish-colored house
that had evergreens laced along the sidewalk and the remnants of a vegetable garden on the right. This time, Jan leaped out first. I turned
back. The rear door was ajar while Jan pulled out a folded wheelchair,
and I heard the sounds of metal hitting metal. Jan transferred the
woman from the van to the wheelchair and took her to the front door.
She was greeted by her husband as I gaped. *We all need somebody!*

I was finally home, sweet home. Jan had the terror of a task of safely
guiding me, with the walker, through the garage to the back door,
holding the gait belt. *Knock, knock. Who's there? Hey, is anybody home?*
Jan then knocked on the door and Mom greeted me warmly. *Hah, I
made it!* Jan cleverly lifted me up one step to the inside of the house.
That first night, I went to the kitchen table and had a cup of coffee
while I read a business magazine. Well, I tried, but my eyes would not
focus together. *Dang it!*

The main thing—I was home. Dinner was the same as always: Dad
returned home from his commute from his downtown Chicago office
at around 6:45 p.m.; Mom, Dad, myself, and, on occasion, my sister
would join us if she wasn't working. *Hey, something is different!* This
time I had the privilege of sitting at the head of the gleaming cherry
wood table instead of Dad, who was seated in my sister's chair, to my
right. I peered through the mini-jungle of a centerpiece, made by my
mother, and could faintly see her, on the other side. *Geez, why am I sitting here?* Mom explained that it would be easier for me to sit at the
head of the table than having to scrunch up at one of the two sides.

After dinner, Dad assisted me, with the walker and the gait belt,
from the kitchen to the base of the stairs, approximately 20 feet. I han-

dled the stairs well, going up step by step, holding onto the railing while Dad was behind me holding onto my gait belt. We managed it.

I sat in the chair in front of the sink. *I do not want to brush my teeth. Why? I can't even smile!* One look in the mirror: I was still broken-out and still bald. *Aah!* I washed my face then spread on a lotion recommended by the nurses to help clear up the acne. *This lotion does not work. I need some Clinique cleanser*, which I frequently used before the surgery.

Dad assisted, with a firm grip on the gait belt as I hobbled into my room. I stopped. He pulled back the blankets on the second bed, next to the window. I hobbled over to it with the walker and plunged into it. *All right, let's go! Adios!* As I was lying in bed, face up, Dad lined my left eye with an oil-based eye drop. (This routine went on for two months, the length of time I was still reliant on the wheelchair and walker.) I was, and am, a very active sleeper. According to my sister, whose room was next to mine, I frequently talked, tossed and turned in my sleep. Since I was no longer accustomed to the size of the bed, I fell out that night. Using all my might, I laboriously rose. Then I scrambled to latch onto the corner of the mattress to hurriedly pull myself back into bed. *Whew! I made it back without having to be peeled off the floor or disturbing my parents*, or so I thought. My mother heard the thump and hurried into my room to make sure I was all right. *Gosh, Mom can hear everything!* (Even when I was a little kid, trying to secretively sneak a cookie out of the cookie jar, oh so quietly.)

The next day at 7:00 a.m., Mom entered to wake me. This time Brenda assisted me to the washroom for the morning preparations. Again, I sat on a small wooden chair as I brushed my teeth and kind of shaved. The doorbell rang. It was Karen, from RAC, who was going to assist with my early morning needs for two months.

Karen helped me put on my stylish clothing ensemble—a sweatshirt and a pair of sweatpants. She then put my socks on my very swollen feet and squeezed them into my shoes. We both laughed at the difficulties. *Ah, finally!* When I was ready, we embarked downstairs. Karen was nervous about this, but I calmly sat on my rump and slid down, step by step, all 14 of them.

When we made it to the kitchen, I filled up on cereal. Karen grabbed the lunch that Mom had prepared for me out of the refrigerator, and placed it in a black vinyl sack with Velcro to close it. Then she loaded me into the back of her car, folded the walker and put it in the trunk. Off to the Center!

When we arrived in the parking lot, Karen scooted out of the car and told me to wait for her while she went to get my wheelchair. The wheelchair was stored at the Center, which made sense, because I used it there more often than at home. Karen transferred me into the wheelchair, and away we went to the entrance. This arrangement continued for two months, until mid-December.

On November 21, Dr. Kent asked me why I was so confident, and I related the story of my automobile accident. "I went through this before; I will come back again." I also explained that I had the support of my interior unit—my family, who had a great influence on my life. Dad was the motivator: "Go get 'em. Take two and hit to the right. Pick yourself up!" Dad had his experience with adversity when he was 18 and was drafted into the Army Air Corps during WW II. He was washed out to be a ball turret gunner, with a five-percent survival rate, beneath a B-17 bomber at 30,000 feet. He flew 35 bombing missions from England to Germany. He often told me, "You had to do what you had to do." I inherited that attitude. As for Mom, she suffered from severe migraine headaches, and taught my sister and me to have grace under pressure while taking control. Mom worked eight hours a day, five days a week and raised the family while going through all kinds of arduous medical testing. I didn't even know about her headaches until my senior year in high school. Talk about grace under pressure! My sister was always on the go and portrayed herself to be in an everlasting happy-go-lucky mood. *I was trained at the outset, and now it is my turn to show what I have inside. Go get 'em!*

I was always a competitor. If I didn't think that way, it wouldn't have been normal. As a youngster growing up in Lincolnshire, Illinois, I was involved in every organized sport, and pick up games on a daily basis. In grade school, I was introduced to the great game and teacher, football. This became the teacher of hard work, dedication and most importantly, motivation to overcome adversity. I remained in competitive sports throughout high school. During my senior year at Carmel, the Catholic high school in Mundelein which I attended, I was the starting nose guard. I was 5'9", 165 pounds. The nose guard position is usually on the defensive line, lined up over the center or in a gap of the center. The object is to hold your own, clog up the middle, and create havoc on the other team's offense, while the 6'5", 240-pound offensive linemen want to smash you out of the way. You have to hold your own! Back at Carmel, I asked the coach, "Why am I the nose guard?" He responded, "Because you are the craziest person on the team!" For example, on a hot summer day during doubles (intense twice-a-day football practices in August), the head coach made the team go through nutcracker drills (a tackling drill). Two players are lined up helmet-to-helmet in opposite directions, lying on their backs. A whistle is blown. The two players rise as fast as they can and pile-drive into each other, while trying to land the other guy on his back (one of the great ideas developed by man). "Aaaa, let's go!" The entire team was exhausted and dragging from the intense workout in the hot sun, and we were eagerly waiting for a water break. The coach belted out: "After the hardest collision during the next drill, the team will get a water break. Didier and Flood, get in there." Boom! We collided. Lying on the ground, dazed, I sat up and noticed that the team was at the water trough like a bunch of pigs. "I guess it was a pretty good hit." *I am still proud of that!*

Another time during scrimmage, I nailed the fullback behind the line of scrimmage. He asked: "Are you from a rough neighborhood?" After sharing these stories with Dr. Kent, I told him that I would come back and I hoped the therapists could help in my recovery. "Well," Dr.

Kent said, "you certainly have a good attitude and that will be a big plus in your recovery."

Every Friday morning, RAC would select eight clients and two therapists to go on an outing. The group was split up into two vans. An outing consisted of traveling to a mall, park, or restaurant with the goal of taking the client out into the community. This was an effective, innovative method for community re-entry—a chance for us to experience something besides the medical world.

A week after my introduction to the rehab environment, I was chosen to go on an outing. *Lucky me!* I thought I was special. It was the end of November in the northern tundra of Illinois. The weather had changed drastically, turning colder and cloudier.

We visited the "Grove," which is part of the Cook County Forest Preserve, a 20-minute trip south on River Road. After the vans pulled into the Forest Preserve's rocky parking lot, we all leaped excitedly out of the vans and cheerfully skipped to the front building. (Just joking!)

Back to reality: The therapist slid the doors open, and the freezing temperature with the high winds quickly filled the van. *What am I doing here!?* I thought the therapists were crazy, exposing us to this frigid weather.

Joyce, a vocational therapist, plopped my 220-pound blob of a frame (from the intake of "Da Pantry") into my hot-rod wheelchair. As I sat there, the freezing winds came howling through the barren Forest Preserves at a 30-mile-an-hour clip. *This is good community exposure?* Joyce then dashed "the load" to a wooden building 100 feet away, along a rocky trail.

The log-cabin style nature building, which is wheelchair accessible, houses many animals native to the area, along with early artifacts of Native American tribes. Some of the artifacts date back to the early 1600s. What really stood out in my mind were the turtles. Naturally, as a kid, I used to catch a few and bring them home as pets. That drove Mom crazy, but I have always been fascinated with turtles because they date back to the dinosaur age. There is a large pond just inside the entrance of the nature building at the Grove, with vegetation, rock and mud, and turtles of all different sizes. I was thinking back to my younger days when I was fascinated with painted turtles, little snappers, mud turtles; even boxers. Those younger days seemed pretty good to me now.

As I maneuvered around in my wheelchair, I noticed interesting displays of flora and fauna. Then I came across a truck-wheel-sized snapping turtle. I was enthralled. It was floating in a small freshwater aquarium. Actually, it was a large aquarium, but it was small considering the size of the snapper. I turned my wheelchair and stared; then I began to ponder. *What a symbol! This strong creature held captive; that's what I feel like. Held captive, not being able to roam freely like I once did. Held, bound. There is no way out! Something has to be done!* After the hour-long excursion, we all made it safely back to RAC.

That Tuesday afternoon, at 1:00 p.m. (the first Tuesday of the month), the Center held "Community Hour." The clients sat in meeting chairs with crutches, walkers, and canes at their side. Two or three others, including myself, finished off the semi-circle in wheelchairs, while the eight therapists sat among or behind us. For the first 15 minutes, a therapist, who sat next to and assisted a blonde-haired woman in her mid-forties, reviewed the notes from the previous meeting, out loud to the group. *I'll bet that client has been here for a while. She seems so relaxed. She has probably done this before.* For the next 20 minutes, each client (15 to 20 of us) shared his or her monthly accomplishments, at times cued with the help of a therapist. For example, "Walking has improved," "Speech has improved," reading, comprehension or cooking, etc. After a client shared an accomplishment, the entire group gave a round of applause. *This place is great!* As my turn came up, I had no idea what to share. *I haven't done anything.* I was clueless. Beth Fazio, who sat next to me, whispered: "You got out of the hospital." *Yeah!* "I just got out of the hospital!" All clapped. As the noise died down, one of the clients opened the suggestion box, a shoe box wrapped in blue paper. Everyone laughed that there was an actual suggestion. The client unfolded the small piece of notebook paper and held it two inches from her glasses. The note recommended that the front doors should be automatic so it would be easier to enter and exit the Center. The idea was received enthusiastically by the clients, but the Administrative Manager concluded that it would be too expensive and the hour ended.

A week passed. I started to get a handle on the various therapies and the therapists' names, even though I was bad at remembering names. I enjoyed rehab, seeing it as a fun task. I shared with Karen that RAC seemed like one big, happy family as everybody enjoyed each other and *I get to go home at 4:00 p.m. I am lucky!* Two weeks after the hospital released me, I became comfortable with the new schedule. In fact, I felt great! I didn't have any chemotherapy treatments; I didn't have any harsh medications, just steroids to keep down the swelling; I didn't have any seizures. I was still partially reliant on a wheelchair, though, and my face was swollen to what seemed, to me, to be the size of a beach ball. My lip drooped; I was bald; I had double vision. *But, what is the big deal?* I started to walk well with a walker during physical rehabilitation. I felt good about myself and began to cheer up and encourage people, other clients.

7

Laugh at Life and What It Brings

November 30, 1990: *Geez, not again! I hate taking tests, especially now! I do not want to sit around! Let's get going!* I wasn't worried about the mental aspect. I knew it was there; I just had to focus it. I was more concerned with the physical and communicative attributes that fed my mentality. Tests were rendered from 11/14-12/3/90:

Wechsler Adult Intelligence Scale-Revised (WAIS-R), Wechsler Memory Scale-Revised (WMS-R), Bender Visual Motor Gestalt Test (BVM GT), Rey Auditory Verbal Learning Test (RAVLT), Trail Making Test, Wisconsin Card Sorting Test (WCST), Shipley Institute of Living Scale (SILS), Test of Nonverbal Intelligence (TONI).

"Darryl's tests indicated impaired mental tracking skills, registration and retrieval of new information (visual and verbal). Darryl's visual perception was significantly hampered by double vision and reduced peripheral vision. These perception problems greatly limited his ability to read; however, he started to make good adaptations. Darryl showed significantly reduced speech due to a deficit in cognitive processing. There was evidence Darryl had impairment of executive functions, including decreased self-monitoring, self-awareness and self-regulation. From the following studies, it was recommended that Darryl partake in cognitive rehabilitation therapy, individual and group 6-8 times per week.

"Darryl's mobility was with a standard wheelchair as he used both his feet and arms to propel. He remained independent with wheelchair mobility on level surfaces, but needed assistance on uneven surfaces. Darryl exhibited tremors in both arms, especially when he was fatigued. His motor skills appeared to be at least moderately impaired and there were right-sided tremors of the upper and lower extremities. Darryl appeared to take a conscientious approach and performed adequate task persistence.

"Darryl demonstrated that he can sit without support and be independent. He needed the walker in order to stand in place and performed fair. He performed poorly when he walked supported by a walker, approximately 100 feet on level surfaces. While he was on unlevel surfaces, he was unable to stand with the walker. Darryl was unable to stand without support.

"Darryl demonstrated environmental awareness with functional limits such as decreased speed and distance. Nevertheless, he was functional for structured setting. He needed assistance with community mobility, due to impaired environmental awareness, due to his visual deficits.

"When Darryl transferred to bed or mat, he needed minimal assistance but when he transferred to a toilet, he needed close help. He reported that he required some help to transfer to the shower bench. Darryl reported he needed assistance on stairs when he ascended, but needed minimal assistance when he descended as he sat and slid down the stairs.

"Darryl had poor endurance and fatigued easily with exercise or ambulation, which resulted in tremors in all muscle groups.

"Darryl had adequate verbal skills and appeared to have compromised as his speech was intelligible. His initiation of speech was adequate. His auditory skills were intact for testing purposes.

"Darryl was pleasant to interact with and was very optimistic. He was highly motivated and was often very hard on himself when he felt that his performance wasn't satisfactory.

Projected length of treatment time for Darryl was 8-10 months, subject to change." **RAC's Initial evaluation. December 3, 1990.** By Marie L. Andres, MA, cognitive therapist and Harry Kent, Ph.D.

I implemented notes which were taken by Harry Kent, Ph.D., psychologist on staff. The notes were his observations of me when I received consultation from him once a week. I have bolded and dated the notes accordingly for the sake of conformity.

12/3/90: Darryl said he was getting down on himself because his attention, concentration, reasoning and processing results were low.—Dr. Kent.

Despite all the negative news, I wanted to stay positive and determined that my situation was something that could be overcome with hard work.

12/3/90:   Darryl has maintained his positive attitude and determination while he has improved his understanding of his condition. Darryl is conversational, pleasant and a good historian.—Dr. Kent.

12/4/90:   Darryl's short-term goals for the month were: 1) Darryl will consistently recall 75-85 percent of information during memory group exercises. The memory exercises consisted of watching a video of the morning national and international news, followed by a test to recall the information presented; 2) Darryl will consistently identify five ways to utilize his memory book (the memory book was a daily and yearly organizer by Day Timers, which RAC provided); 3) Darryl will achieve 90-100 percent accuracy on Level I tasks involved with his reasoning skills and problem solving skills; 4) Darryl will obtain baseline data on computer-based programs for visual and motor reactions; 5) Darryl will demonstrate basic understanding of residual deficits and their impact on social roles, and improve his ability to adjust emotionally and behaviorally to necessary role changes.—Dr. Kent.

What! I am not going to give in and accept a new role! What new role? I am still the same Darryl Didier. I am not going to change, and accept defeat!

12/5/90:   Darryl has a love for life and he said that he was not going to be denied.—Dr. Kent.

The following motto was what was/is behind my drive: *Life is great! There is a lot more that I want to do yet. I am not going to be denied!*

I also discussed with Dr. Kent the tremendous support I had received from my immediate family and from an abundance of friends. I had a very positive social circle, friends from work and from the health club. Dr. Kent then went on to ask if I had a girlfriend, and to his surprise, I responded, "Yes, I do." *He is trying to probe my sensitive side, since he can't find anything that I am depressed about.* I explained how dedicated Vicki had been to me when I was in the hospital. She always tried so hard to visit on the weekends, even though she had a full load of classes and other activities at the University of Illinois, Champaign. She maintained an A+ average. I was frustrated because I could not give of myself to her.

12/6/90:   Darryl's good points are: "Getting things done." His one bad point is that he is not patient.—Dr. Kent.

Get going! How is one going to attain his goal by just sitting around?
Physical therapy was the most interesting to me because of the particular challenges that I faced. I still heard the prediction of a pessimistic nurse rumbling in my mind: "You may never walk again.*" Bring it on! Let's go! I will show her! I will show them all!* On the sixth of December, I was waiting in the gym. I immediately became friends with Julie, the assistant physical therapist, a mother of two preschool children, and who loved sports. I conversed with her about my father's baseball experiences with a minor league club, then about my love of sports: "It gives one the attitude to win." Julie transferred me from the wheelchair to a walker. She followed at my side while holding onto the gait belt as I labored toward the parallel bars. Then she instructed me to walk between the bars while continuously clutching them with every step. *Gosh, my left leg crosses my right leg. What's going on? I have to really concentrate and control it.* I continued the particular exercise two full lengths of the apparatus, about 20 feet. I became more determined after performing terribly. *Come on, Didier!*

Next, Julie had another exercise planned. She instructed me to stand horizontally at one of the side bars and do the Karioke, a balance exercise as one crisscrosses their legs and moves side to side. *I remember this from football practice.* I stood on the right side of the apparatus and firmly held onto the bar and meticulously moved to the right. *Ugh!* That was only the beginning. Julie instructed me to start the entire process over and over again at the end of the bars, five more times. I was exhausted after the session and plunged rump-first into the wheel-chair. *I still have a long way to go! I am so slow.*

Julie wheeled me to a blue mat, three feet away then transferred me onto the mat. I had ten minutes to rest before the next session, so I took advantage of it and conked out. When I awoke, Karen transferred me from the mat to the wheelchair and wheeled me to the next sched-uled event, Speech Therapy. The speech exercises were the same as the hospital's, but more repetitive. After the hour-long class, I had Voca-tional Therapy, designed to prepare the client to enter the work place with cognition, memory, and concentration, combined with motor control tasks.

After the initial greetings, I participated in word association games on an oval table in the vocational therapist's office. I worked on mem-ory recall as she placed a pen on the right side of her desk. She set a timer for five minutes and when the timer buzzed, I had to remember to get the red pen. Five minutes later, the buzzer went off with an annoying fire-alarm sound that flickered. I flunked the test. The thera-pist had to remind me to get the pen. She tried it again. This time, I focused hard on the alarm as I searched for words that started with "B" and ended with "C." I passed, having been determined not to fail again. After the test, the therapist placed a crossword puzzle in front of me. I filled in two words, but it was difficult to read due to blurred vision. The hour ended. The therapist wheeled me out of her office to visit with the psychologist. *Ah, time to relax and have a conversation.*

12/7/90:   Darryl's determination motivated family rapport.—Dr. Kent.

December, 1990. My favorite time of the year was in full swing, the holidays. I just loved all the decorations and the holiday cheer. RAC took a group of eight clients on an outing. I couldn't wait to go to the local mall, as a therapist initially promised, and soak up all of the Christmas decorations, while seeing all the smiling faces. *This is going to be great!*

To my big disappointment, we ended up going to the local Kmart. What a letdown! How boring—everything was so dull and plain. We (clients) all felt the same way!

The next day, Judy, the speech therapist, asked me to write an article for RAC's monthly newsletter, so I said, "Good, on what topic?" "Anything," Judy replied. *Terrific!* This was my chance to really make a mark—I thought.

The newsletter was circulated to current clients and recent graduates of the rehab center. The purpose was to inform the target audience about the current happenings at the Center. The newsletter was also therapeutic for the clients as they wrote articles, which served as a mental challenge.

I took some time to write about the Christmas outing, in a critical tone. I blasted the decision-makers for cutting corners and reneging on their promise that we would visit a mall. I also related that the clients should be involved when choosing a destination and an activity, because I thought: *even though we have challenges set before us and we are dependent upon others to travel, please respect our ability to think independently.*

On Monday following the outing, I excitedly turned in my editorial. To my surprise, Judy rejected it because of the negative tone the article took regarding RAC. What bias? I had told it like it was. *We were excluded from the decision-making process.* The discount outlet had two Christmas trees and very minuscule amounts of garland. *Hey, what is going on here?*

The therapist thought I was off the wall. How could I write anything bad about RAC? At that point, I became very upset with the therapist and administrators, in general, for their lack of humanity. **Keep Going!**

12/8/90:   Darryl participated actively with the group during the community hour and shared the value of a good mental attitude.—Dr. Kent.

The confrontation of the staff members' bias woke up the monster. *I am not going to be taken advantage of and be treated like I do not have a mind of my own because I am disabled! Hey!* I felt obliged to represent the clients by speaking out and sending a message. "Hello! We are not idiots. We can think on our own and make sound decisions!" Keep Going!

12/8/90:   Darryl is frustrated that everybody is telling him to take his time and not rush things. He wanted to be making 100 G's ($100,000.00) within 5 years.—Dr. Kent.

What? How is one going to get things done? I wanted to relate to Dr. Kent that I was a professional, not just a client. *I was and am somebody. I was really living; I was doing it. Then I was taken out of the game, but I will be back!* **Keep Going!**

12/9/90:   Darryl could not wait to see the optometrist.—Dr. Kent.

I was very frustrated due to my double vision. I loved to pick up the paper and read at night after dinner, but now it was very difficult. I couldn't follow along because I would see two different images.

Dr. Margolis had worked extensively with clients from RAC and I'd heard that he did wonderful work. For example, an older lady in a wheelchair who had a brain tumor similar to mine mentioned that the optometrist had used prisms to eradicate her double vision. I asked Dr. Kent and Beth Fazio about Dr. Margolis and I received positive feedback. I was ready to go! I was excited and told Dad about it. "Is he an ophthalmologist or an optometrist?" Dad asked. I replied with much vigor, "He is an optometrist." My dad was not in favor of it. He asked, "Do you know the difference between an optometrist and an ophthalmologist?" "Yeah!" I replied. "An ophthalmologist is a doctor and an optometrist is not." My dad said that an ophthalmologist can perform surgery and an optometrist cannot. So I said, "Dr. Margolis is pro-active and works with prisms (on lenses) to help one adjust and focus on a subject. Here, read this." I gave him all sorts of pamphlets about the work that Dr. Margolis performed. "Even Beth Fazio recommended him." *That should get him to agree since he has great admiration for her.* Dad still did not like the idea, but he sensed my excitement and responded to my persistence. *Ah, I have sold him!* Dad said he would call and set up the appointment. Mom intervened: "Wait, have Darryl do it. It will be good for him." *It will be easy, no problem. I have worked on the phones all the time.* I scheduled the appointment for the following Saturday so Dad could drive.

"Hey, Dr. Margolis!" I knew him and he knew who I was because of his frequent visits to the Center. He was a very outgoing person who made me feel comfortable right away. I went into his office and he administered a variety of basic eye tests. I performed terribly with both eyes. With a patch over my right eye, I could see more clearly as it blocked out the bounding eye. Therefore, when I focused on a letter of the alphabet, it didn't seem to dart in all directions. After the exam was concluded, Dad guided me, very slowly, to the next room. The doctor instructed me to place my chin on a strap, then peer into a Field Machine, an oval eye examination device, which was comparable to looking into a black tunnel with a small image of light that flashed up, down, left or right. *Oh, I understand.* The machine measured my eyeball's movement by frequency sounds. First, I gazed with my left eye and there was no frequency sound. When I then looked with my right eye, frequency sounds were abundant. *Dang it!* Dr. Margolis's assistant began to instruct me to control the movement. *Let's go! Mind over matter.* The sounds were becoming softer and softer. Then they would fluctuate in tone. Up for a while, then down for a while.

The after the test the doctor checked the prescription I'd had before the cancer operation. He found it to be way off-track. He prescribed bifocal lenses to assist with reading and also to allow for long-distance vision. Dr. Margolis was an entrepreneur as he had his own eyeglass shop within the office, to the left of the examining room. His assistant helped me choose frames and installed the lenses. She was very apologetic because there was clearly a line in the middle that separated the nearsighted lens from the farsighted lens. "You will look older for awhile until the permanent lenses come, in about two weeks." *What? Then how can I pick up any girls? (Just kidding.)*

I couldn't wait to see if the glasses really worked. At home, after dinner, I tried reading the newspaper. Using my new glasses, I slowly made out the words, then glanced up to view what was happening on TV. *Hey, they work as prescribed!* Two weeks earlier, my father and I had picked out a pair of reading glasses. They were not prescriptions, but were like magnifying glasses so I could vaguely make out the words. Before, I would read while listening to CNN. When an interesting news flash came up, I quickly took off the reading glasses then hurriedly rummaged for my original glasses to see what had happened on TV. By the time the process was complete, the interesting news item had escaped. *Dang it! Missed it again!* Now, I had a whole new lease on life. I could read and instantly look up and view what was on TV. *All right! Awesome!* **Keep Going!**

12/12/90:   Darryl said his eyes still need to get better.—Dr. Kent.

During the second week of December, I took a day off from therapy sessions. My sister, who also had the day off, was my chauffeur. She drove me to the branch office of Merrill Lynch in the late afternoon. I purposely went later in the day so the office activity would be tame after the market closed. The major reason I wanted to go back was to register my hard-earned Series-7 License with Merrill Lynch. It had to be registered or else it would soon expire and I did not want to take that strenuous eight-hour exam again!

As Brenda drove me in her light-blue sports car, I was very nervous. My main concern was: How would the co-workers and management accept me? I used my wheelchair for this occasion because I did not want to make a mistake. We parked in the handicapped space and placed the "handicapped" card on the dash. Brenda hurriedly readied the wheelchair, then transferred me into it. My heart pounded as we entered the office complex through the heavy glass doors. As we walked through the front lobby, the ceiling towered over us, five stories, with two 30-foot palm trees in the center, decorated with Christmas lights around the trunks. I began to feel even more nervous when I saw the familiar Merrill Lynch sign, with a symbol of the bull encrypted in the center near the office entranceway. Once I gathered enough gusto, I was wheeled in by Brenda. Immediately, the blonde receptionist greeted us warmly: "Darryl, it's great to see you!" She rounded the desk and gave me a hug. *All right! I feel on top of the world! I am being accepted!* I introduced my sister, who was wearing a pale green blazer with a black skirt. As we chatted further, I said that I wanted to conduct some business concerning my securities license. The receptionist instructed us to go across the hall to the other offices. Merrill Lynch leased the entire first floor, and half of the third. As we walked over to the other side, two brokers wearing designer suits quickly walked down the corridor toward us. *Hey, I know them! I hope they do not see me!* I was wearing an exercise suit, a black winter coat, and a hat to cover my bald head. I felt inferior—beneath their class. They both turned: "Hi, Darryl, it's great to see you!" One of the gentlemen, mid-forties, asked, "Did you like the book I sent you in the hospital?" I looked up at the smiling face and said yes, but actually, I couldn't remember what book it was. *I don't even remember his name.*

We entered the reception area across the hall and Brenda wheeled me to the other receptionist. The young brunette smiled at me and gave me a warm greeting. *This is a great place!* I asked to see the assistant to the manager, who had resembled photographs of the Duchess of York in the 15th century, when I worked with her back in July. We waited for a few moments; then the assistant glamorously stepped into the lobby and smiled happily to see me alive! She told us to follow her to her desk. As we went down the corridor, I noticed three young brokers hunching down at their desks with the telephone receiver glued to their ear, *probably making cold-calls.* We traipsed 30 feet down the beige-carpeted hall then took a left to the assistant's desk, where she initiated the process. I signed the necessary documents and was given "fingerprint" cards so I could correctly register and be legally liable. I was to mail the prints back to the assistant; then she would forward them on to the registration department of Merrill Lynch in New York to be processed, then sent to the NASD (National Association of Securities Dealers), which is the governing body over regulations imposed on the stock market industry.

After business was conducted, the assistant and I began to socialize. She told me to hurry up and come back because, "We need your help here." *All right! Let's go!* That was a major concern of mine. Had they liked my work previously? Did Merrill Lynch really want me back? The gracious young woman asked for my address and said she would send me an invitation to the annual Christmas party. *I would love to go, but I am not in the right condition! I look terrible and can't talk right! Mmm! Maybe I should go! Last year's was fun!* It was a successful visit for the hour we were there. **Keep Going!**

12/14/90: **Darryl said he is not happy about prognosis of eyes.—Dr. Kent.**

This time I listened to my father and decided to see my ophthalmologist. *Maybe he can surgically repair the double vision.* There was some hope. Dr. Johnson, a kind, older doctor, had a very good reputation as an ophthalmologist. Again, I had made an appointment for a Saturday morning to adjust to Dad's work schedule.

The office was in the next town to the east, Highland Park, a 25-minute drive through traffic. The five-story office building had an open-air parking garage. We rode the elevator to the second floor. I wore a navy-blue Notre Dame Baseball cap, and noticed another person in the waiting room, an older man, wearing a Notre Dame Football sweatshirt. I was embarrassed. I felt that I was not in the same intellectual class as he was. *I didn't attend Notre Dame and he probably did!* Dad, being friendly as always, struck up a conversation with the other gentleman about Notre Dame's football chances in the upcoming Bowl game. Dad has always been enamored of Notre Dame's football team and the university. As the conversation went on, Dad mentioned the challenge I was up against. *All right, Dad! Spread the word! I feel good inside. My dad and the fellow have respect for me!*

While I was waiting, I took notice of the "Color-Blind Test" on the wall, with its three rows of six circles. A multitude of different colored spots filled each circle and were arranged to depict a hidden number. If one was not color blind, he/she could easily pick out the numbers, but if you were in my shoes, you had no chance. Heck, I had flunked the color-blind test in grade school.

The receptionist called my name and Dad wheeled me into the examining room. Dr. Johnson placed an eye drop into my eye then he instructed me to read the general vision test, which was five feet away. The results were the same as when I was examined by Dr. Margolis.

After the eye test, the doctor used an ophthalmoscope, a small device with a microscopic light beam that reveals the inner workings of the eye. With the office completely dark, he held the scope centimeters from my face, and peered deeply into my eyes. "Aah, okay, interesting," the doctor mumbled as he focused, changing the scope's lenses with his thumb on a circular adjuster, lightly clicking with every movement. Once he viewed the optic nerves, he concluded that it would just take time for my right eye to settle. The left would improve slightly, but would never create natural tears, due to the left facial nerve being severed. The doctor stated that I should keep using the eye drops, and he handed me a cellophane bag with a special eye patch inside. The silver patch was riddled with pin-prick holes to allow the flow of air to get to the eye. He strongly recommended that I wear the patch at night to protect my left eye's retina from being scratched by the bed sheets as I slept, because my left eyelid did not close. The doctor went on to say that the bifocal lenses, which were prescribed by Dr. Margolis, were fine for now, but my eyes might improve over time. Then he suggested that a way to combat the double vision was to tape my right lens so I could see straight without any interference. *I cannot believe it! I will look like an idiot with tape over my lens. But maybe I should do it. I can get stylish tape. Mmm!* I was perplexed.

That night when I readied for bed, Dad coated my left eye with the oil-based solvent. As the doctor proposed, I placed an eye patch over my left eye. When Mom woke me the following morning at 6:30, the eye patch was nowhere in sight. *I still toss and turn!* When I went for therapy sessions that day, I used regular tape on the left lens of my glasses. It was so pleasurable. I could look at an image and see only one, instead of two. *One! All right! But I still feel foolish.* **Keep Going!**

In mid-December, I returned to the University of Illinois at Chicago Hospital (UIC) for a check-up with Dr. Stone, the rehabilitation staff, and Dr. Goodman, the ophthalmologist. Dr. Goodman's office was situated on the south side of Taylor Street, just to the west of the hospital in a one-story medical building. All I recall was that the office was dark and devoid of people as Dad wheeled me into the large examining room.

Dr. Goodman rose from his paper-riddled desk as the sounds of the El-train rumbled by. I sat in the examining chair and the doctor performed the same optical tests I had had previously. There was no change. Dr. Goodman concluded that I should wear the protective eye patch to protect my left eye while I slept and that I should continue wearing my current eyeglass prescription, with the right lens taped to block double vision. *Well, I will try to wear the protective patch when I sleep, but I am too restless!*

We were preparing ourselves to brave the cold, windy weather when an exciting incident occurred. A medical student, Dr. Goodman's assistant, who was reading my medical reports, suddenly yelled out: "He worked for Merrill Lynch! Wow!" *I am somebody!*

As we left Dr. Goodman's office, the weather slapped us in the face with a cold rain and blustery wind. Dad guided my wheelchair as we rapidly trooped along the sidewalk to visit Dr. Stone—the doctor who had performed my initial surgery—and the rehabilitation staff. The building was two blocks to the south, across the street on Taylor. As we approached the building, there was a slight diversion in our path. The sidewalk led into an alley, and we maintained the rapid pace as my dad pushed my wheelchair. We approached the break-off point and angled down a small slope, picking up momentum. It was raining harder. Water had built up in the alley so we couldn't anticipate the terrain confronting us. With full force, we entered the zone. *Ugh, ugh, ha, what are you doing?* The left wheel snagged in a pothole and I catapulted from the wheelchair. I landed with my arms outstretched to brace the landing and then rolled onto my back to take the fall. *Hahaha! No big deal. I am not hurt,* as I lay in a puddle of water. I was amazed by my reaction time to take a tumble correctly and so was Dad, who was greatly relieved that I hadn't been hurt. I was proud at that moment. *I can take it!* I was fine.

Once inside the building, we traveled down the hallway to the Rehabilitation Department. We encountered a therapist, who instructed us to go into the gym for an evaluation by various other therapists. It was like going into a rehab antique shop, filled with century-worn rehab fixtures, even down to the old musty smell, combined with drab milk-glass windows. *How depressing!*

What ensued was like a reunion, but instead of a high school reunion, it was a neurological-rehab veterans' reunion. We patients gathered in the front of the gym, 20 of us, with every assisting device imaginable. *Hey! How ya doing, Buddy?* I remembered the guy who walked in with a quad-cane and, at his side, a woman, whom I presumed to be his sister. Boy, was I jealous as I remained in the wheelchair with Mom and Dad at my side. *He is doing better than me! Already! Hey!* He was the same age as me, had been operated on for a brain tumor and had taken part in rehabilitation with me during my last month at the hospital. We had often crossed paths in the corridors of the hospital or while waiting for physical therapy. We seldom talked to each other, but when we did, it was a motivational tidbit: "Keep going!"

I heard a sexy voice: "Darryl! Hi!" I recanted back with a boisterous, "Hello!" *Hey! It's that really cute speech therapist.* The therapist said, "You look great!" *I wish I would have met her before! I would have had a better chance.*

My rehabilitation follow-ups for the two hours were: standing, sitting, walking 100 feet (with the walker); reciting various word combinations, and interviews about my daily activities, which consisted of rehabilitation, rehabilitation and more rehabilitation. When the hour ended, we departed for Dr. Stone's office on the murky fourth floor, riding in the box-like 1930s elevator. Once on the fourth floor, we waited in the dark hallway on a brown bench that bore the worn memories of 60 years. Class pictures of medical students and residents since inception, 1896, lined the wall of the waiting room. A new soul entered and sat down next to me. The lady, in her mid-twenties, asked us about Dr. Stone and his credibility. Dad and I sang his praises, stating that he was the best doctor when it came to brain tumors. The desperate woman said she had searched many states. She had a brain tumor and was in dire need of a good surgeon. I assured her that he was the best doctor in his field then shared some motivational thoughts. I kept encouraging her and she responded with motivational thoughts. She was a fighter. **Keep Going!**

8

The Power of Commitment

Since early December, Mom had been picking me up at the Center at 4:30 p.m. every other day and we took the 40-minute drive to Lake Forest Hospital. Dr. Stone prescribed that I take blood tests in order for Dr. Shah, my oncologist, to monitor my blood count to make sure I remained cancer-free. Dr. Stone was cautious because the type of tumor I had, medulloblastoma, tends to spread down the spine.

The good news of the blood test was consistently announced on our answering machine—until Christmas weekend. The morning of Christmas Eve, I awoke to admire the day, and remained enthralled that I was home. As I peered out the bedroom window, watching the birds and squirrels scurrying around the back yard, I heard the phone ring. Dad answered in his usual tone: "Hello, good morning." There was silence; then I heard him mumble: "*Mmm*, okay, mmm, okay. We will be there right away." Then I overheard him talking with Mom in the kitchen (his voiced carried). He said Dr. Shah had called and that my last blood count was off due to a dangerously low platelet count. *What?* Dad then told Mom that I must go to the hospital immediately and take another blood test. "They want to check it again; there could have been a mistake when the first reading was taken. But this could be an emergency situation.*" Darn it, I do not want to go to the hospital with the possibility of being admitted! Not the day before Christmas!*

On the way to the hospital, Dad explained to me the seriousness of the situation. He said it was very dangerous to have a low platelet count. "If you fall and hit your arm or leg on something, your entire vascular system would collapse: arteries, veins, corpuscles." *What? Hey, what is going on?!*

The nurse captured a sample of my blood in a vial and I nervously waited for the results. Half an hour later, the nurse said my count was low, so I had to stay overnight. As she cautiously helped me into a bed, I lamented my frustration: "Dang it! I cannot believe this! There is no way I am going back into the hospital!" *This is my favorite time of year! Tonight is Christmas Eve and tomorrow is Christmas Day! I had better get some stollen (German pastry) to eat tomorrow!* (It is a family tradition on Christmas morning to feast on Stollen.) Looking out the hospital window in disgust, I saw a fully-grown pine tree surrounded by brown grass and I noticed small snowflakes beginning to fall. *Great, we are going to have a white Christmas for the first time in years and I am stuck in the hospital again!*

An IV dripped plasma into my system overnight, Christmas Eve. On Christmas morning, they checked my blood count again. Dr. Shah would allow me to leave if the count was good, and I would be home in time to celebrate Christmas Day with my family. *All is not lost!* I recited a prayer.

The test showed that my count was normal and I was free to go in the late morning, but I had to be careful. *All right, I will be able to enjoy Christmas at home with my family!* Christmas was celebrated in the usual way: we spent the entire day exchanging gifts around the Christmas tree and sharing laughs, maybe more laughter than usual out of relief. However, Dr. Shah was still worried that my low platelet count meant I had bone cancer. He wanted to set up an appointment to drill into my hip to obtain a sample of bone marrow for analysis.

I was distressed, not by the possibility of bone cancer, but at the thought of having my hip invaded by a drill. I consulted with Dad, who said he had heard many people say that Dr. Shah was a very gentle doctor. We made the appointment for the following Saturday morning.

On the appointed day, Dad helped me into Dr. Shah's office. I anticipated the pain, so the only way to deal with it was to be charged up and ready to go! *Come on, get it over with!* I hobbled with the walker, assisted by a nurse, into the examining and procedure room. "Hey, Dr. Shah!" I said, with a vigorous handshake. I sprawled out on the surgical bed on my right side, took deep breaths, and maintained a stern face. Moments later, the doctor administered a shot of Novocain. He began to drill with what seemed like a Sears Black & Decker power screwdriver. The drill was loud, and it hurt with the sting of grinding pain, even with Novocain. As he drilled deeper, I bit my tongue and remained quiet. I imagined that I was John Wayne biting a bullet as I was having an arrow removed from my hip: *Just grin and bear it!* The procedure lasted for only a minute, but it seemed like an eternity. Dr. Shah retrieved his sample.

I remained hopeful and kept on doing my thing—living—even though Mom and Dad were concerned. The results were called in by the doctor's nurse two days later, to Dad, and were negative. *Yeah! I knew the test would turn out fine!* I had faith, and believed in my immune system to overpower any cancer trying to metastasize.

Soon after this procedure, I had a visit with my primary care physician, Dr. Pickard, to find out the reason for my low platelet count. Dr. Pickard, a good-looking, middle-aged doctor who spoke very rapidly, had come to a conclusion. He said the hospital had taken me off the steroid medication too quickly, which had caused the low platelet count. He prescribed steroids again for a month. *What a disappointment! The swelling in my fat face was starting to come down!*

The blood tests continued for two weeks. Every time the nurse pricked my arm, I watched the healing process very closely. *All right! My blood is coagulating.* A nurse had told me earlier that was a sign of a good count.

1/2/91:   **Brenda, sister, helps in the morning along with Karen, nurse, and Sandy, physical therapist. His mother wakes him.—Dr. Kent.**

1/3/91:   Darryl started on a bike at RAC during physical therapy.—Dr. Kent.

In late December, when I was going through a physical rehab session in the gym, I noticed for the first time there were two stationary bikes. *Let me at 'em. I know what I can do. Ha! But, the way my balance is now, if I ride, I will probably tip over! I will have to wait and improve!* I watched with envy and anticipation as a client hopped on the apparatus and rode off "into the sunset."

I walked and walked and walked between the parallel bars. On the second day of January, in the late afternoon, Sandy, the physical therapist, made a tough decision that I was capable of riding an exercise bike without tipping over. *All right!* The therapist carefully assisted me onto the seat. She supervised during the intermediate period. My feet went into straps on the pedals in order to latch my feet in place during the arduous journey. I started to pedal, *aah! What?* My arms started to move back and forth in conjunction with the movement of the pedals. It was as though I was practicing jabs on a punching bag. *Come on, Ali!* (Mohammed Ali.) It was an Air-Dyne exercise bike. Sandy felt that I would be alright unassisted. She walked into the therapists' offices in the back of the gym, 20 feet from me, after emphasizing the point that I should maintain a minimum pace: 72 rpm (revolutions per minute). A small computerized monitoring system mounted between the two handlebars kept me on track.

I rode for 10 minutes and upped my speed to 100 rpm. *All right, this is fun!* Hearing the sound of wheels churning rapidly, Sandy shouted my name and ordered me to slow down. *How am I going to exercise?* I knew no other way: either do it or don't do it. I was thrilled that I could do something for myself. At that point, I knew what to do to overcome the challenges confronting me. *I have to lose this excess weight. The entire pantry is stored in my stomach. My sweatshirt does not even cover my protruding abdomen! I have to combat cancer and increase the flow of blood to help in the healing process. Something has to be done!*

1/4/91:   Darryl started an exercise program for weight-loss in his home.—Dr. Kent.

On January 6, Dad and I lounged around and watched the college basketball games in the family room. I became very bored as time ticked by. *That's it! I need to exercise independently! I need the flow of blood. I need to get out of this mess!* I asked, then urged Dad to go over to our neighbors' house to borrow their stationary bike. Back in early December, on a Sunday, we were at the home of our friendly neighbors, Mr. and Mrs. Charger, who had three grade school children. We watched the Chicago Bears' playoff game and had dinner. During the meal, I asked Mrs. Charger if they still had their stationary exercise bike, and she said yes and that I could borrow it. Well, it was time. At first Dad didn't want to bother the Chargers, but I kept up the pleading, with Mom's influence, and he finally agreed. *See, persistence pays off!* **Keep Going!**

Every weekday, when I returned home from rehab at 3:30 p.m., I descended very slowly and cautiously down the 14 basement steps, holding onto my mother's arm for dear life. We did not want to have any accidents, like tumbling down the basement stairs. *Hey, what an idea!* My powerful stereo that I had during college was down in the basement behind the bike, on an old green cabinet, ready to blare out motivating, rhythmic Hip-Hop music. After Mom made sure I was steady on the bike, I asked if she could turn on the stereo and tune it to 96.3 FM, with high volume. The music aided my motivation: I rode as hard as I could with high resistance. *Come on, let's get it done! There is no doubt in my mind now that it must get done! The cancer is out of here and it will not come back! All right!* I was soaked with sweat and drenched with positive thoughts circulating around and around in my blood. With messages like that, how could one lose the battle? How could anybody lose? There was no possible way. I had the exercise mind-set. I had competed all my life, that's all I knew; pick-up games at the park or in the street; baseball, touch football. I took part in organized baseball and football from grade school to a short stint in college. My sophomore year in college, I weighed 220 pounds and pressed 365 pounds, all natural, no "roids" (steroids). I always trained (exercised) every chance I could. **Keep Going!**

1/8/91:   **Therapist said Darryl needs a hearing test because he is loud and impulsive.—Dr. Kent.**

Speech therapy was (and still is) a great need of mine. If I wanted to get back into the social scene again, I would have to sound as if I was with it. My goal was to return to the selling business, the talking business. Why? I love it and love the contact with other people. I love to "cold-call"; it is a challenge and it's fun to semi-meet people (on the phone that is).

During speech therapy, Judy asked me to recite a group of sentences. I read through them as fast as possible, chopping everything up, and ruined the entire exercise. "Slow down," Judy instructed me, as everyone else suggested. I tended to fly through things. Well then, on the other hand, how are things going to get done? Be precise. I could no longer speed through the syllables or I would sound choppy and totally unclear. Concentration is the key to E N U N C I A T I N G properly, and especially, to keep up the energy level. That was the biggest challenge.

Judy strongly suggested that I schedule an appointment for a hearing test. Apparently, she thought I had some hearing loss that caused me to be too loud. Other therapists agreed.

I was really burned up! They had their Masters' degrees in therapy and the books told them that the after-effects of a brain tumor can result in loud and verbose behavior. But I had always been that way. That's Darryl Didier! This pronouncement still irks me very much, as it does my immediate family and friends. Why? I actually believed the therapists! Hello, my name is Darryl Didier. Would somebody listen to this little person? *How do you think I did so well at Merrill Lynch?* I spoke up and communicated. *Come on!* If you are going to say something, say it with power and authority. Be convincing. I set up the appointment with Dr. Block, the ear/nose/throat specialist, at Lake Forest Hospital on a weekday afternoon after rehab with mom.

During the appointment Dr. Block, who had a broad smile and a large oval reflector on his forehead, cleaned my ears. Pop! *Wow! Everything is so loud! This is great! Maybe I will talk more clearly.*

Dr. Block then told me that I had to take a hearing test in the next room. I rose with the walker from the examining chair and made my way to a soundproof room, right down the hall. I stepped up into the room, holding on to both sides of the doorway, with Mom's assistance. I took the main seat, while Mom sat behind. The assistant placed a set of headphones over my ears—the kind that pilots wear—and instructed me to raise my right hand, or my left, according to the toned beep. *I hope I get through this. I have to really concentrate because there is no way I am going to wear a hearing aid. It will ruin my striving to be normal. But, again, what is normal?* After the half-hour of tests, Dr. Block concluded, with the aid of a computer printout, that I had a slight hearing loss in my left ear. He said it was so slight that there was nothing to worry about. He wanted to see me again in six months. It was important, he said, for him to clean my ears routinely since there weren't any cilia to protect them from invading particles in the air, an effect of radiation. *Ha, total therapeutic bias! I was always loud.* The following day, when I returned to the rehab center, I continued being myself—Loud! **Keep Going!**

1/10/91:   Darryl is feeling better.—Dr. Kent.

I was very comfortable with rehab, my fellow clients, therapists, the administration, and the transportation department personnel. For example, I was in a van with four other clients on our way home at the end of the fun day. Ron, the driver, and I conversed about life after he dropped off the other passengers. He told me how motivating and encouraging I was to him. "Wow!" I said. "You have got to be kidding! What is the big deal? To act this way is normal." Later, Ron, who was middle-aged and soft-spoken, told me he was on a sabbatical. He said his managerial position at an accounting firm in Chicago had caused him undue stress. Ron and I became great friends.

I began to kid around with the therapists and the other clients; in other words, I was becoming myself again. I started to grasp the environment of the Center in terms of how to act and how not to act. For instance, a fellow client, with whom I had become comfortable, was in the gym resting on one of the mats during the lunch hour. While two rows of ten chairs were in the gym for the aerobic hour (clients and therapists took part), I raced around in my wheelchair before it began. I noticed that it was almost one o'clock. I flew by the fellow on the mat and decided to be a smart-aleck: "Hey, wake up!" I wheeled quickly around the corner into the kitchen to hide. As clients and therapists began to fill the room with the murmurs of an audience filtering into a theater, I quietly eased the wheelchair back to the gym. I tried to look innocent, as if nothing had occurred. I came across the older man sitting in his chair. He belted out his disgust at being disturbed and then hit me on the head with his four-pronged cane. Immediately, a therapist rescued me. What I had thought was a joke turned out to be almost disastrous. Luckily, I have a hard head. However, I felt bad and was distraught over the incident, blaming myself. At the end of the day, on the way home, Ron told me that the guy who lashed out had done that to others. Ron did not fault me.

1/24/91:   Darryl established goals: Walk with a walker more independently one month; walk with a quad-cane the second month; walk with a straight cane the third month.—Dr. Kent.

The healthy effects of exercise fueled my determination that I would meet those goals.

1/24/91:   Lost memory at first, but just scored 100 percent on the memory computer test.—Dr. Kent.

See the power of exercise and the effect that it plays on the mind and the body? **Keep Going!**

1/30/91: **Darryl said he was riding the bike in the basement on the days after therapy and on the weekends. Darryl said: "Work hard and test yourself!"—Dr. Kent.**

I believed in testing the waters and going a step higher. If I failed, work harder and then try it again. I took wider steps and sometimes lost control while I tried to maintain my balance with the walker. *I have to do extra in order to succeed! Work more on the weekends.* As Mom often drove me and walked with me at Northbrook Court, a large shopping mall on Chicago's North Shore, for a short stint, 100 yards as a few shoppers dashed by. **Keep Going!**

1/30/91: **Darryl said he received a letter from Vicki. "Keep fighting. Love always."—Dr. Kent.**

February, 1991. After dinner with the family, at around 7:00 p.m., we usually read and watched the CNN news channel. At 9:00 p.m., my dad helped me get ready for bed. I walked with the walker to the middle of my bedroom, between the two beds, and planted myself for a short time while my father pulled down the bedding. Once all was ready, I moved the walker to the side and took a deep breath. I focused on the bed: "Hey, Dad, I'm going to try to walk from here to the bed without the walker, three feet." "Be careful!" Dad warned. I dashed and picked up speed, then dove into the safety net, my bed. I laughed and laughed boisterously. *Hey, pretty good, ha!* Dad moistened my eye with the oil-based eye drops and I went off to sleep. Internally, I smiled; I was improving. Keep Going!

February 5, 1991. It was decided by the RAC team and my family that I no longer needed the assistance of the nurse, Karen, in the morning, due to my improvement. My sister would minimally assist me to get ready in the morning, which was a great help to Mom and Dad. They could remain on their early morning work schedules without hiring an in-home nurse for an outrageous price.

The following morning, at 7:00 a.m., Mom entered my room to wake me. As I was in the washroom brushing my teeth with my head over the bowl, two physical therapists from the Center invaded my peace and tranquility. I glanced up and saw Mike and Sandy. Mike was holding a video camera. *All right, it is my time to shine!* I was being taped in the bathroom for the purpose of evaluating my ability to groom myself independently and dress safely. Of course, I had to do something off-the-wall to liven up the situation. It is rather boring videotaping someone brushing their teeth and shaving. "Hey," I said, as I looked into the camera half-naked, with no hair and a swollen face. "Look at this soap; it can clean, clean and clean while lathering up very well." I held up a bar of soap and gave a half-smile into the camera. My sister burst out of her bedroom and laughed with the two therapists. I love trying to market something. I passed the early morning management test and moved on to the next step of becoming independent. **Keep Going!**

Back at the Center, I was humoring myself, which is a very important part of recovery. For example, in the afternoon, I was with three other clients during occupational therapy. The occupational therapist's goal that day was to introduce the clients to the kitchen and observe their safety while preparing a meal. The clients worked together as a team; for example, preparing the salad, mixing the sauce, boiling the noodles, etc. As the crew (three clients and I) set out to prepare a hearty Italian meal, I was designated to prepare the salad—slice and chop all the salad fixings. Due to the tedious task, I tried to entertain myself by mimicking Julia Child. In a high-pitched voice, I recited: "Today we are going to prepare a salad. We will cut the tomatoes, onions, celery then grate the cheese." I heard laughter, which only egged me on. I bellowed louder and louder during each task. It echoed through every crevice at the rehab center. I heard laughter throughout the building from other therapists and clients. We all need to laugh at life and what it brings. It will make the world a better place. Keep Going!

2/5/91:   Darryl is positive and constructive, but denies cognitive deficits and social implication of his condition.—Dr. Kent. (*Why be realistic and limit yourself?—Darryl.*)

Another cold, blustery Saturday morning in February; Mom and I journeyed off to the Northbrook Court Mall again. I walked further this time—approximately 1,000 feet—with more confidence. I was very focused on my control. Mom and I were about to exit, when an uplifting, motivating incident occurred. An older gentleman, apparently a regular mall-walker, whizzed by. "I have seen your progress; you are looking good; keep it up!" *What support! All right! Let's go!* That provided so much power and energy for me to keep fighting. *Somebody else has compassion!* Keep Going!

2/19/91:   **Darryl said: "Live life like a bandit. Do the best you can do at every-thing you do." Darryl meant, get out and live life with energy and verac-ity.—Dr. Kent.**

I had not been to church since Easter, 1990, before my surgery. I was one of those parishioners who developed the habit of going to Mass on the two most important days in the Catholic faith, Christmas and Easter. However, I felt the need to give thanks and praise to God in His house and I felt comfortable at that time going to Holy Cross Church, even though I relied on the walker and had a weird appearance. The church was familiar to me because I had been educated at the adjoining grade school for eight years, and Dad was a regular usher for the nine o'clock Mass.

Dad slowly guided me to the front pew on the left side of the church, facing the altar. I sat in the right corner, with the walker placed directly in front of the pew. I knelt and stared at the large crucifix of Jesus on the wall behind the altar. I was deeply touched by just being in His presence. Tears filled my right eye. I was emotionally moved by the spirit as the large gathering of people came together to give praise to God!

During the sharing of the Eucharist, the Ambassadors of the Holy Eucharist, servers of the bread and wine, were situated in the front of each of the three aisles. (The Eucharist represents the body and blood of Jesus when it is consecrated by a priest and is offered as bread and wine.) The usher approached the front pew and waved the servers to come forward so I could receive the holy bread and wine. At the end of the Mass, the congregation stood and praised the Lord with a hymn led by the church choir. *Wow! I want to dance! All right! I feel it!* My right eye began to tear again from exultation. *Hey!* My grade school basketball coach, Mr. McCarthy, offered his comfort. I could not say much. I was so moved by the spirit, I had a lump in my throat.

I felt great. I was so comfortable with my surroundings at the Center. I began to walk from therapy session to therapy session without the cane. I was still unsteady, but, *hey, I am ahead of my goal #3: to walk without a cane! All right!* I was as motivated then as I am now: *let's get it done!* In between therapy sessions, I walked around the octagon-shaped reception area. I was out of control. All excited! I pranced around like a child chasing butterflies.

I wanted to help other clients step in the same shoes I walked in. I wanted to motivate the clients. I wanted to share my success. The following is an article I wrote for the RAC newsletter.

"Willingness of the Soul"

Whoever is reading this, ask yourself, what is your goal? What are you doing right now to achieve that goal? How could you have a dream and not do anything to achieve it? The main idea of this article is the human will, determination and the soul.

If you don't mind, let me ask you another question. How many of you (clients) will continue therapy once you leave here? Well, it should be continued. Why? I will give you an example: I came here in mid-November, glued to a wheelchair. I had neither the desire, nor will, nor determination to improve. I was going nowhere fast. Then I did something. I set three realistic goals in January: 1) Walker to a quad-cane by February; 2) Quad-cane to straight-cane by March, which I have achieved; 3) Walk unassisted by July. What happened was, I committed myself. I developed determination to complete my goals. I worked overtime. I worked on therapy daily after 4:00 p.m., and on the weekends. A person must work hard to get where they want to go. Have a pro-active attitude. In other words, the individual soul and heart can do more than what any book says.

9

Don't Be a "Wimp." Get Up and Adapt!

One Saturday afternoon, Chris my good friend and motivator stopped by for a visit. "Hey, buddy," I said. "Look at this, no cane!" I was in the kitchen facing the front door when Chris entered. "Watch this!" I ran around the kitchen like a two-year-old. "All right!" Chris was thrilled and he remarked: "Seeing you like this brings a tear to my eye."

5/17/91: Darryl walked two blocks without a cane and is elated. "Needs a girl-friend."—Dr. Kent.

I had just completed a huge task, yet I felt lonely. Sure, there was stupendous support around me, but it was not the same as sharing it with a female companion. Nothing can compare to when the heart speaks. I thought about Vicki often. She was behind my energy; she was my prime motivation. I wanted to climb the mountain for her. It had only been one year before that we had become friends. I still had the burning memories of love. I was down. *What if nothing had happened? Would we still be involved in a close relationship?* I even thought about dating anyone who came along—someone just to share thoughts with. Before the surgery, I had been a regular guy; I had relationships; I was a romantic. I found myself thinking back to the summer of the late '80s. I had liked to go to the sandy beaches of Lake Michigan with Maritza, a Venezuelan friend from college. She and I would have a bottle of champagne and look at the stars. We discussed everlasting thoughts, dreams, while smooth rhythmic patterns were orchestrated from waves caressing the shores. *I miss that!*

I had often imagined Vicki walking down to my basement to witness my determination while I exercised on the stationary bike. That was so real to me. *I will date, but, I am not ready to date yet. Come on, let's go!* To combat the lonely feeling that dared to intrude upon my positive frame of mind, I told myself that I needed to concentrate on me. *I have nothing to offer a woman anyway—at least not now!* I didn't have much opportunity to make social contacts. I rationalized to myself about why I didn't go out: A majority of my friends were now married or heavily involved with their "significant others." You know, they were busy. I wanted to leave Vicki alone, and when I became brave enough to call her, she was busy filling out applications to medical school. Apparently, she had other things on her mind. *Hey, Didier, do not get depressed! Don't lose the edge! Remember what brought you here!*

As a result, my confidence soared. I felt so good with my overall ability. I started to venture out of my room in the morning very discreetly to the bathroom, independently! I didn't want to wake Brenda. Then I slowly climbed into the tub, using the wall as a brace with my right hand, stepped down, and sat on the shower seat. *All right!* I took a shower independently! Dried myself off independently! Climbed out of the shower independently! *Mmm. I will sneak downstairs, then walk quietly into the kitchen and make my breakfast, independently!* I opened a box of Wheaties and filled a bowl to capacity, then fixed rye toast and I *buttered it myself!* I even ate the meal, myself, in total, utter peace until I was caught a minute later by Brenda. I wasn't surprised. When I walked, the entire house shook. I was like Frankenstein. "What are you doing?" Brenda asked, her hair frazzled in all directions. "I did it all on my own, with no problems!" That was the start of doing things on my own in the morning without my sister's assistance.

This pretense went on for a week before Brenda brought up the subject with my parents. They were pleased. *All right, I will have some independence!*

Along with my growing independence, I developed growing concerns: Return to Merrill Lynch; attain Master's Degree in Business Administration; complete job therapy. I was still hurt by Vicki, who no longer seemed interested in me. She ran out on a modern miracle! I had brain cancer, was dragged through the dirt, and rose to the occasion. I was winning! That thought is what kept me sane.

I loved Vicki so much! I was motivated by her. I wanted to take her up on the three-mile marathon she had challenged me to the day after surgery. But Vicki didn't call and I was too nervous to call her.

5/24/91:   Darryl said he has an idea of writing a book.—Dr. Kent.

The support staff encouraged me to write a book about my recovery, with the "I will come back!" attitude that was maintained throughout. It could help other people.

5/30/91:   Darryl shared more thoughts: "Focus on what you want. How badly do you want it? How hard are you willing to work to get there?"—Dr. Kent.

Again self-responsibility. Come on, what are you willing to do to achieve your goal? Do you want to walk, get out of the predicament you are in, whatever it may be: Education, building one's career, getting over alcoholism or drugs, any challenge with which one is faced. If you want it badly enough, then you can do it. Don't cry about it and blame it on someone—or something. Take self-responsibility! Don't be a "wimp" and hide in the corner. Adapt; get up and go. Mow down the obstacles that lie ahead of you!

6/4/91:   Volunteer work at Farmers Insurance.—Dr. Kent.

Thank goodness for RAC. The Center had an excellent philosophy. The main goal of rehab was to heal the client in such a way that he/she could re-enter the workplace—make contributions to society and build self-worth, self-confidence.

Kim Hogan, OT, was preparing me for a work re-entry program. I was asked to update my resume and write a cover letter. *Ah, I am used to this. Heck, I sent out 200 resumes before I graduated from college.* She encouraged me to find a volunteer job where I could work on my previous job skills. *Cold-calling. Go get 'em!* I knew from recent conversations with Frank, the flamboyant van driver, that he did cold-calling on a part-time basis at Farmers Insurance in Park Ridge, a northwest suburb of Chicago. I decided to do some networking and seize the opportunity. I asked Frank if he could get me in and I gave him my updated resume to pass on to the office manager. The following day, Frank came back and told me the good news: "The office manager and the insurance agent welcomed the idea. They want you to call." I called Phyllis, the office manager. We set up the work re-entry program scheduled for every Thursday, from 9:00 a.m. to 12:30 p.m.

Primed and ready, I walked into the Center. I felt good; I felt important. As soon as Kim was ready, we drove in her car to Park Ridge, a 30-minute drive southwest on Rt. 83.

When we arrived, Kim parallel-parked the car in front of the Farmers Insurance office, which was in a separate one-story building in the small-town-like strip. Across the street, resting on a 30-foot platform, was the Park Ridge train station from which many people commuted downtown. Kim opened the passenger door and cautiously assisted me while I tried to get out of the car. I lost my balance and left my handprints all over her window. I leaned on the cane, then up the curb to the sidewalk, then to the office entrance. What a task! What a reality check. *You have to deal with curbs and sidewalks in life!* When Kim and I entered the quaint, two-agent, two-secretary office, we were greeted very warmly by the administrator. In my loud voice, I said: "Good morning! How ya doing today?" Kim introduced us. I was not surprised by the enthusiastic reaction. When I had spoken with Phyllis the week before and had mentioned Frank's name, she was energetically accommodating. She immediately told me that the other gentleman in the office specialized in pension accounts. Phyllis hinted to me that he might need assistance with marketing the pension accounts to local businesses. *Hmm. Maybe I can work with him in the near future. I can see myself in this suburb.* Phyllis led Kim and me to a small office, which housed a desk, chair and the main tool, a telephone. I was handed a list of dental offices to call and was instructed, with a script, to cold-call dentists in the area and probe them about when their current dental coverage was up for renewal. I felt great! *I am getting closer to the game!* I concentrated when I dialed. It was difficult to distinguish the numbers; my eyes produced two different images. But, *my eyes are getting better! I do not need glasses to see within close proximity! Well, next time I will bring my eye patch to block out the double vision, so I can focus quickly!*

After I made a few calls, Kim graded my work-trial performance. She suggested that I hold the receiver on the undamaged side of my face. She thought I would sound more intelligible to the person on the other side of the phone and she was right: The first form of adaptation in the real world. I called down the list. *Hey, I am understood! I'm making some key contacts! Yes!*

After two hours, the visit concluded. Kim and I were invited back for the following Thursday, so it was a success. Back outside to the jungle to do some more rock climbing (having to deal with the sidewalk obstacle course).

6/6/91:   Darryl is working on the PACE application with the OT.—Dr. Kent.

The occupational therapist, Ann, was working with me to be able to go out into the community independently and safely. PACE operates van/buses for the general public in the suburban townships around Chicago, and has a Special Services Department. The main purpose is to offer independent travel at a very affordable price, 35 cents one-way, for the elderly and disabled. *Isn't that great? I'll be able to go out on my own!*

6/8/91:   Darryl is positive thinking and motivational. Wants to share a video with the whole group.—Dr. Kent.

I was very desperate to fire up the entire group of clients at RAC that I was seriously considering showing a motivational video of Lou

Holtz, the inspiring coach of the Notre Dame Football team and the subject of the made-for-TV movie, "Fighting Back," circa 1981, about Rocky Blier. *Gosh, what an inspirational movie!* Rocky Blier was the star halfback on Notre Dame's Football team his senior season, 1966, when they won the National Championship. He was drafted in the 16th round by the Pittsburgh Steelers and was considered too slow and too small to be in the NFL as a halfback. The following year, he was drafted into the army to fight in the Vietnam War as an infantryman. In 1969, during an ambush, a hand grenade landed next to him while he was in a hut dodging the enemy. The grenade exploded and severely damaged his legs. Doctors doubted his ability to walk normally again, but he worked and worked and worked. He went back to the Steelers' training camp in 1971. His 40-yard-dash-time was too slow. Although he made the team, he had only limited playing time, but he did not quit! He came back and became the team's starting halfback in 1974, helping the Steelers win four Super Bowl titles: 1975, '76, '79, and '80. He had that determination to fight back! He did it with valor and greatness. *Gosh, that video will challenge everybody to succeed! If he could do it, I can do it. We all can do it!* I looked for the video at "Blockbuster," but they couldn't locate it in their massive archive of videos. I went to the local library circulation desk, but they could only locate a video about the Revolutionary War that had the same name: "Fighting Back." So, I never had a chance to show the film, but two years later, I did find the book, Fighting Back, written by Rocky Blier with Terry O'Neil. What an inspiration that book was to me!

6/10/91:   Darryl said he went to a Medjugorie party.—Dr. Kent.

My family and I were invited to a Medjugorie party at the home of a Mr. and Mrs. Rio. Mr. Rio was a good friend and colleague of my father's when they worked together at Continental Bank in Chicago. Two weeks prior, I had met the Rios when Dad and I visited them in their home. It was a one-story cozy house in a nice middle-class neighborhood in the suburb of Arlington Heights.

What is a Medjugorie party? I found out that Medjugorie is a mountain in Yugoslavia where it is said, the Blessed Virgin Mary has appeared several times. It is believed that many healings have occurred there. The Rios, with their two daughters, around my age, had gone with a group of 10 on a pilgrimage to the holy city a few months before. The party's purpose was to unite the people who had gone on the trip together. When we arrived at the Rios', I was anticipating a very friendly group and my expectations were met. There was a close spiritual feeling. One could sense that all who were present had great camaraderie. Laughter resounded throughout the cocktail hour. The people were tremendous. Even though Mom, Dad, and I were outsiders, we were immediately accepted. Before dinner was served, a Mass was said by the priest who had journeyed with them. After the two-hour filling dinner, everyone formed a circle on the brick two-level patio. On the top tier, people sat at a wooden picnic table that was lightly covered with maple seeds that had drifted down from the mature tree that canopied over us. On the lower tier, six of us were sprawled out on lounge chairs. As I sat there, I peered through the branches and saw that the sky was star-filled. There was a constant hum from the crickets. It was very calm—a perfect summer night. The pilgrim shared the personal, spiritual experiences they had witnessed at Medjugorie. For example, a story that sticks in my mind was told by Ben. He owned his own medium-sized advertising agency, and when he started out, he had been very skeptical of the stories he had heard about Medjugorie, and he said he had wanted to witness it firsthand. During the pilgrimage, he took a hike with Ann, Mr. Rio's fun-loving daughter, up to the mountain top, where a large cross was located. As they were climbing the mountain, he looked up at the cross. He once again expressed skepticism about the holy witnesses, then continued on. When he looked at the cross for the second time, he saw it rising. He said he shook his head in disbelief: "No way, I am not drunk. This can't be!" When he looked up a third time, as the cloudy skies opened up, the cross was aflame and rising. *Incredible!*

When we returned to the present, the party ended in silence. Mrs. Rio gave my father two small plastic containers of holy water, some soil and a Rosary from the holy city. That night, after we got home, I was about to enter my room, but I stopped. My dad was flicking holy water on my bed. *Now I know I will make it. I have divine power on my side*, as I was looking towards heaven.

6/12/91:   **Darryl feels that the Center should create a team atmosphere.—Dr. Kent.**

I told Harry, the psychologist: "We are all in this together." Harry agreed and said that we needed to create a chant and bring everybody together once a day. MMM! A minute passed. The motivational chant was born:

"WE ARE ALL HERE AT RAC! WE ARE ALL GOING TO FIGHT BACK! WE KNOW IT IS GOING TO TAKE TIME, BUT WE ARE ALL GOING TO BE FINE!"

In-between therapy sessions, I gathered up as many people—from clients to therapists—as I could see fluttering around in the Center. I rushed up and instructed them, a total of 10, give or take one or two, to form a circle in the middle of the gym, and place their hands together, in the middle, then call out as loudly as possible the "RAC Chant." It worked! **YEAH!**

6/26/91:   **Darryl said: "No Chemo." Dr. Vick said, "Okay."**

Dr. Vick reiterated his earlier stance of two months before. Mom, Dad, and I (this time with a straight cane) proudly walked into the check-up room at the Kellogg Center. To my surprise and initial concern, three medical students were present. *Well, I don't know. They look pretty serious. Oh, shoot! Now what's wrong?* Then I was flabbergasted. Dr. Vick, who taught neurology at Northwestern University—one of the top, elite medical schools in the country—proudly shared my case history and how far I had come. The he asked me to share what I had been doing regarding rehabilitation. Realizing that I was a unique case, I threw my shoulders back and spoke with confidence, over-enunciating. I said that while I was receiving various structural therapies every day, all day, I also took it upon myself (self-responsibility) to exercise resolutely, on a stationary bike while listening to motivational "hip-hop" music. The music provided positive thoughts as a result of endorphins—the euphoric feeling (the "second wind") one gets from exercising vigorously. I went on to tell them that I walked and walked and walked. I kept talking and talking. "I am going to win! I treat cancer like a enemy. Go after it." The medical students turned their attention from the doctor to me, staring at me with respect. The doctor placed before, during, and after MRI readings in slots on a roll scope (a fluorescent screen). He explained the medical terminology in detail. *Oh, my gosh! He might find something!* I was nervous looking at my own brain scans. But Dr. Vick just reiterated that I should have another MRI in three months. *Time to eat healthy food and work out as much as possible!* We shook hands and I happily left. I would like to note here that Mom is a great cook. No fatty foods. Each night for dinner, she fixed a stupendous salad with onions, tomatoes, broccoli and, very importantly, fresh herbs. I always had seconds and whenever I snacked, it was fresh fruit.

6/28/91:   **Darryl said that he was trying to adapt his personality, but agreed to be himself.—Dr. Kent.**

I wondered why people didn't like me and thought that I was so weird. Was I too loud, too aggressive? I like to make teasing comments. I couldn't regulate my facial expressions, so a person I would be clowning around with couldn't tell if I was joking or serious. *Mmm! Maybe I should be more laid-back and passive. I wonder if I should listen to the therapist and not be so loud.* I did change for a day, but found it terribly boring. The effort sapped my internal energy and was debilitating. *Hey, what are you doing? Let's go!* "Hey, Harry, what is going on?" I asked, as I strode unsteadily into Dr. Kent's office to share my views.

7/31/91:   Darryl had an appointment downtown at Paine Webber to see his bosses from Merrill Lynch.

After a grueling day at RAC, I was in the kitchen with my family at around 7:00 p.m. I was getting ready to claim my place at the table, to chow down on a delicious dinner. The telephone rang. I scurried to answer the phone. "Hello! Hi, Mr. Watkins." I began to over-enunciate; this was a very important call to me. It was George Watkins, a man I respected in business as a high-flier (one who gets things done by leadership). I also respected George for giving me the chance to flourish at Merrill Lynch. George and John were the men with whom I had smoked the stogie. As we talked, he forwarded a vote of confidence by stating that I was speaking much clearer than the last time we had spoken. He threw me a verbal proposal, telling me that he would like me to come downtown to the Paine Webber office where "the partners" had moved their business. (It is very transient in the financial community.) He wanted me to seriously consider "cold-calling" (smiling and dialing) for new pension business, as I had done at Merrill Lynch. "You still remember what to say?" George asked. *Yes!* "Hello, Mr. Smith. I am aware that you are very busy, but may I take a few moments of your time? I understand that your company has a retirement account already established for your employees...etc." I knew the pitch down to a T; I had said it 100 times a day. *How could one forget?* George and I made the appointment for July 5, 10:00 a.m. *All right!* I immediately shared my delight with my parents. *I feel important again! Yeah!* The added incentive was that the office was downtown in the financial district on Madison Avenue. The area was so competitive. *People have places to go; people to see; goals to achieve! Let's go!*

The next day, when I went to the Center, I proudly told the therapists about the appointment. It was decided that Judy would go with me, to make sure that I got there in one piece.

The day arrived and boy, I felt proud. I wore my black suit with a silver-trimmed dress shirt and an aqua-blue tie. *I look good in aqua-*

blue. Two middle-aged female clients, in wheelchairs, reinforced my confidence. Judy scheduled everything to coincide with the appointment. *Hey! I could have done it!* I was insulted, taking it personally. Did the therapist think I was an imbecile, and just not say anything about it? Nah—I was being overly sensitive.

We took the 9:00 a.m. train from the Mt. Prospect station. We had to cross two tracks to get to the southbound commuter. I pranced like a petrified kitty crossing the path of a doghouse. I hated tracks. I imagined my foot getting stuck between the rails while a train was pile-driving down the tracks. *Whew!* We made it. When the car doors opened, I was faced with a new challenge: how to scale the three high steps to enter the train. Ah, but there were railings that I could latch onto and pull myself up and away. Ha, no problem!

When we arrived at Union Station, I exited the Metra commuter car down the steep three steps while grasping the middle railing for support. Judy waited down below, ready to catch me if I missed a step. But I didn't. As we walked through the long underground depot, there was no room for a mistake. *I am glad I am wearing my black high-top basketball shoes, for support and control.* One had to really hustle. *What an adrenaline pump, just coming to the downtown area.*

Judy and I walked the two blocks to the building. I paid the utmost attention to the curvatures in the sidewalk and the edges. I certainly didn't want to tumble, then be trampled on or fall over the edge out into the middle of traffic. We walked eastbound on Adams for two blocks. *There it is!* The glass office building towered over the competition, gleaming silver and light blue over the city as the summer sun emphasized its radiance.

We hurried across the street at the crosswalk, me, with cane in hand. I did stop to analyze how I could manage the four cement steps leading to the entrance. There was a railing to hang onto. We walked 100 feet to the doors and swung through. Judy and I located the correct bank of elevators that took us to the 43rd (out of 100) floor. The elevator was lined with mirrors so one could view oneself from all angles. I didn't look because I didn't want to lose my self-confidence by seeing a different image than what I thought a confident young executive. We were scrunched in tightly with a group of business people. *Way too close!* I wanted to hide; I did not want to frighten anyone. Not a word was spoken during the ride. Everyone was fixated on the floor-counter above the doors. Then I said to myself: *what a bunch of robots. Do I want to be like this? Mmm!* People filtered out according to their designated floor. Judy and I were the last ones in the elevator. Finally, as my ears popped, we reached the 43rd floor. We darted directly to the reception desk. *The entire floor was leased by Paine Webber.* I was nervous—so nervous that I didn't return the "hello" from the friendly receptionist.

As we started to make our way into George's suite, George's and John's administrative assistant peeked her head out from her credenza to say hello.

While in the office, the two partners began to discuss the opportunity of working for them as a prospector for institutional accounts. George told me that he had talked with the manager of Paine Webber's main Chicago office. He explained to him my condition to him and told him that I had a speech impediment. George said the manager had no problem with the idea and thought that it would be great to have me around. *Wow!* I glanced out the windows and soaked up the magnificent view, overlooking the city towards the east. I took pleasure in noticing that "Taste of Chicago," the fantastic annual food festival, was in full-swing at Grant Park. I loved overlooking the dark-blue waters of the lake from way up high. *Beautiful! I have always wanted to work in a high-rise office! Mmm!* What about logistics? *I could take the train and flag down a cab.* George said that John could provide a ride on the two or three days a week he drove into the city. *Mmm!* But I had to think about it. When the meeting ended, I said that I would call in a few days to give my answer. That call was never made. I was very concerned that I could lose my insurance with Merrill Lynch. I had visions of being followed by a Merrill Lynch special agent, trying to find out exactly what I was doing. I did not want to take a chance on jeopardizing my safety net. Without the insurance, the family would be out on the street somewhere. I also felt that I wasn't quite ready to be a cold-caller; soon, but not yet.

7/6/91: **Darryl said that he still wants to be a success: "Get out in the environment again."—Dr. Kent.**

This cancer sidestep is not going to stop my climb! It may alter it, but it will not stop it! I am not going to be held back! Get out there and live! I was highly motivated by being in the financial district of Chicago. I wanted to return to that highly competitive environment when the time was right.

7/10/91: **Darryl shared that he went to a concert.—Dr. Kent.**

Wow, all right! as I dressed myself. It wasn't that hard, really. I simply sat on the bed. I had limited balance; so what? It would get better. In the meantime, I listened to my clock radio, which was tuned in to a smooth jazz station. During a break, the disc jockey announced that Otmart Liebert was going to perform a concert that weekend. *All right! I love his style of playing the upbeat, rhythmic Spanish flamenco with smooth jazz!* I had just started to be an awed fan when Vicki and I became friends in June of 1990.

I immediately called and ordered five tickets via my Visa card. *All right! What initiative. I am not all washed up.*

I began to recruit team members who wanted to go and enjoy the show. My mother happily agreed; my father reluctantly agreed; Chris Larson very joyfully accepted, since he was an avid fan, like me. Ron, the van driver, also wanted to go. Ron was in his mid-thirties, medium height, slender, with a soft but authoritative, caring voice. He and I had become good friends. We had thought-provoking, philosophical conversations during our many drives to and from the Center.

Gosh, I really wish Vicki would go, but I am not going to risk asking her! I did not want to call and put any kind of pressure on her, afraid to lose what little contact we had. When Vicki and I went on our first date, I bought Otmart Liebert's very first tape called "Nuevo Flamenco." I played it on my car stereo because I wanted to make an impression. That first date was great and when I dropped Vicki off.

We decided that all parties should meet at my house at 4:30. Dad drove our maroon 1990 Oldsmobile to the Park West Hotel in Lincoln Park (Yuppieville). The area was lined with old brownstones, with vines sneaking up the front and sides of the classic dwellings.

On the drive down, Chris and Ron became the navigators in the back seat. They knew the area and we reached our destination around 7:00 p.m. Dad pulled the car up to the entrance of the theater. Ten feet of concrete led to the five-door entrance at a 30-degree ascending slope. Mom went to the ticket window to claim the tickets with the order number given to me over the phone. It seemed to be taking Mom a long time. Had I transcribed the wrong number? *Darn it!* Luckily, they had the tickets by the last name. As we walked into the cozy theater-lounge, Chris latched onto my arm to make sure I wouldn't take a dive. We scanned the theater to locate the most strategic table for five that had the best view of the stage. It was general admission seating. As we roamed around, I took notice: *wow! Look at all these attractive people dressed in fashionable black clothes. There is no excuse! I have to get back!* We were also "hip" with our clothing.

We took our seats—Mom, Dad, Ron, Chris and I—at a table on the second level, 200 feet from stage-right. The theater was tiered by five levels with tables on each one. At the base of the stage were a number of banquet-like tables that comfortably seated parties of 10. Smooth jazz was played softly over the intercom to set the mood. One could hear the cling-clang of glasses, along with the chatter and laughter of the festive audience. Our whole group was in eager anticipation, except for my dad. He was very skeptical and never has been a great fan of any kind of music. He is not musically inclined in any way, shape, or form, resulting from damage to his ear that he received in WW II. What little music he tolerate were sounds that rapidly sang out from the Spanish guitar. I knew that I would never win the debate, but I decided to play-up Otmart Liebert as the best flamenco-with-jazz combo in the world. "Come on! It is interesting and different."

Anyway, as the crowd was anxiously waiting for the concert to begin. A young woman, sitting behind our table, tapped me on the shoulder. She asked if I was the brother of someone she knew. "Well, no, but people always seem to associate me with somebody they know." Chris took notice of the inquiry by the woman and said: "Hey, Dids, you still have it." *What? All right! I still do! A sign of improvement!*

The music started. The percussionist played a smooth, rhythmic jazz beat accompanying a bass guitar, and Otmart Liebert strummed flamenco. I turned and noticed my mother's enjoyment. When I stretched my neck and turned more to my right, I saw that Dad was tapping his fingers on the table.

The concert lasted for three hours, with three encores. We strategically waited until the majority of the happy fans filed out, so I could plow through. I held onto Chris's shoulder; he was the fullback leading me through the hole. We made it! Dad retrieved the car from the parking garage across the street. In conclusion, we all enjoyed ourselves immensely. I became more determined than ever to make it back into the norms of society. *Come on!*

10

Do the Best with the Hand You Are Dealt

7/11/91: Darryl is concerned about returning to the work environment.—Dr. Kent

After giving it a great deal of thought, I decided that it wouldn't be in my best interest to re-enter the work environment at that time. *I need to exercise my legs. Motivate the nerves! I cannot sit for any long duration of time! If I do, I will go back to ground zero:* Back to the wheelchair! *All the hard work would go for naught.*

7/12/91: Darryl said he has to be one step ahead of everybody else. He has to work harder than everybody else.—Dr. Kent.

Downstairs, in the basement, where my glistening thoughts were generated while exercising to the rhythm of music, I told myself over and over: *just get it done! Just get it done!* Ten minutes elapsed; sweat began to permeate through my skin cells, then poured down my face. *All right!* When the rhythm picked up, my pace picked up. *Just get it done! Just get it done! One has to work to get where they want and I have to work harder than most people to meet my dream!*

7/14/91: Darryl said his friends are telling him that he is very driven and motivated.—Dr. Kent

The support staff (my friends) called on the phone. Naturally, they were concerned. They inquired about how I was doing. I resounded: "Great! Great! Why, do I sound sick? You have to do the best you can with the hand you are dealt." That is something else that Dad says.

7/20/91:   Darryl is clearly frustrated. He said: "To overcome the frustration, I talk to myself and pump myself up with motivational sayings or messages."—Dr. Kent.

I immediately went outside and walked up and down the driveway, but I would not dare to venture down the six-foot 40-degree slope at the end of the drive. Because the surgery had damaged my VIII cranial nerve, my muscles had limited ability to combat gravitational forces. I was steady with my balance for the first 50 feet, from one side of the driveway back to the front turn-around. I then began to sway like a sailing ship on the wavy sea. I stopped and counted 30 seconds to gather my bearings. *Come on!* I kept going back and forth. An hour later, I called it quits. I took part in a stretch program, on the front lawn, for my legs. I had read an article in a fitness magazine stating that it is very important to stretch your legs after you have worked out. **Keep Going!**

The first in a series of the facial nerve reconstruction:

Middle of July, 1991. Mom and I traveled to Glenbrook Hospital, where I had an appointment with Dr. Casis, an attractive female plastic surgeon who was recommended by Dr. Vick. The purpose of the appointment was to test my seventh nerve that controls my left cheek. After being led into an examining room, where I was instructed by the nurse to climb up to a hospital-like bed and lay face-up, Dr. Casis entered the room and offered a warm greeting. Then she placed electrodes on my left cheek to detect any life in the nerve. The results were very conclusive: no activity, no impulses; in other words, the nerve was completely dead and the left side of my face was paralyzed. *Oh, well. At least I am still around!* Dr. Casis recommended that we consult with

Dr. Penslers' reconstructive surgeon, at Children's Memorial Hospital in Chicago about his procedure. We seized the option. The appointment was set up for September 16, 1991.

I was still trying to figure out a way to make my wish become a reality—to be able to smile all the way across my face again. I had dreams in the wee morning hours that my lip was just like it used to be. *Yes! My lip is straight across. I can see it in the bathroom mirror. I will be able to speak normally!* I awoke in a daze and scooted out of bed. I went frantically out of control to the washroom, bashing into the antique black cabinet in the hall. The family was disturbed by the high-pitched clanging of the lamp as it swayed above the cabinet top. A yell came from the master bedroom; of course, it was Mom. She could hear everything. "Darryl, what are you doing?" I always replied: "Nothing." I flipped the switch, held my breath and peeked; then peeked some more into the mirror. *Darn it! I was dreaming again! Well, that's good. If I can dream it—imagine it—then it can happen.* The "smile dream" occurred frequently. I remembered that while I was on the "Step-Down Floor" back at the hospital, Brenda told me that the mother of a close friend faced a similar situation. Brenda said that the woman massaged her paralyzed cheek for months. "It all came back after a year." My loving sister stocked the dresser by my hospital bed with packs of gum. I didn't grab the opportunity. I was lazy then. But not anymore! I now chew five pieces of gum per day, hold up my cheek whenever I talk on the phone, practice smiling exercises, and read out loud from a newspaper.

7/28/91: **Darryl said: "Marie Andres, vocational therapist, included divided attention tests."—Dr. Kent.**

On a hot summer afternoon, in my physical therapy class, three other clients and I were getting prepared for a walk around a lake. The small lake was a design fixture of the modern 15-story office building across the street from the Center. In the gym, Sandy, PT, guided us through stretching exercises before the journey. *Ha, number one: I can't stand up and do stretches like the others, so I will do my own thing. Besides, my way is more effective. I know what I am doing. I played ball and always worked out, so there! Mmm…(what a snob!)*

The group made its way through the parking lot, and crossed the barren street, to a sidewalk that encircled the office building. The walkway around the lake was the length of a 440-yard high school track. I figured that it was used by the employees for a walk or jog during their lunch break. Since it was 2:00 p.m., it was quiet. The sidewalk had a slight slant towards the lake for water runoff. The slant posed a problem, and one also had to dodge the little bombs strewn all over (goose droppings). I was doing pretty well without a cane, or so I thought. Karen, who was walking with me, said that I'd make a good drunken sailor in a movie. "You would be a natural." *What? What do you mean?* What goes around, comes around, I guess. I deserved that for being a smart-aleck when she assisted me in the mornings after I had just started at RAC.

That's what I look like out in society? As we continued, Karen asked a few questions. With every response, I stopped, planted my feet then spoke. I could not perform two challenging activities at one time. My balance needed utmost attention when I walked. My speech needed utmost attention when I talked. So much energy was involved in each task. I could not walk and talk at the same time or else I would fall, although sitting and talking was no problem at all.

Another example: A few weeks earlier, during the PT session, I walked outside in the parking lot with Sandy. I tried to stay balanced along the yellow lines, but every time we talked about an interesting topic, I stalled my momentum and then jabbered. The therapists were concerned about this lack of double concentration. As a result, Marie, the vocational therapist, instituted double concentration tests. A list of mixed numbers was placed before me. I was instructed to circle the numbers that had a multiple of 5; then, at the same time, listen carefully to a tape of a person rehearsing singular nouns. Words starting with "N," for example, had to be counted and marked on a separate sheet. My performance was timed. The higher the grade, the faster the words would be announced. The first trial was difficult, but once I kept on taking part in double concentration tasks, they became challenging and fun. I scored in the high range, and I actually looked forward to the tests. Please note: When these tests were administered, I was sitting, which is quite different from walking and talking at the same time. *Wait, no excuse!*

8/1/91: **Darryl went on a vacation to Maine.—Dr. Kent**

Mom and I took off from O'Hare Airport, while Dad stayed behind to tend to business. I hated planes. If there was a mistake, you were doomed. One does not have control. *I have much more living to do!* The purpose was to visit my Aunt Betty and Uncle Dick at their summer camp in Belgrade, about 40 miles to the south of Augusta, the capital of Maine. All right, I was excited to go back again even though I didn't want to fly. I had many fond memories of the last time I had visited there, 20 years before, when I was six years old. The camp (a "camp" in Maine is known as a "cottage" elsewhere) was situated on hundreds of feet of lakefront property amidst the dense forest. I recalled that many camps were hidden by the foliage. Each one was very secluded.I remembered that when I was little, Mom, Dad, Aunt Betty, Uncle Dick, Brenda and I piled into their speedboat. We crossed the lake, about a mile, pulled into a marina, then wandered into a general store, where they had great homemade doughnuts. *Yum!*

I continued to reminisce. One could smell the pine, hear the birds—the loon's lonely echo across the lake—see the fish swimming in the crystal-clear lake; the clear-blue skies; the multitude of twinkling stars at night, with the occasional shooting star gliding across the sky. Nature at its best! Oh yes, and I remembered that the eastern rocky coast had an abundance of fresh lobster, for only $1.00 a pound. *Mmm!* I love seafood. I really missed the camp and I wanted to hang out with my aunt and uncle. We landed at the Augusta airport and I took notice. We were actually landing in the woods. *This sure is not like*

O'Hare, with the hustle and bustle of planes; ant-sized cars crawling along the freeways and toll ways. I am glad I am here.

I was able to get all the exercise I needed, being closely assisted by Uncle Dick. I worked on a rowing machine in the camp garage for 20 minutes, walked in the lake, waist high, often having my feet nibbled by a sunfish, and performed twisting exercises with floating Styrofoam barbells. I had the laborious task of walking on the camp road, well behind Mom, Aunt Betty and Uncle Dick. Why? So I wouldn't weave into one of them. The camp road dipped, swayed and turned in all directions; it was a well-traveled car path. I tried to stay in-between the tire crevasses because this was the steadiest terrain. *Ah, what a challenge! Darn it! Waah! I almost lost it! Thank gosh I am wearing my high-top black sneakers for support.* Mom viewed my struggle and told me that after this trip, I would be able to handle level ground in the Midwest with ease. I was determined to have a good vacation, though—to enjoy the natural beauty and not be hindered by balance impairment. I was not going to succumb to any limitations. I tried everything during the trip. Since Mom and Aunt Betty loved to browse through old "things," I even dared to sneak around in an antique shop located in one of the many small towns we visited. I was like a "bull in a china shop." *Man, if I lose my balance and weave into a bunch of old antiques, I could be liable, and end up owing a bundle. I do not want to take that chance!* What to do? Well, at every parking lot, I walked around on the grounds without straying too far from the car, with Uncle Dick supervising. Or I sat in the station wagon, grabbed a magazine and read aloud, practicing my diction, enunciation.

All in all, it was a great vacation with my artistic Aunt Betty and very comical ex-jazz drummer, Uncle Dick. I even learned how to devour a lobster like a real Maine native, by strategically removing the outer shell to enjoy the delicacy. How could I be foiled? I was instructed by a native, Uncle Dick. Keep Going!

Back to reality.

8/15/91: I was ready to return to Merrill Lynch; I was sure of it. My speech was intelligible and I looked better than I had during my last visit; I had better mobility and my handwriting was more legible. I could certainly cold-call on a part-time basis or even work in the mailroom. *All right. This is it! Now or never!* I was a nervous wreck, wishing, hoping, praying that Mr. Davis, my former manager, would offer me something—anything, like cold-calling, just to show them, *again,* that I could do it. *I know I can.*

The appointment was set for late morning. It was a beautiful, bright, sunny day, but that didn't make me feel any calmer. Kim, the occupational therapist, who had coached me for successful work re-entry therapy at Farmers Insurance, drove me to the complex. *Oh, man!* I was ready to jump out the window and run all the way there. *Will I be accepted? Will I be tolerated? I hope I don't talk like an idiot, blah, blah, blah.* Twenty minutes later, we reached the office parking lot half an hour early. *Ah, here we are!* We had time to kill. *This is going to give me more time to think about it! That will make me more agitated.* "Kim, I am a nervous wreck," I said as we waited in the car. She had me do various speech exercises to calm me down. She told me to breathe deeply then say the alphabet, slowly. *It worked! Let's get 'em!* I rushed out of the car then charged to the entrance with cane in hand. *I am going to get some exercise and feel as high as an air balloon, (everybody else says kite!)*

I was warmly greeted by Wendy, my former manager's secretary. "Hi, how ya doing?" I asked. "How is the new baby?" I recalled that in late June, 1990, she was expecting. I assumed she'd had the baby by now since it had been a year. After telling me that the baby was great and saying how surprised she was that I had remembered, Wendy led me into Mr. Davis's office. As I sat across from him, I felt very nervous again, but soon Kim entered the room and introduced herself. She explained the therapeutic role she had played in my recovery. Mr. Davis' authoritative tone shifted and became accommodating. I remained very attentive to his dialogue, waiting to hear his decision.

He said that he had given much thought to the idea of my rejoining the company, and decided that the best way to bring me back into the firm would be to designate me as a "floater," to assist other stockbrokers whose regular assistant was sick or on vacation. He said that I would work three or four days a week, depending on the need. *All right! Wait a minute; don't start cheering yet!* I had worked on the institutional side (corporations) where the big dollars were. I had never learned how to process the individual accounts. *I will be in a sink-or-swim situation again. If I sink, I could really sink, with the entire family on board! Mmm! Could this be a set-up? I am sure they would love to get rid of me and the added cost.* Without the medical coverage, our family would be liable for 100 percent of the cost. Mom and Dad would probably have to sell the house and the majority of their assets.

At ease! A big sigh of relief! The meeting concluded with the same message, "Don't come back until you are ready to come back." I gleefully shook Mr. Davis's hand and wobbled with the cane to exit the premises. As we departed, I began to reflect: *These are the same footsteps that I took after a normal business day.* I replayed the scene in my mind: The sun was descending; I was feeling elevated, while riding the tides of success right in my grasp, only a few days before the infamous day, July 16, 1990. It was hard to handle the emotions now, but I became more determined than ever to re-enter the game. *I will rise again and be the best I can be!* Kim and I drove back to the Center for a few more rounds of rehab.

I decided not to return to work at this time. I felt that I wasn't ready yet because I needed more surgeries on my left cheek so I could communicate more effectively, perform my job well and also keep my health insurance intact. *If I am too hasty and go back and don't perform well on the job, I could get fired, and therefore, lose my insurance.* Keep Going!

8/15/91:   Darryl said he is stuck, due to insurance. He wants to get an MBA.—Dr. Kent.

8/19/91: I went on vacation again. *What a traveler!* Mom and I decided to fly out to San Diego to visit my grandmother. Grandma resided in a mobile-home park for people 55 and older, named "Mission View." Mission San Luis Rey was up in the hills, overlooking the park. Again, I did not like the idea of flying, especially to San Diego. I had read that it was the most difficult airport to land in because of the towering office buildings in close proximity to the runway.

Dad dropped Mom and me off at United's departure area. We flagged down a Skycap to check in our luggage then went on our L-O-N-G walk to the terminal. I enjoyed the walk because of the level floor, and the quick pace one had to maintain to stay in the flow. *Come on! You have somewhere to go quickly!*

All right! We made it to our gate, number 32, the last gate! I used the cane for support and guidance so I wouldn't bowl anyone down. Mom and I boarded the plane first because older and less able people were allowed to board first. We had to go down a walkway that connected the airport to the entrance of the plane, approximately 50 yards. It was difficult, because there was a 40-degree declining slope. I literally ran out of control to meet the pilot and his crew at the entrance. "Hey, what's going on?" I shook their hands, sternly, and offered them good luck. I took notice of the little kids on the flight. *Their time is not up. I am in good hands!*

I enjoyed the flight as I sat in the middle seat, reading. Once in a while, I peered anxiously at Colorado's interesting topography, especially the Grand Canyon, from a view of 30,000 feet. We landed safely, rented a car, and went on our way to see Grandma. I observed the very attractive people walking along the streets of San Diego and I began to wonder if I was attractive. *Mmm! Let's find out!* I lowered the front passenger window and poked my head out to take a peek in the rearview mirror. *Geesh! No way! I need more hair!*

I could not wait to see Grandma. I hadn't seen her for a year and four months, which had been the April before the cancer bout. I had talked with her on the phone, unintelligibly at times, and had the feeling that she didn't quite understand what had happened.

"Grandma! Hi!" I said, as we exchanged hugs. She took one look at me and began to analyze my facial impairments. "You are completely frozen on that side." She witnessed my UNSTEADINESS. "You're crippled like me." *No way, far from it!* She revealed her remorse. "Oh, Darryl, why did this have to happen in the prime of your life? You have a long way to go. I feel so sorry for you." I quickly responded, "There is nothing to worry about, Grandma. Everything is fine. There are many more opportunities out there in life." *One of my pet peeves is to have people feel sorry for me! I do not want sympathy. Only respect. I know I will get better! I am not afraid to work as hard as possible!* **Keep Going!**

The vacation was exercise-oriented and leisurely at the same time, which frustrated the heck out of me. *Oh well, I'll just take advantage of what is around me.* At the mobile-home park, there was a medium-sized pool that had a shallow end and a deep end, which was only five feet deep, so I was able to incorporate the same exercises that I performed in the YMCA's therapeutic pool. *This is great! I am able to exercise and soak up some vitamin D, sunshine.* But I used sunscreen that contained SPF 25. *I am not a sun god! I am Scottish-German, with red hair.* When I finished the swimming exercises, I walked along the streets in the small, quaint mobile-home park. *Hey, there are no angles, slopes or gravitational pulls.* There was little traffic, and if there were any vehicles crossing one's path, they went very slowly because the legal speed limit in the park was only 10 miles per hour. It was quiet! *Hey, everybody, what is going on?* When I walked past Grandma's neighbor's mobile home, Nelly, who was in her nineties and very fragile, came out on her front porch and called out my name. *Huh?* She told me that she and my grandmother were close friends, and when her husband went to the local grocery store, he would pick up some doughnut holes to share with my grandmother. *All right!* I had a friendly conversation about my grandma, the park, and me. She was interested in my medical history and I proudly shared it. I did not hesitate to say the word,

"cancer." She did not run away and hide like people in their twenties and thirties tended to do. Nelly was very considerate and told me that she had a great deal of respect for me. *Gosh! I notice the older generation does have more respect for what I have accomplished than most people of my own generation. Mmm! I wonder why!*

After the hour-long visit, Nelly and I hugged and agreed to visit again. *Let's go!* HEY, I AM MORE STABLE. The streets were level, so I kept going and going and going. My legs were getting very tired. *Where in the heck am I?* I was lost in the small park. My legs were literally out of control. I had to S-L-O-W-L-Y inch along, wishing I had my cane. I had overdone it again, as I often did. *All right, where is "Lynn Lane?"* I searched desperately for the street, even though it was right around the corner. I limped in the opposite direction, to the right. An hour later, I made it back. *Geesh! Pay attention! Concentrate!* Thank goodness the streets were empty. *Everybody is hiding in their mobile homes; the shades are pulled down; the doors are locked! "There he is!"* (Stupid, huh?) Mom and I visited with Grandma for two weeks. I was ready to move to sunny California. Everybody was so friendly. But since that was out of the question, I wished my grandma would come back with us. She lived alone. My grandfather had passed away 10 years before in his sleep, but she wanted to remain independent. She was/is one heck of a lady! She drove her Ford Pinto down the San Diego Freeway until she decided, on her own, that she was unable to drive safely and revoked her own driving privileges back in '91 at age 86. Grandma lives in the most ideal climate in the U.S. It is always sunny and 72 degrees year-round. My grandmother has never been sick; the climate has been good for her. I think I inherited her Scandinavian genes, to deal with this cancer. I don't blame her for staying in California. It was a good break, but I was ready to return to the enjoyable grind.

9/6/91:   Darryl's view on vacations: "Vacations are inhibiting. I am not challenged enough, leads to errors. Goals are reduced and the progress is
diminished." Darryl feels he has plateaued. "Will not get better."
Expressed frustration: 1. Can't drive. 2. Reduced visits by friends. 3.
Realization that Vicki is gone.—Dr. Kent.

I had thought that the vacations had provided enough exercise to
keep me from falling off the progressive path. Well, reality set in.
When I returned to the daily travails—the high peak performance
environment—I was not the same. *Geesh! I am back to ground-zero
again.* I could walk, but I struggled. The leg muscles were tight. My
legs crossed. The fluidity of my stride was gone. *Dang it! I have to start
all over again. I have to ride! I don't like vacations.* I was emotionally
down. *See, vacations make one mentally lazy!* I did not have the same
euphoric feeling after my exercises. I felt more dependent again. Everywhere I went during the trips to Maine and California, I had close
assistance, like a hand and a glove. Before the vacations, I was able to
carry out simple tasks on my own, like making breakfast, walking along
a sidewalk alone, etc. But while on vacation, every time there was a
hindrance in the way—a step up or a step down—I was always
reminded, then closely assisted. I felt like a little kid. I knew it was out
of love and concern, but I had lost the little independence I'd had. I
actually started to focus on the negatives of my situation, not the challenges set before me. I started to give in.

Vacations are okay if your job is completed. At the initial stage, I
liked getting away, but when I returned, I realized the debilitating
effect it had on me. *It was not the same as going down into the basement
to ride the stationary bike like a madman sweating profusely!*

9/7/91:   Driving on Sundays with Dad.—Dr. Kent.

The therapists shared with me the difficulty of the driving review
exam, which is in accordance to Illinois State Law and states that a person with any physical disorders must report it to the Secretary of State.
They said the exam is conducted at Marinjoy Driver's rehabilitation in

Wheaton, a far west suburb at a cost of $400.00 and offered once a year per person. They went on to say that the examiners test you with computer simulators for vision, and reaction time. If you qualify, there will be comprehensive drivers' evaluation by a police person. The results are sent to the Drivers' Medical Review Unit at the state. A team of doctors will make a decision if you are medically able to drive. If they decide in your favor, you can take the book and driver's tests at a local Secretary of State's office and hope you pass to legally obtain your license.

On that Saturday morning, my friend, Paul, and I were on our way to the local mall, Hawthorn Center. Paul was driving my beloved car. On our way, I was expressing my frustration that I could not legally drive, but I knew I was capable of driving. "All right," he said. He pulled into the Daniel Wright Elementary School parking lot, which was vacant. We switched seats. I shimmied over; he walked around. The car coughed and coughed while I shifted from first to second. *But I did it!* "See, I told you I could to it," I said, grinning at him. Hey, I have an idea! "Hey, Dad!"

I wanted so badly to practice driving; to become independent again. After Mass on Sunday, Dad and I practiced various driving techniques. My father drove to an office complex, "Lincolnshire Woods." Nobody worked on Sundays, so the place was totally deserted, resembling a ghost town. Close your eyes and imagine an old western "ghost town." The wind is blowing dust; four ravens are circling above, searching for the last inhabitants. Then, out of nowhere, a red hatchback Acura Integra goes pile-driving through an old wagon and comes to a screeching halt. Two shady characters perform a "Chinese Fire Drill": Dad the driver, and me the passenger, changing places. *Ahh, let's go!* I was confident that I could handle the 5-speed stick with ease. "What, you have not driven in over a year. You lack the coordination to handle a stick," the team of therapists had logically said. *Uh! That's what you think! I know I can do it!* Positive attitude!

I plopped into the seat and put on my seat belt. I placed an eye patch over my right eye (swimming eye) to alleviate the double vision. I turned on the motor; I placed my foot on the clutch, and shifted into first. *All right, here we go!* I slowly tried to time the gas with the release of the clutch. I remembered how hard it was, and how easy it was to stall. The car shook for a few seconds then died. *Geesh! Dang it!* This happened over and over, five times. Dad's knuckles turned white as he braced himself against the dash. I finally drove forward, trying to coordinate the flow of gas while easing the clutch. First...second...third...fourth...! *There! I knew I could do it!* The ravens above multiplied. Were they anticipating something? *Let's try it again!* I pulled the car off to the side and tried to time the clutch with the gas with perfect symmetry. The car coughed and faded out. *Let's try it again!* First, second! The car strained and finally forged ahead.

We went down the road, *a red octagon-shaped sign; ha, a stop sign!* It was like second nature. Another signal that I was not off the wall! I slowed down the car with the use of the gear shift, gradually reducing the rpms. I actually made a full stop behind the line. Not a "California Stop"; a rolling stop. *Oh, no! I have to start out in first again!* I glanced around slowly as my eye moved into focus. I looked to the right, then to the left, wanting to make certain I could make my attempt. I made the left turn. The car shuddered. I cruised into second; then third, doing a good 30 miles per hour. I turned right, into a cul-de-sac to the parking lot of an office complex. I tried to park the car in-between the lines. *Ah, I did it!* Dad was critical about my alignment—more critical than a driving instructor would be. Dad corrected my every driving move. With a frustrated burst, "All right, Dad."

I wove slightly to the left, not crossing to the other lane. As I clamped the steering wheel with full force, sweat balls formed on my forehead. *I have to concentrate hard and look straight ahead. Gosh, Dad sure is brave!* The two-hour excursion ended. It was only the beginning.

9/9/91:   Completed a successful work trial at Farmers Insurance. Seriously considering returning to Merrill Lynch and working in the mail room.—Dr. Kent.

9/10/91:   Took PACE bus for the first time.—Dr. Kent

All right! I felt great. I was making good strides. I had heard that there was talk among the therapists that my hours might be reduced as a result of my progress. My goal of independence was beginning to unfold. The PACE application was approved and I received a wallet-sized PACE Special Service ID card in the mail. (PACE is the suburban transportation service.) What a handsome card. It was yellow, with the blue insignia of PACE, and it had an April, 1990 picture of me, smiling.

This was a dual-edged sword. I wanted to be independent, but I did not want to be alone, either. Deep down inside, I wasn't that thrilled about it. Sandy, physical therapist, set up a trial run for me on the PACE bus to find out if I could handle it. I had been putting off filling out the registration form to qualify me for PACE Special Service. Reality hit on that pivotal, cloudy mid-afternoon. "Darryl, let's go! The PACE bus is here!" "Oh great." DARN! I waddled, with the cane, down the sidewalk, resisting gravity.

The mini-bus was like those rental vans at the airports, with the diesel engine humming. I grabbed a bar, like on the train ride, and pulled myself up the four steep steps to the entrance. I proudly displayed my ID card then clunked 35 cents into the coffer, a collection receptacle between the driver and the door.

I reluctantly took my seat, facing vertically, and began to scan the hollow shell and the vacant surroundings. *There is no one else on the bus.* I was all alone. I'd had some type of caregiver by my side since surgery. The diesel engine rattled. The bus was so empty. No music. *Nothing!*

Ah!! I took notice of the wheelchair lift and other adaptations for physically challenged people. *Oh, man! Reality hit hard. It is not fun and games. This is serious stuff. My life has really changed—180 degrees.* I was down in the doldrums. *After 10 months of rehab, I am still stuck! This is my life! I am disabled! Worse, I am more dependent!* I cried for the second time since July 17, 1990, that fourth evening before surgery when I broke down in Vicki's arms.

As the van took off, I was still whimpering. I held onto the straps so I would not be vaulted to the center aisle. The van bounced over potholes in the road. *Geesh! This bus does not have any shock absorbers.* I flopped up and down like a rag doll, so much that I sang out a note and automatically created a rhythm that flowed according to the terrain. *All right!* Reason entered the scene: *hey! Pick it up, Didier! It is not so bad. This offers some independence! Let's go!*

After the half-hour journey, I was dropped off at the Center to meet Sandy, PT. She inquired about my fun-filled experience on the PACE bus, and guess what I replied.

11

Keep Up the Intensity!

September 11, 1991. The days at the Center diminished to three days a week due to my progress, and besides, the insurance "nest egg" was running thin. The cost was $400.00 per day for rehabilitation at the Center. It was decided by Beth Fazio, Case Coordinator, that it was time for me to move on to bigger and brighter things. But I felt lost, like I was being abandoned—excommunicated.

After the family meeting at the Center, Mom, Dad and I were gathered around the dinner table. I voiced my concern about the drastically reduced hours. Mom was very adamant, and told me to volunteer, get out of the house. She said that I should write a long list of possible places. *Mmmm!* I thought hard and recalled that various RAC clients volunteered at a local hospital or at their local public library. Well, I did not follow through with either of these suggestions. At the initial stage, I was all right going to the Center three days a week.

On the off days, Tuesdays and Thursdays: *Mmm! Wow! Keep going, Didier!* At 5:30 a.m., I awoke and heard the chatter of Mom strategically instructing my father to wear a tie that matched his shirt. Times had not changed! I wanted to get a good start in the morning; I wanted to KEEP GOING, keep up the pace and not fall back to the basics. I put on a pair of worn-out shorts and a T-shirt, then charged down the stairs into the kitchen and shared a friendly good-morning growl with Dad when he was getting ready to leave for work. I carefully scaled down to the basement, clutching the railing with my right hand and bracing my left hand on the left wall for support. *Yeah! I have to get it done!* I didn't know what I had to get done, but I had to get it done. *Keep the blood flowing and clean out your system! Keep the right attitude!* After 20 minutes on the stationary bike, I performed 100 sit-ups, three sets. I was full of sweat and ready to start off the day with a bang! I took a shower, on the shower seat, and performed all the morning rituals. Then I dressed, and prepared my own cereal. *On my own!* At 7:00 a.m., as I was sitting at the kitchen table reading the morning newspaper aloud, to work on my enunciation, Mom was preparing to leave for work. She was very concerned about my psychological state because she knew that it would be a difficult adjustment for me to be in the house, alone all day. Do not worry, Mom; I'll be all right. Besides, I need to work on my enunciation. Reluctantly, she went out the door—then turned back for a last glimpse.

I didn't like to sit for long periods of time, so in the mid-morning hours, I'd go outside and walk. I'd struggle up and down the driveway four times. Then I tried to do balancing activities like the ones performed at the Center, in-between parallel bars. But this time, there were no bars to hang onto. *Haaaa! That was close* as I tried desperately to balance on one foot. *I almost went over! Remember, there are no bars to catch you.* The tension was relieved as I shifted my weight to the opposite side and immediately stomped my other foot down. *I am doing something to counteract the problem.*

As the day wore on, I sat at the kitchen table and read out loud some more, using the cassette recorder to gauge my performance. I was running my own rehab center for me. More self-responsibility! Hey, Mom, what is going on? My day of being alone ended at 4:00 p.m.—the beginning of a journey you could only do alone. *I was and am a communicative guy! Friendly, open! It is very hard on the off days!*

On Mondays, Wednesdays, and Fridays, the days I went to the Center, I walked rapidly through the corridors, with a cane at times. The only way to stay on balance was to take swift strides. I could only steady myself on one leg for a fraction of a minute, until I had to take another step to support my balance. On the way to occupational therapy with Kim, I saw Judy, the speech therapist. I quickly interjected: "I got it! My speech is down pat. Hey, don't I sound good?" Judy then forwarded a question: "Is it good enough for Merrill Lynch?" In a wishful-thinking mood: "Yes, I am ready to go. I sound good." Judy then asked her client, who was standing next to her, what she thought. "It's all right. It could be better." *Dang it! I am ready to go back to work!* That quickly deflated my balloon and I set off on a personal quest to correct my speech and adapt. Practice, practice and more practice!

As the week passed, the mornings went by so quickly at the Center. *Already?* I returned home before 1:00 p.m. I became frustrated because my hours and days at RAC had been cut so severely. While my entire family was off performing their work, I was home alone. *Aaahhh, this is driving me crazy!* I was even excited about folding the laundry. Heck, it was something to do. I could rehabilitate by standing, folding underwear at the same time; *great,* after that activity, *what next? Find something to do that's beneficial!* I read a lot, to work on my comprehension skills, while also reading aloud to practice my diction, enunciation. *Ah, it is 4:00 p.m. Time to work out and stimulate those endorphins!* I quickly jumped up from the kitchen table and marched down the basement steps like a soldier, pounding my feet on every step, still using the railing and wall for support. I turned in the stereo to my favorite station that played "Hip-Hop" dance music, and I rode as hard as I could, feeling as high as an eagle soaring through the sky because those endorphins were in full force. I assured myself that the battle would be won. I felt great, and even greater that I had the self-responsibility to do something to kill the cancer cells that might be trying to grow. I also fantasized about Vicki visiting me one day, witnessing my determination and being so proud of me. Wishful thinking! With my left hand on the railing, and my right hand on the wall, I climbed the basement steps. When I reached the top, I quickly turned left, then motored off to the bedroom stairs, managing to bang into the closet door on the right. I took a shower, putting on fresh clothes, and the afternoon was over. This was my schedule every other day when I returned home from limited rehab, until graduation. I was by myself too much, getting lonelier. *That's it! I need to get involved in something. I need to get out of the house!*

All right, something different! September 16, 1991. The visit was made to see Dr. Pensler, reconstructive surgeon at Children's Memorial Hospital. "Hey, he looks just like Inspector Jacques Clouseau from the 'Pink Panther.'" Ha, I liked Dr. Pensler already. He was very gentle as he examined my seventh nerve palsy. Then he went on to explain the procedure. He said a limited functional nerve would be removed from the leg I decided upon: the calf muscle, left or right. *Hey, wait a minute. How serious an effect is the loss of that nerve going to have on my balance?* I was quite concerned, since I was already impaired. I asked the question and Dr. Pensler said it would be a very limited functional nerve that was not involved with balance. *Good!* The nerve would then be attached to the good facial nerve in my right cheek and would be moved across the lip, then attached to the dead facial nerve on the left. Dr. Pensler made an analogy: "It's like jump-starting a car battery." He then stated that once the nerve grew across my face to the left side, the next process would begin. Nerves take a long time to grow, so the elapsed time would be eight months. "Once the nerve stimulates to the other side," explained Dr. Pensler, "a muscle called the Gracilius muscle will be transferred from the inside of your thigh, from the groin to the knee, on whichever leg you choose. The muscle will then be inserted in the left cheek. Eventually, the nerve and the muscle will come together and eventually have ninety percent movement in your left cheek." *The "Bionic Man"! All right! I will look normal and speak clearly again!*

The doctor then showed a slide presentation revealing "before" and "after" photographs of one of his clients. It was a young boy whom I estimated to be between the ages of six and eight. Wow! What a difference! In the first photo, the left lip was noticeably drooping, just like mine. In the "after" picture, the lip was straight across.

After the "show and tell," Dr. Pensler was going to show us the entire process of the boy's surgery. "No way," Mother called out. We just wanted to focus on the positive, as we were accustomed to doing. Again, I remained naive. I didn't want to see the gruesome surgical process; it might have scared me off.

As any good salesperson would do after making a solid presentation, Dr. Pensler went for the close—with gusto! He used the dialogue of a good closer who had great conviction about his product. He knew my wants and needs, and I was ready to buy. "When do you want to have it done?" the doctor asked. *As soon as possible. I do not want to be 40 years old and say "What if?"* I said, "Let's go and get it done! Today! I will go down to the operating room right now!" Dr. Pensler looked stunned then smiled. Gosh, I was impulsive again! The surgery would be 10 to 12 hours long. I was very concerned about the use of the ventilator! AAHH, NOT AGAIN, NO WAY! I didn't want to deal with that "Wrestling Match" again, as I'd had a horrifying experience being weaned from the ventilator tube three previous times after surgery. I told the doctor about my ventilator experience and he quickly assured me that there wouldn't be a problem. I liked the doctor, so I agreed to the surgery.

I wanted to get back to work. I wanted so badly to be able to communicate and be normal again, but, after all, what is normal? *Mmmm.* One week later, Dr. Pensler's secretary, Penny, called to schedule the surgery. The only day the doctor could do it was Saturday, October 31, 1991, Halloween morning. *What?* I couldn't believe it. *Halloween day! What are you, nuts? Surgery, no way!* What an omen; could it be a sign? I was still worried about the ventilator and every night at the dinner table, I expressed my concern. Mom kept reassuring me that the surgery, in the long run, would make a difference. "You will be a lady-killer." *All right! It's about time!*

My parents remained very concerned about my current lifestyle of limited rehab, and more time of being alone. My brain started to ooze out of my ears. Well, thank goodness for PACE. I had to keep going. I called the PACE dispatcher at the Vernon Hills Community Center. "Good morning! I would like to schedule a morning pick-up time as early as possible for tomorrow, Tuesday morning!" The coordinator, Mrs. Peterson, whose son I played basketball with in high school, recognized my name and, to my surprise, knew who I was. One had to call a day ahead to schedule a time to be picked up, where to be dropped off then the time to be picked up again. All of this had to be coordinated with the other riders' schedules and destinations. I wanted to be hauled off to the healing place, a place where I could be independent, a place where I could do something to help myself. That place was the Bally Total Fitness health club in Vernon Hills. I was a member and frequent visitor at the club before the brain surgery. I am still a member. Want to hear a nice story? Before the debacle in June, 1990, I had taken out a new membership to the club, owing a $400 contract to be paid off in two years. It was the Presidential Membership, so I could travel anywhere in the world and still work out at one of the affiliated gyms. Well, the payments stopped abruptly for four months. Someone from Bally's billing department called to inquire about the problem on a Saturday morning in late November, a few days after I was released from the hospital. I was just waking up, 9:00 a.m., when the phone rang. I overhead Dad talking about my case history, and later that morning, he told me that I no longer needed to worry about paying my membership at the health club. The debt was cancelled. For seven years, I had not paid a single cent until I updated my membership in March.

September 18, 1991. I awoke early that morning, 6:00 a.m., and leapt out of my bed with excitement: *I am going to the health club!* I ate breakfast—a banana and a bowl of oatmeal. I then downed a cup of coffee so I could be energized, which increased my enthusiasm. *Wow! This is great! I feel better! I am acutely alert!* I was ready. *All right, where is PACE? It is 8:20! They are late!* I grew impatient as I gazed out the front window with anticipation. *That's it!* I grabbed the phone and called PACE. Fran answered the phone, the other scheduler. I barked out a strong good-morning and inquired about why the bus was late. *What's going on? I do not like to wait!* She replied confidently that the bus would arrive soon. The very second I hung up the phone; I saw the bus turning into the driveway. I grabbed my exercise bag, cane, and the garage door opener so that when I returned, I could easily make it back into the house through the garage. The doors of the bus opened just like a school bus. I offered a good-morning and with a Spanish accent, the driver responded in the same manner. I claimed the front seat and plopped into it. I noticed other riders on board. Six young women on their way to work (or college, perhaps) sat near me. *Aaah! I want to hide.* I was self-conscious about their thoughts. That's when reality hit again. I sat and stared through the window as we made our way down River Woods Road, the main two-lane road just to the east of my neighborhood. *You know, this kind of reminds me of the ambulance ride to UIC. Life goes on! People are going places, getting things done. Come on, Didier, pick it up! Make the best of it!* I suddenly became tense and started to visualize myself going through the exercise routine. My blood started to rise and boil over. *Now what! I cannot believe this!* I was getting frustrated that it was taking so l o n g. *Finally!* The last person was dropped off. I asked the driver his name in Spanish. He actually understood what I said and responded, in Spanish. "Me nombre es Edwardo! Hola." ("My name is Edward, hello.") I saw the bright side and tried to converse in Spanish and have fun with the tour. Tour? Well, there were more stops on the way; apartment complexes, private homes, and retirement communities. *Grandmothers!* Instead of being somber about the whole situation, I told myself to be nice to them and respect my elders. But the other key thought in my mind was: I *had better be nice to them because one of them might have a good-looking granddaughter. Hahahaha!* I had to make light of the situation; there was no other way. The moral of the story: Take the positive side. Seek it out!

Five grandmothers were picked up and two of them seemed to be good friends from the same apartment complex. They were both

Ukrainian and spoke broken English with an accent as they debated about the price of a pound of pepper cheese. The grandmothers, God bless them, had their own challenges, but they did not care what you looked like. All they cared about was that you were a person with inner feelings.

"Hey, Edwardo! You need a radio in here, and new shock absorbers," I said as I bounced in all directions. Finally, I was dropped off at my destination. *It is about time:* 10:00 a.m.; an hour-and-a-half excursion which normally takes 20 minutes by car. *Geesh! I lost my drive and focus!* I slowly rose and embarked to the exit without paying the fare. I still needed to be picked up; I would pay then. I cautiously walked down the three steps, holding on desperately to the side railings. I sighed; another challenge. I had to step down, a foot, to the concrete block that led to the entrance, without falling. *I have been in the sitting position for so long! That's not good!*

I called out a loud, energetic good-morning to the personal trainer working the front desk. Members usually have their card screened by a computer to see if they are legitimate. Well, I was never confronted; I guess they just knew.

Let's go! I claimed a computerized stationary bike, one of many, to ride with force. I was confident; after all, I rode hard every day for 20 minutes. On the bike next to me was an attractive, petite woman who was sizing me up and then hurriedly ran into the women's locker room. *Mmm!* To my surprise, she returned 10 minutes later. *Mmm!* I kept going. I completed that exercise with the lovely feeling of sweat rushing down. She looked over at my bike and took notice that 20 minutes had elapsed. She remarked, "You must have strong legs." "Yeah, I ride every day. It is the only way to come back." I was living by my statement. I said to myself when I looked around the huge workout room, *I must work harder than anyone here! Harder than anyone who doesn't have a physical disability.* I rode; I stretched and stretched—the same leg-stretching exercises that I performed at RAC before a long walk: thighs, hamstrings, and groin. I went through the same exercise routine that I had always done before the cancer: push, push, pull, pull routine; pecs and triceps, back and biceps; then shoulders, on the third day. I worked out on the Universal machines for safety reasons. The repetitions I instituted were as follows: five sets, 10 times each, while increasing the weight 10 pounds after each set; then back to the original weight, and performing a burnout set, doing as many reps as I could, until I couldn't do anymore. It is very important to remember to rest only 10 seconds between sets. *One has to keep up the intensity.* The most important aspect was to get in and get out. *Yeah, I did it!* I felt elated, euphoric after every exercise session. *Cancer is out of here!*

My gym bag was strategically placed in the back corner by the locker room, by the rest room and next to a brick wall in the back corner. The area wasn't used much by the other members. I could take my time and make mistakes without falling on top of some other man. I did not use their showers. I never have; it takes too long and I don't enjoy seeing other men floating around in their birthday suits. I changed, grappled with the cane and hobbled out of the locker room to the front. I had to wait for PACE, 20 minutes. So I sat on a couch, watching the swimmers in the large pool. Seeing the members trudging in and out gave me a sense of independence. *I am doing something on my own!*

I felt great. The legs were loosened up, motivated and ready to go! It was a simple task to hop, skip and jump into the bus. *Yeah, the power of exercise!* As the bus departed, we retraced a small portion of the early-morning ride and picked up three women at their original drop-off site. *All right! Let's go!* I was ready to run home. *Let's go, Ed!* But I had to cool my heels. The sightseeing tour lasted one hour. Ed was a great guy. Two of the elderly women had six bags of groceries each. Ed carried the bags into the bus and after he dropped the ladies off, he carried their groceries at no extra charge. When we made it back to my house safely, I paid the fare, and suddenly found myself wondering whether the woman on the bike at the health club was hitting on me.

I had to think about reality again. 9/22/91: I had an MRI scan. I went through my same Catholic traditions in preparation—saying the "Our Father" prayer, and spreading holy water from Medjagorie on the back of my head where the cancer was. The technician again asked if I had a metal plate in my head. "No." A few days went by. "Well, no news is good news." I was less anxious, but still concerned. A week and a half later, the report came in as clear. *Yeah!*

Hit on Spanish

In mid-September, I enrolled in a first-year Spanish class at Deer-field High School Adult Continuing Education. I wanted to take the class to increase my human databank. I had to do something to enhance my strengths and keep my mind motivated. *"Mmmm!"* International Marketing could be a good idea because of the serious talk and debate over the NAFTA agreement. (National Free Trade Association between the U.S., Mexico, and Canada.)

I loved it! I loved being in the classroom, learning something of interest, being in the educational atmosphere made me feel good inside. *I am doing something beneficial for me!*

Spanish came easy to me. I had been an enthusiastic student of beginning and intermediate Spanish for two years in high school, where I was fortunate to be instructed by a unique teacher. His name was Father Pierce Gillmartin, a Carmelite priest of Irish descent. For many years, he had established Catholic schools in the South American country of Peru. Every morning, he conducted the Catholic Mass at Santa Maria de Poppolo Church, a few blocks from my high school. Padre Pierce, as we called him, a man in his sixties, liked to tell about the beautiful women in Peru and about the overall culture. He was very personable; he was our friend. But he was strict. If any of the guys acted up in class, he instructed them to kneel on the hard tile floor with good posture, at the front of the class, with their nose only inches away from the chalkboard during the entire class. That looked very difficult to me, so I kept my mouth shut. Wanting to perform well, I studied hard and fell in love with the language and the food.

I felt comfortable in the Spanish class at Deerfield High School. It came very naturally for me to speak the language. *Hey, I realize something. I speak better in Spanish than I do in English.* My tongue was much more active and I was able to increase my rate of delivery! *This is great!* And it carried over—outside the class. When I read a newspaper article out loud in English now, I sounded better. My tongue was activated, so I went nuts every morning just like with physical exercise and recited Spanish phrases over and over from my text book.

9/23/91:   Darryl said exercise on your own. Why pay someone else?—Dr. Kent.

I came to the realization that my initial thoughts of total rehabilitation coming via the rehab therapists would not do the trick. *I have to take matters into my own hands! Go after it!* The height of someone's personal character and determination is the key. Exercise was/is the root. On my days off from the Center, I did everything I possibly could do for my own rehab. I noticed gains in my balance and energy level. I awoke at 6:00 a.m., of my own free will, and went to the health club of my own free will; I put myself through rigorous paces of my own free will. I rode the stationary bike nine miles in 20 minutes, lifted weights on self-guided exercise equipment for an hour, and walked in the pool at the club. When I would return home, two hours later, I kept going! I performed balance-challenging activities in the kitchen in-between the two countertops as though I was on the parallel bars at RAC. The right counter was eight feet long and three feet wide. The left countertop was a small five-foot square that was used as a placemat for an old-fashioned telephone with a spice rack behind it. I would try to balance on one leg and focus on some dried flowers that hung on a post 10 feet away, where the family room started. The two countertops served as a brace. *Come on, nerves!* I stood on my right leg. My nerves trembled as though an earthquake was unfolding in my legs. They tried to guide my leg in all directions. *Ah! Just in time!* I placed my right had on the counter to brace and control the calamity. I had more control with the left. My nerves trembled in my left leg, but not with the same brute force as with my right leg. A record! I stood without toppling over for three minutes. *Come on!* After three sets, each encompassing 40 minutes, I ventured out in the hinterlands (neighborhood streets)—all on my own free will.

I had minimal control when I walked; I was all over the road and my right leg crossed over the left. The road had a constant 30-degree slope (to drain the rainwater). I was stopped by a policeman who thought I was drunk. Two days later, someone rang the doorbell. It was another policeman telling me that a neighbor reported that somebody was walking around disoriented. "Don't worry, it's only me." *What? That's it! I am going to write a letter to all the neighbors and tell them: I am the drunk walking around. Come on! They don't know. Under these constraints, what is one to do? Go into a shell and hide? No way! Get out there and get it done!* I didn't write the letter, but my mom and a neighbor went to the local police department to explain to Chief Larson about the challenge set before me and to alert the force. *Ha, all right!* By the way, my senses of hearing and sight were intact. The neighborhood streets were usually empty during the day because the majority of the residents worked. Sometimes a service truck or van would enter the scene. My sensors detected something and relayed a message to the brain, posting a warning that there was a vehicle approaching behind me, 30 yards away. I went to the side of the road and desperately held my ground (*hold steady*). I allowed the vehicle to move by while I offered a friendly neighborhood wave. After a few days of rehabilitating the neighborhood streets, the neighbors drove cautiously by. They waved with respect or even rolled down their windows and offered a motivational greeting. *People are great!* It kept me fired up. **Keep Going!**

9/27/91:   Darryl became a volunteer at the Chicago Health Club, Vernon Hills.

That's it! You can only work out so much. I needed to do something with my mind—something that challenged my deficits. I wanted to find an opportunity and seize it. Steve was still the manager of the health club, as he was before my surgery. We were buddies; we respected each other. As a matter of fact, he was my boss when I had worked there on the weekends the summer before the surgery, 1990. After the workout, I stopped in his office and candidly inquired whether I could volunteer at the club. *I wanted to stay out of the house longer.* He enthusiastically agreed with the idea.

Two days later, I was given a list of new members with their phone numbers to find out if they had signed up for an orientation to the club, which would introduce them to the operations of the computerized exercise equipment. At the same time, they would be told the advantages of having a personal trainer customize their individual exercise programs. I felt important. I was doing something that was needed and I was part of the team. There was a 32-day grace period during which a new member could legally terminate his or her contract. Thirty percent of new members never actually used the club then canceled their membership, and, in turn, the sales rep lost his/her commission. *Oh no!* The calls were important.

My days out of the house lasted longer now. Instead of 8:30 to 11:30 a.m., it was lengthened from 8:30 a.m. to 2:00 p.m. *All right, the day is almost done.* The longer I stayed the more old acquaintances I saw. They knew what happened to me, and were happy to see me out and about. For example, Karen, the friendly blonde personal trainer whom I had always respected, walked into the office where I was making calls. She gave me a bear hug and said she was thrilled to see me looking so well. *Thanks! Now I have more energy!* My hair had grown back; I was wearing stylish exercise clothing and cool-looking sunglasses to hide my crossed, drooping eye. Steve said he thought I looked pretty good with the sunglasses on. "Hey, Darryl!"- another old acquaintance. *What a power booster!* I volunteered at the health club for the following month, until I began to volunteer at Condell Hospital as Chairman of the History Committee.

12

Keep Up the Pace!

10/1/91: **Darryl said: "Therapists always say that I am in denial. The therapists want me to think about reality. No way! I know the challenges before me. I know what I have to do."**

Geesh, the therapists are still trying to influence my way of thinking! I shared with Dr. Kent that if I thought about reality, I would not be around.

One evening, as I was driven home by Ron, he said, as he'd said before, that I should write a book. *Mmm! Maybe he's right!* I charged ahead. I needed a computer in order to write the story of my recovery. *I don't want to be 40 years old and say, "What if?"* I had no idea what kind, or where to look for a computer, never having bought one. I had worked with the technology in high school, but more frequently in college for doing term papers and at work for Merrill Lynch. I thought that Maureen Mulkrone, my friend and fellow client at the Center, could advise me on where to turn, because I recalled that her mom was a computer consultant. Taking advantage of Mrs. Mulkrone's expertise, I called her at home one morning and told her that I needed a basic computer at the most affordable price. Mrs. Mulkrone suggested a Magnavox PC and told me there was going to be a sale that weekend at CDW (Computer Discount Warehouse). The warehouse was only 10 minutes from my house. I was ready to spend $1500 for the computer and a Laser Jet printer.

The parking lot was full and many cars were parked along the side of the road. Dad said he would drop me off at the front entrance, but I refused. I could walk with the cane. Besides, it was a crisp, beautiful fall day and I wanted the exercise. We found a place to park approximately 100 yards from the warehouse. I wiggled and waggled to the front door. Dad and I went into the entranceway, where a long line of people were waiting to get into the warehouse for the great deals. The sale was very well organized, as only a certain number of people were allowed to shop at one time.

When it was finally our turn, 30 minutes later, I saw boxes and boxes of computer equipment stacked in 30-foot-high metal storage bins. I had no idea where to turn. Finally, a mid-thirties salesman assisted us, and I purchased a Magnavox PC and Hewlett Packard Laser Jet printer. What a deal! The total cost was $1500. Later that day, we bought a computer desk that had a drawer just for the keyboard. The following week, I was introduced to Dave Sause, the son of my mother's friend, Norah, whom she worked with at the high school. Dave was a computer whiz. He set up the computer in operating form in my basement, next to the stationary bike. *Great! Now I have to learn how this thing works!* Dave helped me to become acclimated to the software, "GeoWorks," so I could begin to write my story. I was happy to get started because so many people—Mom, Dad, Brenda, relatives and friends—provided me with encouragement to get going while everything was still fresh in my mind. I did not keep a journal of my experiences; it was all in my head. I had to write down the story before I lost it.

◆   ◆   ◆

On the afternoon of October 7, Dr. Kent and I took a trip to the Randhurst Mall for physical therapy. As Harry and I walked around, I picked up the pace with a fancy laminated cane. "Hey, you are walking fast," he said. "Yeah," I responded, and laughed. "The quicker I walk, the better my balance becomes." *Let's go!* My hair was blowing in the wind. *Whoops!* My left leg uncontrollably crossed in front of my right. I just about lost it. I skipped to the right, then to the left. *Whew! I'm safe! The athletic ability is still there.* When I looked up, I noticed that I had crossed the path of an older woman. Instead of hiding in my shell, I wanted to make light of what had just happened, so the woman wouldn't think there was something wrong with me. "Just practicing some tap routines," I said. *Ha, ha!* It eased the stress. Harry laughed, too. He had to fill out a report when we returned, which was customary. Beth Fazio received Harry's report and subsequently had a meeting with Harry and me in her office. She said that I was a hard person to read, because people couldn't tell if I was serious or joking since my facial expressions had been severely affected by the surgery. Beth went on to say that I shouldn't embarrass other people. Harry, in the background, gave a small smile because he thought my comment to the lady was funny.

10/9/91:   A fellow client died and Darryl turned his grief and frustration into determination.

Allen, a friend, a colleague at the rehab center, passed away from a heart attack. He was only in his mid-forties, with three youngsters and a wonderful wife. Allen had suffered a stroke one month before. As far as I could judge, it seemed he had all his faculties, with a slight imbalance challenge. He looked like a healthy fellow, standing 6'2", 240 pounds. Allen had a perpetual laugh that encouraged my crazy habits even more. He laughed at every silly comment I made. *"Hehehe."* It just grew on you. For example, Allen and I frequently attended physical rehabilitation together. In the late afternoon session, we had to do a highly demanding balancing activity in the gym. Sandy, the physical therapist, placed an eight-foot ladder on the carpeted gym floor. The ladder had straddled steps at every foot, so the person climbing up or down had to take controlled steps, shifting his/her weight to the right or left while remaining in a four-foot-wide boundary. I needed assistance or else I would take a "digger" (tumble) in each direction. *This is crazy!* Allen did it with ease until I ruined his concentration by making a silly comment. We took on three sets of that challenge. Then we performed another number. Sandy instructed us to place our feet shoulder-width apart, bend our knees slowly to where the rump almost touched the ground, while maintaining our balance with good posture, and then slowly spring up. My nerves jumped around in my legs, throwing me off balance. *Come on, control it!* I used my leg muscles. HA! My nerves jumped too much; I was ready to eat the rug. Natural instinct took over and my hands braced the fall, just in time. *Hey, I hear my sister.* Brenda stopped by for a visit and since she is a dancer, I threw out a dumb comment as Allen and I were bending our knees: "1…2…3…*Perrier,* 1…2…3…*Perrier.*" I knew it wasn't the right ballet term, but it sounded right. Plié is the correct term for that exercise. *Perrier* is a brand of bottled water. We all laughed. Two days later, when I returned to the Center for therapy, I received the news from Harry Kent that Allen had passed away. *What? No way!* I was distraught. The entire Center was subdued. *He had a great family.* I had met them at the Center after a recent family support group meeting. When I worked out on the bike that afternoon, I rode hard, really hard. I cried over my lost friend for the first 10 minutes. I became even more determined the second 10 minutes. *I am going to work as hard as possible to come back, in dedication to Allan and his family! Come on!* **Keep Going!**

That evening, the telephone rang. I hastily grabbed it; I love phone calls. Dr. Vick's secretary called with the report that the results of the scan were clear. *Yea, the cancer is gone and it will not come back! Thank you, God!* I gave a thumbs-up sign to God. I immediately shouted and cheered. I was so-ooo thrilled. I rushed downstairs to the kitchen and shared the great news with Mom and Dad, who were ecstatic. I wanted so badly to pass on the wonderful news to Brenda, but she was teaching dance at a local studio. I called Grandma, who lived in San Diego, and she expressed her pleasure. I then called everybody else I could think of. I was even brave enough to call Vicki. I glided up the stairs to my parents' bedroom to use their phone because I wanted privacy. I was a nervous wreck. During the dialing process, my right hand, holding the receiver, shook in all directions. "Hello, Vicki, this is Darryl." With her enthusiasm, she greeted me warmly. I, on the other hand, flubbed it. Uh Uh Uh! Guess what? With gusto, I shared the exciting news. But that was it. I tried to think of a conversational piece, but to no avail; nothing came to mind. She had to hang up. *Dang it! I had her interest, but I could not go for the close! Ask her out, dummy!*

The next day, Saturday morning, Dad had a dental appointment with Dr. Rodbro at his large office off of Lake Cook Road in Deerfield. Dad shared the news since Dr. Rodbro was our friend as well as our dentist. Dr. Rodbro knew the implications and was thrilled for me. He told Dad that the first six months to a year was the most critical time regarding recurrence in my case. *Okay, all I have to worry about are the residual effects.*

◆ ◆ ◆

October 10, 7:30 p.m.; family meeting with the RAC therapists in the conference room. Each therapist shared his/her observation. Their combined opinion was that I had made significant gains during the time I had been at the Center. Judy, the speech therapist, even said that I had 90 percent clarity in my speech. But it was concluded that on a month-to-month basis, I had hit a plateau. It was time to move on and get out into the community.

Mmmm! I have an important message to get across. I was succeeding with rehab. I was ready to break out of the rehab shell. The more I entered into the community, the more I witnessed how naïve and uneducated the general public is about people with disabilities. People either stared, or looked away to simply avoid contact. *Hey, I am a person, too! We are all people!* I had told Harry that I was seriously considering law school. I wanted to obtain my law degree in order to effectively represent people who qualify for the "Americans with Disabilities Act." I believe that we all deserve a shot and shouldn't be ridiculed by society. I wanted to be outspoken; besides, I was already inherently loud and verbose. I had met the first criteria. *Mmmm! What should I do? Get on the Oprah Winfrey Show!* I shared the idea with my family and friends. They liked it. *Now, how do I get on?* I dialed information and asked for the number for the "Oprah Winfrey Show." The operator told me the correct name of Oprah's company, "Harpo Productions," and gave me the phone number. I was thrilled. *Yes!* I was certain that the production team would *jump out of their chairs when I called!* I gave the receptionist a grandiose good morning, shared my name, background and rehabilitative success from brain cancer, and was told, "Write your request to us and let the production staff look at it and they will decide if you should be on the show." *What? My written plea to be on the show will get lost with the million other requests! I feel that my experiences are so important to share with others and give the message that yes, you can overcome!* Later that night, I shared my disappointment with Brenda and she said that I would have to get my book done in order to get on the "Oprah Winfrey Show." *I am working on it!* Keep Going!

10/16/91:   "Darryl began to do volunteer work with the American Cancer Society."—Dr. Kent

I was still bored and even more frustrated. I felt that my calling had not been met. I needed to touch base with someone. I called Mrs. Pat Rodbro at home that afternoon. To my surprise, she answered. She is a very busy woman, as she works as a receptionist at her husband's dental office and, at the time, was the Chairwoman of the American Cancer Society, Lake County Unit. "Hello, this is Darryl Didier." After some small talk, I said, "I need to help someone else; I need to get out of here." In her caring voice, Mrs. Rodbro said, "Okay, I have an idea…"

That very evening, I received a phone call from Mrs. Rodbro's son, Mike, Jr. Mike, who is my age and a friend of mine, was a local football star. He had received a scholarship to the University of Miami, Florida. Mike asked whether I would like to go with him to the ACS office in Waukegan, Illinois, where Ed Rodbro, his uncle, was the Executive Director of the Lake County Unit. Mike is a free-spirited type of guy and comically drove us as loud rock music was played. We shouted at each other to be heard as the windows were down on that cold, dreary day in October. Mike reiterated the respect he had for me: "You were always a tough guy."

We arrived in the front parking lot and screeched to a halt in one of the many available parking spaces. It was a four-story office complex that looked as though it had been built in the fifties. I was nervously charged-up. I grabbed my fancy wooden cane and marched, with momentum, to the entrance.

A receptionist greeted Mike and me cheerfully. It was a small office with a yellow shag rug and brown paneling. It was so gloomy. The receptionist lead Mike and I for Ed Rodbro's office. Ed sported a nice fall-colored suit, shook our hands warmly. Mike started out by saying that we were going to do some volunteer work for Dorothy Small, a field representative, and since we were here, he wanted to stop by to say "hello!" Ed invited us to take a seat in the two large leather chairs facing his desk. Mike introduced us by saying that we had been friends since grade school and then bolstered my ego in his usual way: "Darryl was a great athlete at Carmel; he played football and baseball." Mike went on to say, "he is a real tough guy. He had a brain tumor two years ago and has beaten it." As I was floating off the chair after that affirmation, Mike asked me to tell my story. I proudly talked about what had happened to me, emphasizing I wanted to help others directly or indirectly by volunteering for the ACS. From his facial expressions, I sensed Ed was in my corner. "We will definitely give you opportunities to volunteer."

After about half an hour, Ed had to get back to his tasks so Mike and I walked along the yellow shag rug to the next large office to work with Dorothy Small, who had short, wavy white hair and reminded me of my first-grade teacher. Dorothy set Mike and me up with a list of people to call to try to find out their views about the ACS.

Two hours flew by. When I stood up, my legs were tight; I had little control. *Geesh! It is not good to sit for so long!* As Mike and I walked down the hallway, I weaved to the right, then to the left. This time, I had to accept help walking down the outside steps to the parking lot. *Dang it!*

10/22/91: I took the PACE bus to the Vernon Hills Public Library, a small one-story building. I was thrilled to be out of the house again. *I will be smart today. I'll read and study the markets.* The library has always been a lifesaver for me. It heightens my awareness and concentration because it is so quiet. No telephone, no TV or stereo. There is no tendency to get hungry and mosey on down to the fridge. It was also motivating for me to witness other people working hard, like at the health club. I gratefully claimed my seat, choosing a private desk so nobody could see me as I read. I wanted to be hidden because when I read, I had to move my head from the left to the right like a typewriter carriage. My eyes could not simply scan. At times, I tried to silently read along by coordinating my eyes together without shifting my head from side to side.

Mental stimulation is key! Exercise the mind along with the body. I looked at my watch and two hours had elapsed. *Wow, already?* As I was making my way to the exit through rows of shelved books on either side, there was no room for a mistake. The shelves were separated by only two feet. I had sat too long; my legs were not in coordination with my brain. They did not want to go where I told them to go. *Dang it!* I bounced from one side to the other, knocking over a row of books. *Uh-oh!! The librarians are not going to be happy with me.* I stacked the books back on the third shelf in complete disarray. *Whew! No one came by to observe the scuffle.*

I furtively dashed, like a house cat that hadn't used the litter box, in-between the card catalogues and through the front doors. It was 1:00 p.m. I waited for PACE. *Ugh, Edwardo is late!* As I glared at my watch to focus in on the time (1:05 p.m.), I stood holding my backpack's left strap that was draped over my right shoulder. 1:10 p.m. No sign of Ed. *Dang it! I hope he didn't forget me!* I grew more impatient by the minute and sighed heavily. As I lifted my cane and tried to maintain my balance, my nerves jumped in my right leg, which jerked out. I just about lost it. *I knew I should have worked out this morning!* I grabbed the wooden cane and threw it down on the cement. It broke in two just below the handle. *Good job, idiot!* What to do? *There is no way that I am going to travel around and sport one of those aluminum canes!* Edwardo finally came. I sat on the bus thinking about what I could do to repair the needed assisting device. A lightning bolt zapped in my mind. I could use brown masking tape—it would match the cane. The moment I was dropped off, I salvaged the breakage.

13

Shoot for the Moon

The girlfriend issue came up again during counseling with Harry. *What is he trying to do?* I still had challenges before me. "I am not ready for a girlfriend. I can't give of myself yet. I have to pay attention to myself."

During the week before the reconstructive facial surgery, I told everybody I knew about it, including all the therapists at the Center, the clients, my friends, even Jellybean, our cat. Heck, it was a way to gain comfort from others. During the monthly family meeting, during which the client, family, and the rehab team meet and review the client's progress over the past month, I began to feel sorry for myself because the doctor had said that I would have to stay home for a week to recover. "What will I do for seven days after the 13-hour surgery?" Beth Fazio, the case coordinator, said that I should read some good books. "Well...maybe..." Gosh, I was already anticipating the misery and anxiety of being "Home Alone."

10/23/91:   Darryl has long-term goals.—Dr. Kent.

I was in a challenging position, still walking with a cane for steadiness; my legs tired easily; my speech was semi-intelligible, my eyes still didn't focus together; I still received curious stares from the public, but *hey, I will only improve. Just wait until 10 years from now!* I knew there was a good outlook ahead of me. I was so confident about returning to the work environment and becoming a success. I knew the cancer was *out of here!* My long-term goal was to ultimately return to Merrill Lynch in some capacity and contribute positively to society. I pondered the thought of going back to school for an MBA, and I wanted to get married and have a family—like a normal human being. I had another goal: to return to the original haunted house. I wanted to go back to the hospital where I had the initial surgery: the University of Illinois at Chicago Medical Center. I was hoping to see the medical staff that helped me during the traumatizing period after surgery, to show them firsthand that their hard work had paid off. I wanted to become re-acquainted with the nurse who had ordered-in the chicken wings for me, but I especially wanted to see the one who had denied my courage to fight—to be able to walk again. I wanted to stuff it right back in her face! I also wanted to see Dr. Desalvo, the oral surgeon intern who assisted Dr. Arnold during the first surgery to drain the built-up brain fluid. I wanted to tell him of the time when he changed my head bandages the day after surgery and I heard every word he said when he talked to a nurse, "Poor guy, I really feel sorry for him." I wanted to tell him that now I had a chance to verbally rebut that statement: "Don't feel sorry for me!" I wanted to see my speech therapist, physical therapist, vocational therapist, the medical staff that cared for me, and the nurse I met when I was initially brought in, "Mai-Tai." I wanted to thank them all for their help and to show them what the power of the human spirit can do! I shared this personal urge with Dad. With sensitivity to my needs, he agreed to take the day off from work on Friday to drive me down to UIC. As he looked for a parking space, I stared at the dark grotesque beast. It brought back bad memories of being controlled and confined to a place where I hadn't wanted to be—jail! When Dad and I had first left the house, I was excited. I wanted so badly to show off my progress, but once we arrived, I was faced with the ugliness of reality. I wanted to turn back and not face it. "Come on, Dad, let's go home!"

Dad combated my resistance by saying that it would be good for me to go back to the hospital as a visitor. *Ah!* I reluctantly agreed. As we walked in, and I relied on my cane, I once again felt a loss of personal control. At the rehab center, I always focused on the future: goals to knock down, bright prophesies, a positive outlook. *I have been blessed!* But now, I returned to the ugly past. I relived the negative feelings—the setbacks: collapsed lung, pneumonia, trachea, the battle with the ventilator. Memories! I saw the exact area in the main entrance where I had sat in the wheelchair, waiting with Mom, while Dad went to fetch the car the first Friday evening when I was allowed to go home for a weekend visit. I felt sick to my stomach when I recalled the horrible times in the rehab gym. I thought about the time when I had struggled to walk 10 feet with the walker. I saw the hallway and the actual room where I had the memory-recall tests administered; the daily photograph sessions with the X-ray machine. *Gosh, such bleak times.* I observed a whole new batch of therapists and patients. This was no homecoming; just bad memories. Even that cute, lively speech therapist was nowhere to be seen. Just like in the brokerage business, positions in the medical field are highly transient. We went by the hallway where I had waited and waited for the radiation treatments. On the rehab floor, I remembered the day when I thought I was in the psycho ward. I remembered the time I ate most of the huge can of popcorn while watching the Notre Dame Football game. In the ICU unit, I hoped to see "Mai-Tai," the friendly Cambodian nurse, but to no avail. The only homecomings were beeps and the dreadful silence.

Hah! Finally something good happened. I met up with that loony redheaded nurse from the step-down floor. She was thrilled to see me and welcomed me with open arms. I was satisfied at that moment. *I stuffed it right back in her face! She thought I couldn't make it through the challenge. Well, look at me now! My hair has grown back; I am walking on my own. I do not take any medications! I am free as a bird.* I felt great, even though there were still many obstacles: left facial palsy, speech not 100 percent, walk unsteadily, slumped posture, stationary eye, swirling eye. *But hey, I am making gains and I am doing something to get back in the game again; not sitting on the couch just wishing and crying about it!*

As we talked, our sounds were muted by the rushing roar of the El-train swiftly making its way to its next stop. Another old memory over-took my thoughts. Immediately, I recalled the week-long waiting period before the surgery. It was a time warp. I was taken back. *Let's get out of here!*

As Dad and I left, I realized that it was the worst mistake I had ever made; such terrible memories. *I am never coming back here again!*

10/30/91:   Convinced he is doing the right thing, but is clearly distracted.—Dr. Kent.

I was torn in half. I wanted to return to Merrill Lynch so badly. I wanted to study every day about economic events and their influence on debt and equity fluctuations. I wanted to commit myself to it, just like when I had studied for the Series-7 exam to be a registered broker. I had committed to all-day sessions (7 hours) for a month in my base-ment. On the other hand, I needed to increase my endurance and mobility. *I have to walk and exercise!* I wanted to spend more time exer-cising at the health club, taking frequent jaunts around the neighbor-hood, and doing stretching exercises. I really had conflicted feelings; I wanted both. *Hey, Didier, you can't do anything unless you have your health!* I kept repeating to myself over and over. *I am doing the right thing!* You have to be dedicated. *I am sticking to what brought me this far! Exercise!*

10/31: The day came. I still could not believe that I was having sur-gery on HALLOWEEN! I was very nervous, but also anxious to get the process going. Mom, Dad, and I arrived at Children's Memorial Hos-pital, in the Lincoln Park area of Chicago. We parked across the street in a parking garage owned and operated by the hospital. We had a handicapped card so we were able to park on the ground floor of the three-story garage. It really wasn't a major deal. My balance felt great that morning. As we stood there waiting for the cars to zip by, I noticed medical students hurrying across, dodging the traffic. *Geesh, I can't do that!* Although I used to take calculated risks, I was now very cautious. "Come on, Darryl," Dad said. I finally took the plunge. I literally ran to the other side, carrying the cane in my right hand. *Ah, I made it! See what motivation can do?* My balance felt great from all the working-out and walking exercises.

After the task of crossing the street, I faced another challenge. The entrance walkway had an 80-degree, 200-foot-long incline—going up. *All right! This should be a fun task. It will really challenge my leg strength! Let's go!* I climbed

After entering the hospital grand reception area, we were instructed to go down one floor to check in at the admissions desk. *Come on, let's go!* The wait was long, and I was so hungry! According to the pre-op rules and regs, I wasn't allowed to eat or drink anything for 12 hours prior to surgery. That was a huge feat for me! I love to eat, especially breakfast. As I nervously and impatiently waited, I scanned the room. Directly behind me were a mother and her baby, who was wearing a red mini-jumpsuit with a red hood over its head. The hood had little red horns, with black tips, pointing straight up. What a little devil. He or she was so cute. This eased the tension for me, when I focused on something besides myself. *Hey! I am not alone! Poor little tot is going through this on Halloween, too!*

After I was admitted, we were instructed to go to the pre-operative unit so I could change my garb to a light-blue hospital gown. The unit was much like a typical emergency room. There were surgical beds with the engineered drapes that slide to close for privacy. The anesthesiologist entered the enclosure, a male in his mid-thirties. He asked the general prep questions. When he asked if I took any medication, I very proudly said, "No!" I told him that I exercised like crazy every day, that I had taken things into my own hands. "Good for you!" he said, nodding approvingly. Then he left the room. Once again, I sat in the surgical bed like King Tut, straight up with arms crossed at my chest, waiting to be taken away for the 13-hour operation.

When I woke up in ICU, I was amazed, and very elated. *They didn't use a ventilator!* I'd had a colossal concern that the medical team would have to place the ventilator tube down my throat again. *All right! I am breathing on my own, unaided!* In a weakened voice, I said, "Hey, Dad, the doctor didn't use the ventilator! All right, it's over." Mom and Dad were right there in the ICU room, providing support again. Soon, Brenda entered the room with a bunch of flowers and provided a happy greeting that the surgery was over. I spent four grueling, painful days at Children's Memorial. The day after the surgery, when my father called to see how was doing, I said, "I wouldn't wish this on my worst enemy!" *Why did I agree to do this?* The pain was so severe—it felt like a semi-truck had driven over my face.

Dr. Pensler made remote incisions along both sides of my jawbone so the scars would not be noticeable. I would have to be very patient; the nerve would take from six to eight months to send impulses across my face to the impaired (the left 7th) nerve. *How can I speed up the pace?* I had been expecting a miracle. I thought I would leave the hospital a new man, with a normal face, not a droopy left cheek. Not only wasn't my face normal yet, though, but I had lost ground from being laid up for a week. My balance was terrible. In fact, I was close to where I had been back in November—unable to walk. *This is baloney!* I was disgusted. Before the surgery, I was well on the way back. My balance was improving along with my endurance. *I have to keep up the pace! I have to keep going!* I was completely immobilized in the hospital for four days. What a traumatic experience. I hated hospitals!

I was released, on November 6th. When we got into the house, I wobbled haltingly to the bathroom and looked into the mirror. *Aaahhh! Ha ha!* I looked hilarious. My head was the size of a basketball, totally out of proportion to the rest of my body. I looked like a "Puffer Fish" on the defense! I moved my mouth as though I was a "Carp," and the worst thing about it was that I looked just like one. *How am I going to attract a woman? There is no chance!*

I was home recovering for one week and felt like I was going out of my mind. I was so bored. *I have to get out of here!* On the fifth day, Jill Krueger, our next-door neighbor's sixth-grade daughter, stopped over to see the miraculous change into normalcy—or so she thought. I was in the basement working at my newly acquired personal computer. Dad brought her down to the basement to see me. It was like "Phantom of the Opera," only I was typing on the computer instead of playing the organ. The pretty young girl approached from behind, expecting this handsome prince to turn and smile. But *aaaah!* A misshapen creature offered the greeting: "Hi, Jill!" She took one look at me then dashed back upstairs.

11/8/91: I returned to the Center. Some of the swelling had gone down, but my head was still too big for my body. *Oh, well! What does one do? There is no way I am going to hide in the corner.* Later that afternoon Sandy, physical therapist and I traveled to Hawthorn Mall in Vernon Hills. The mall is a large two-level structure, about the width and length of two football fields, anchored by the Marshall Fields department store on the West End and Sears on the east. I had on those black high-top basketball shoes for support.

We took the escalator to the second floor, which offered no problem. After one lap around, I improved as the kinks were worked out. I felt confident until the escalator incident. I was too stubborn to take an elevator—I didn't want to act like I was disabled; I did not want to give in. (I always told Dad not to park in the handicapped area. *I can walk.*) Anyway, as Sandy and I approached the escalator to go back down to the first floor, a young woman walked in front of us. As four steps went down, I stepped confidently onto the descending ride. *Whoops! Aaah!* I stood in-between two steps so that when they descended, they separated to become two different steps. I was thrown off-kilter. I was going straight down! I had gripped onto the rubber railing for dear life, but my grip started to go. I saw myself tumbling eight feet to the bottom and getting seriously hurt. Suddenly, the young woman in front of me turned and reacted quickly. She held my waist and Sandy, two steps behind, latched onto my shirt, so the accident was averted. *Wow! I was saved! A miracle! Somebody is on my side!* Since it was mid-morning, there was very little traffic in the mall. It was a mere coincidence that someone else was on the escalator. That incident really made me think that I should be more cautious. I needed to be aware of my balance deficit and take the safe route.

The time was dwindling down. I knew that graduation from the Center was near, two weeks away. It was a bittersweet feeling. At the beginning, I had wanted to get out of the Center. But since I had been there for just about a year, I had made some good friends: clients, therapists, and transportation employees. Actually, they were my psychologists, and they were very real to me. You could explain your likes and dislikes about the Center or you could gossip, share funny jokes, exchange information about current affairs. You could actually make mistakes, feel at ease, and listen to music. I had the chance to chat with an individual or individuals going through the rehab process as human beings, not just as other clients. Jan, the driver who reassured me on my very first day; Ron, who always provided strength and the energy for me to keep going with simple respect; Frank (one of the RAC van drivers), the comedian, the jokester, the disc jockey—the one who had opened the doors for the Farmers Insurance work trial, and always kept things light; Dave, the middle-aged manager of a large corporation that had recently been downsized by a major "500" company, who made me realize that there are other challenges out there besides medical ones—like adjusting to a new way of life. I felt a close bond with the people at the Center; they were family to me. They had taken me in when I was in dire need of help. They had coached and encouraged me. Now, I was ready to be launched and to return to society on a full-time basis. But I was afraid to leave the safety net—to make new friends and acquaintances. *People my age are working, married. They do not make the time to do things with me—talk to me.* What a total rationalization. Face it, I was different. I had a small group of true friends who stood by me; the rest were just transitory; non-believers.

November 14, 1991: I graduated as Mom, Dad, and my dear sister, Brenda, plus my friend and hers, Heidi, and Lisa, a former girlfriend, were present. During the community hour, there was a brief announcement recapping the reason I was at the Center and the progress I had made over the year. Beth Fazio, the Case Coordinator of the Center, who originally interviewed me at the hospital, presented me with a graduation certificate. *Out of here, done with, complete.* Here is the copy of the certificate.

14

No Guts, No Glory

11/15/91: *hey! What did I study? Where is my cap and gown? I am still not where I want to be!* I still had challenges. I walked with the straight cane; I swerved; I slurred when I spoke; I could not drive; I could not work at a regular job. I still needed more surgery to repair my face. *I still look stupid!* What was I to do? My life was completely different. I loved competition; I loved to take part in sports: baseball, softball, basketball, golf, riding a mountain bike, etc. *I can't participate now, but I will do it later. Besides, I have a competition with cancer and what it left behind. Come on!*

I was introduced to the Rehabilitation Institute of the Chicago Department of Handicapped Sports Program by Sandy. I scanned the offerings in their monthly publication. I immediately had a vision of participating in Wheelchair Olympics and winning! I was excited about the chance to compete. I called the number to get involved. An enthusiastic-sounding woman answered the phone. I told her about my current dilemma and the fact that I worked out—exercised—every day. She suggested the weight-lifting competition for me. *Mmm! That could be an idea. I'll do it.* Well, I never did. I thought about the drive to the Rehabilitation Institute, which was located in Chicago near the Magnificent Mile on Superior Street (about 30 miles from my house) and decided that it would be too much of a hassle.

Five days per week, Monday through Friday, 8:30 a.m. to 11:30 a.m., with the use of the PACE bus, I went to the health club, Bally Total Fitness. On the weekends, my parents drove me there and picked me up. Sometimes I talked Paul into exercising with me. The health club was my place, my sanctuary, my chance to mingle with people who were healthy, felt good. Some of the members offered support. They told me to keep going: "You're doing well; keep it up." *I will! Gosh, what an energy boost. I'll work out again. Oh, here is PACE!* When I returned home around noon, I walked and walked on the neighborhood roads swerving to the left or right as residents drove cautiously by offering a friendly wave or a nice comment, while I stopped to control my balance. I continued. *Dang it! It will get better one of these days. No guts, no glory!* One of the male members at the health club who had challenge with walking often shared that observation with me.

Once inside my house, I performed stretching exercises and had lunch, which consisted of water-packed tuna and mayonnaise, no bread. I didn't want to be stuffed. I sat at the kitchen table and took small bites, drinking two glasses of water to help swallow. When I finished, I scanned the dishwasher, hoping the dishes would be clean so I could empty it. I wanted to do something more. They were clean. I was extra cautious with the plates and glassware. The last thing I wanted to do was break something. That task (which once would have taken me 10 minutes) took an hour. Now what? *Oh, yeah!* I beamed with excitement. *There should be some dry clothes in the dryer!* Making my way into the half-bathroom, took a breath, and checked the dryer to see if the clothes were dry. *All right, they're ready!* I gladly jumped at the chance to carry the clothes to my parents' bedroom and fold them as I blasted the radio on the Hip-Hop station. *This is fun*, I thought, while folding Dad's underwear. *Ha ha ha haaaa!* I folded to the rhythm of the music.

I was finished an hour later and was very proud of myself. *All right! I am contributing to the household and getting some rehab in!* I recalled that when I was in grade school, Dad had said, "You want to eat, don't ya? Well then, do something to help the family." All right! Cut the grass, split wood, clean the garage, rake leaves, wash the cars. I have always done something to contribute. Well…so I could eat.

Work, work, work; balance, speech and the mind; read, study, quiz yourself. I didn't feel at ease if I wasn't working on any one of those projects. I knew I had a deficit in those areas and they needed my utmost attention—every day.

Mid-December, 1991. I needed some semblance of order to my life. I pleaded with Paul and he bailed me out. I worked, for no pay, at his store, "Paul's Fish House." The fresh fish store was 2,000 square feet, located on the main drag of Glencoe's small, quaint business district. The store was all white inside and there was a constant humming of the ice-maker. Because of the poor acoustics, every little pin-drop echoed.

On one wall was a large sculpture of a sea bass, a work of art. The fish was seven-feet-high, 16-feet-long, had perfect fins and tail, and the eyes lit up.

The fish store was a dream comes true for Paul. Ever since I could remember, he'd wanted to run his own fish business, and he did it with the backing of a silent partner. In May of 1990, I'd helped him gut out the store space from the previous owner, his partner's wife, so he could move in. He had garnered up six years of experience by working at a fish counter in a nearby supermarket. He knew his stuff. He knew how to dress up a fish case to entice every shopper's appetite. He knew how to order fresh salmon flown in from Norway every morning, clams, shrimp, calamari, etc. He filleted with elegance and called all the customers by their first names. He could de-vein and clean shrimp in record time, with gusto. Figure that one out! He loved people. What a talker he was, and he always made people laugh. He should have been a stand-up comedian. He was also a fisherman; he fished every chance he could get—even in his sleep. He conversed about the theories and techniques of fishing with every person he met, and he went on fishing trips. "Paul's Fish House." What a fit!

I did fish with him, but whenever I did, I became bored stiff if I didn't catch anything in the first 10 minutes, I was always too impatient and wanted to do something more important. "Come on, let's go!" Well, I do have a fishing story to tell. It happened back in February of 1990, five months prior to the tumor episode. On a Saturday afternoon, Paul called and asked if I wanted to go ice-fishing with him because he wanted to try his new power augur, a gas-powered drill, to dig a hole through the thick ice. My first reaction was *no way!* but I hadn't gone out on a fishing adventure for three years, so I decided, why not?

We ended up in the middle of a frozen lake, way out in McHenry County, sitting on two small barrels, holding our fishing rods, with the line and hook baited with live minnows that were wiggling around in the bucket-sized hole Paul had cut out with the power augur through five feet of ice. As I sat for an hour, moving my pole up and down every few minutes, dangling the minnow to entice the large northern pike lurking in the area, the winter wind whirled across the frozen lake and I felt like it was 20 below zero. "Come on, Paul, let's get out of here. This is crazy!" "Darryl, we are just getting started. Isn't this fun?" Paul was very enthused as he set up two "tip-ups" (unmanned fishing poles) which are horizontal rather than vertical, and when a fish is caught, a red flag tips up as a signal. A half-hour went by then I yelped, "All right, my line is moving; there's a nibbler." I waited a few minutes more and the nibbles became bites as the line moved solidly to the left. I flicked the rod up and set the hook. Then I reeled in my catch, which turned out to be a five-inch sunfish. I took off my gloves to unhook the small fish and my hands practically froze. I plopped the prize catch onto the ice and it flipped around. Paul said that if you got enough of them, they were good eating. He soon sat down next to me on his white barrel and was completely content. In fact, he was in all his glory, not bothered at all by the cold because he was equipped with the proper gear: a heavy down snowmobile suit with a mask and snowmobile boots, so he was cozy. I, on the other hand, was outfitted with a heavy ski jacket, jeans, tennis shoes, and a winter cap—not enough to handle the cold. As we continued tweaking our poles up and down and peering into the round hole with anticipation, a tall man wearing a brown winter outfit and green hat stepped onto the ice from 40 yards away and walked towards us. I asked Paul who he might be and Paul said he looked like the game warden. "He probably wants to check our fishing licenses!" "What?" I said. The man did ask to see our fishing licenses. As we were huddled together, Paul dug his out of his pants pocket and flashed it to the warden. The warden looked at me, cocked his eyebrow, and in a deep, authoritative voice asked, "Okay, where is your license?" I quickly responded, "I left it at home today; I didn't think I would need it." Then the man asked, "What color is it?" I came back confidently, "Beige!" The wind howled. "All right, what did it cost?" he asked, crossing his arms. "Mmm, twenty-one fifty." "All right, come with me!" he ordered. *I guess I was wrong!* Paul laughed softly and whispered to me that it only cost seven dollars for a license. He remained behind as I went off to the warden's truck across the frozen lake. The warden filled out a citation and told me to post a bond of $50.00 or I would go to the local jail. "What? I don't have fifty bucks on me!" We walked back to the lake to see if Paul could help. Luckily, he had the cash on him and I was bailed out, but I was issued a ticket to pay a fine of $12.40. After the warden left, I thanked Paul and, out of relief, we laughed. Paul barked out, "Hey, you caught a sunfish for fifty dollars! That's ten dollars an inch!" In a way, I was happy because I assumed we were going to leave the frozen tundra, but despite my expectations, Paul didn't want to leave; he was a die-hard fisherman, so we stayed two hours longer even though I didn't try to fish because I didn't want to be caught without a license. (Paul later told me that he had never been checked for a license when ice-fishing, especially way out in McHenry County. *Just my luck!*)

Back to mid-December, 1991. Every morning at 8:30, Paul picked me up in his red and white pick-up truck. "Hey, Darryl! What time did you wake up?" I responded, "Five-thirty, without an alarm!" "Idiot," said Paul, "by noon, you are going to be wiped out." "Me? No way! The heart is going and the blood is flowing. I will be energized all day! I am more mentally alert!" *I wish I would have discovered the early morning "pump" when I went to RAC.* We drove due east on Lake Cook Road for 20 minutes. Paul told me very emphatically that I was not going to be treated like a wimp! I would mop the floor and fill and move a 150-pound, 30-gallon container of ice for the front case. I would answer the telephone and ring people up on the cash register if necessary. I was thrilled. Paul introduced me, with respect, to all his customers and friends when they stopped in. I felt like a champ! When business was slow, I straightened the shelves, neatly arranging the various boxes of food. I was in the game again!

This was my first contact with society outside, on my own, with no caregiver around. I thought I was normal. *Wrong!* As I rang up a sale on the cash register, a young child shrieked and said, "Mommy, part of his face is frozen!" The mother was clearly embarrassed as she fumbled through her purse for the correct dollar amount, while shying away from a straight facial glance. *Hey, thanks a lot! I didn't know it was that noticeable!* Well, the only way around it was to have fun with it. I mimicked a cartoon character with high voice, as I said "H E L L O" to the little boy. This created laughter and eased the tension; just the beginning of being blessed by little children. You know what is funny about it? People say little kids are the worst. Yeah, they stare at you, but a simple wave, half-smile, or a higher-pitched remark and they are more accepting than their parents. Little tots are so truthful. They are so enthralled! I looked like a cartoon character; someone from "Loony Toons." I was "Bugs Bunny" brother Darryl Bunny. *Ha ha ha!*

I loved working at the fish store. Paul and I wouldn't close up until everything was immaculately clean, which was usually at seven p.m. Paul took pride in cleanliness. *Wow, how pretty!* During the Christmas season, the entire town was lit up. The streets were lined with street lamps that were heavily entwined with Christmas lights. The shop owners decorated storefronts in coordination. Every night was festive. I felt radiant with joy! Paul often drove his pick-up around to the front of the store; I'd toss the cane in the back of the pickup, then climb in. *All right! I am back into it!*

The work at the store became minimal during the month of January, so I began to call and look for other volunteer options. Sadly, Paul's Fish House shut down at the end of February, 1992, due to the high rent. Paul returned to his previous job at the local supermarket's fish counter, and I was lost. *Now what?*

February 5, 1992. I still was not ready to jump into the mainstream at Merrill Lynch. I didn't want to blow my insurance; more reconstructive surgery needed to be done. But I certainly didn't want to stay in the house, either. I wanted to Keep Going. Challenge the mind. Contribute to society in some way. I loved to be around people; I loved to work—be active.

I called Condell Memorial Hospital in Libertyville, desperately wanting to volunteer. I pleaded my case. "I need to get out of the house more often." Mary Francoeur, Director of Volunteer Services, heard my plea. I shared my medical background with determination: "I exercise every day. The cancer is out of here and won't come back." Then I shared my professional background with pride. "I am on long-term disability with Merrill Lynch."

Once at the hospital, I filled out an application in the Volunteer Office. Mary and I then drove around the campus to the building, separate and adjacent to the hospital that housed doctors' offices. Once inside the building, we moseyed over to a vacant corner office space, where there were piles and piles of "stuff." Boxes upon boxes were strewn in disarray all over the yellow shaggy rug. A few minutes passed then in came this smiling, tall, energetic woman, Darlene Leonard, Director of Customer Service at Condell Medical Center. She was a very vivacious person who seemed to accomplish everything set before her. A mover and shaker! The three of us took seats in brown leather chairs next to the main desk. We introduced ourselves then Darlene explained a project she had been working on for the past two years—to develop a Condell Hospital Museum. (It seems to have become very fashionable for hospitals to develop museums about their history.) Darlene presented a historical summary of Condell. I was fascinated when she said that Sam Insull had donated land for the hospital to be built on, back in 1917. Sam Insull was secretary to Thomas Edison. *Wow! What an eye-popper!* Darlene went on to say that Condell is a non-profit hospital and was developed according to Elizabeth Condell's will, and five thousand dollars raised by the town of Libertyville. Darlene then emphasized that she always started and finished projects. My eyes lit up and my heart thumped like a little child's on Christmas morn. She asked if I would take charge and help them organize the historical items. *I will do it!* I was charged up and shared my goals of inter-relating the growth of Libertyville with the growth of the hospital, and then relating it to the needs of the people. My big mouth got in the way and I even said that I would develop a flowchart for the organization, to keep the committee on track. Darlene and Mary loved the idea and handed me a baton—a manila folder filled with notes taken over the past two years by the history committee.

At 2:00 p.m., I was driven home by a man in his forties named Chris. He walked slowly and talked with a slow tongue like I do when I'm tired. He was amazing—a medical miracle and a model volunteer. He had more volunteer hours logged in, per year, than any other volunteer. He was a lot like me—a fun-loving guy, a good sense of humor, loved music, women, and was a fighter—he didn't sulk about his handicap, but was determined to overcome it. He was a top advertising salesman in Chicago, who had a near-death car accident. He came back and was winning!

What am I doing? I have never created a flowchart! I do not even know what one looks like. Way to go, Didier! I looked up "flowchart" in the dictionary. No help there. I went to the local library with Dad that Saturday morning to learn what a flowchart looked like and how it was developed. I was still stumped. I flipped through notes in the manila file at the hospital and found a report called "The Evanston Hospital Centennial Retrospective, 1891-1991." I studied the report and noticed that it was organized by department; for example, nurses, doctor, facilities, etc. This titillated my mind to organize by category and decade while placing a timeline on each. *So, it will get done!* This reminded me of the times with Merrill Lynch. I had a mission; I was excited. That following Monday, I called Mary and told her that she had created a monster. Two weeks later, I showed the flowchart to Mary and Darlene in the hospital cafeteria. To my surprise, they were impressed. *I guess I did it right!* Mary called the History Committee members to set up a meeting.

I was given a title: Chairman of the History Committee. Through the great help of Mary, she organized a meeting with the committee to discuss the historical significance. I now had a purpose with goals to achieve.

A few weeks past and the organization was coming along. *Yeah! What a laugh! Here I am, trying to clean up a mess, while my bedroom needs utmost attention!* But I felt active again, being in touch with society. Every day when I came home in the afternoon, I walked and walked and walked. I read and read and read. *What can I do to better myself?*

That's enough practice. Now it is time to find out what's going on! Obtaining my driver's license was so important to me; it created the independence I craved. So on Saturday morning, March 28, 1992: Dad drove me to the Marianjoy Rehabilitation Hospital and Clinic in Wheaton, a 30-mile drive, for my 10:00 a.m. appointment. It was a very impressive-looking place, surrounded by pines on many acres. I felt as though we were entering a prestigious university.

We found the Drivers Education Department. *Wow, look at all this stuff!* I saw a computer, a car simulator, and an eye examination window. *Geesh!* Denise, an occupational therapist, was the examiner. First, I was given a thorough eye exam—the same tests as those administered by Dr. Margolis to test my peripheral and night vision. The results were the same as my previous exam: I was slightly nearsighted and I needed to use an eye-patch over my left eye, which slanted inward, to block the double vision.

Following the eye exam was the reaction test in which Denise instructed me to go over to the car simulator. There was a movie screen about five feet ahead, and a film was shown, circa 1970. The film was shot from a driver's perspective as if you were driving down a country road, and then all of a sudden, *ah!*, a dangerous thing happened: A car pulled out of the driveway in front of you. *Uh-oh, I missed the brake! Hey, this simulator is baloney!* This occurred for a half hour.

After the simulation test, I was qualified to take the road test with a different examiner, a local policeman named Bob. I drove a 1986 light blue, two-door Cutlass. The steering wheel was loose, unlike my car, which I had practiced with. It was like navigating a large ship through rough waters on a small pond. We drove, stopped, reversed, three-point turned and parallel-parked on side roads. I liked that. There was no traffic to contend with. Then I was instructed to travel out onto the main drag. *Oh, man!* I gripped the steering wheel at the desired 10-10 slots. It was hard work to keep the car in my own lane, especially when another car approached. After an hour of driving elapsed, Bob had had enough. I swayed too much. I did not pass the evaluation. *Damn!!!* I was ready to cry. My dream of independence had been destroyed in an instant.

On the journey back, I shared my frustration with Dad. "Everyone who has their license renewed should take the same grueling tests! Well, at least I have another chance." I wanted to practice with the family car because it had the same loose steering as the one Marianjoy used for the drivers' tests. "Hey, Dad," I said, "let me practice driving with the family car." He immediately said no because I was not insured under their auto policy. But he really didn't trust me, so we continued with my car on the weekends.

April 15: Dad and I returned to Marianjoy. I was to be re-evaluated again, but on the road. I was more focused than before. I knew what to expect and how to adjust. From my perspective, I performed 100 percent better than the last time, with more control of the Cutlass and Bob Simons, Driver Examiner, recommended that I was good to drive but in daylight only. That was one goal met, but now I must be approved by the state to legally take the exam.

Early May, 1992. The historical organization at Condell was complete. *Okay, now what?* Develop the historical display? The historical committee's funds were limited, so we had to hold off. *Now, what to do!* I kept up the pace of exercising. That was my job and my life but was bored again. I'd had a small taste of a partially filled day, scheduled with outside work. I loved it. And now I missed it.

15

Do the Best You Can or Don't Do It at All!

My goal was to spread the insurmountable spirit. The American Cancer Society, Lake County Unit, provided the means. So, at the same time that I volunteered at Condell Hospital, I became heavily involved with the ACS thanks to Mrs. Rodbro, and subsequently to be voted to the Board of Directors, Lake County Unit (May, 1994).

Pat Rodbro, Chairwoman, called me on May 12, 1992. She asked whether I would like to be the guest speaker at the Lake County ACS's annual Board of Directors dinner meeting, which would be held at the Holiday Inn, on May 20. She told me to just share my story. *Wow! What an honor!* I was a nervous wreck. With only a week to think about it, my heart raced; I rolled and rolled around in bed at night as thoughts flooded my mind. Wanting to be prepared, I wrote an outline on the computer, then on index cards. I recited my speech over, over, and over again, for days on end, that whole week. *I want to make an impression. I do not want to mess up!*

May 20. *Ah, the day is here. What can I do to calm down?* I went through my regular workout schedule at the health club. As I made my way out of the locker room, I stopped near the exit to the massage room and told my friend, Neal, the masseur at the club, how nervous I was. He was a gracious, philosophical person from India, who calmed me down when he said: "God will be at your side." *Yes, I will have someone by my side! Go get 'em!*

That evening, I dressed in my navy-blue suit with the tie that I borrowed from Dad's tie rack (never to be returned). *I want to look professional!* I made sure I placed the index cards with the tickler notes in my shirt pocket so I would stay on course. My parents and grandmother, age 87, went with me that evening. Grandma usually visited us during the month of May to see the season change. They don't have that in San Diego.

When we arrived, the convention hall was chatty with top professional people—doctors, lawyers, business owners. You name it, they were there! I sat at a large, round convention table that seated 12 people, including Mrs. Pat Rodbro and her husband, Dr. Mike Rodbro. I sat there quietly, eating slowly, taking small bites. *Come on, Divider, talk! Don't just sit there like a crumb on the table!* I finally joined in the conversation with the group about the current economy, concentrating on keeping my tongue directly behind my front teeth. I seemed to come across better that way. (At least I thought so when I listened to myself on the micro-tape.)

Mrs. Rodbro called everyone to order. For the first 40 minutes, the business agenda and verbal voting took place—the "Yeas" and "Nays" for people to be appointed to the board, a board member to be promoted to director, and implementing new by-laws. I became nervous again, but I kept repeating to myself what Neal had said. *Yes, God will be at my side!* Then, Pat Rodbro gave a resounding introduction about my background. I quickly put a small piece of gum in my mouth to keep it moistened, or else it would dry out because of the effects of radiation.

It was my turn. With cane in hand, I scrambled to the podium. I was a ball of nerves, looking at the crowd of 50 attractive people, all focused on me. I noticed the microphone on the podium and remarked, "I don't need this microphone; my voice is loud enough without it!" The crowd laughed. Then I said that I was on long-term disability with Merrill Lynch (I wanted to develop credibility among all those professionals). As I began to blurt out my story, with emphasis on developing goals, I didn't even use the notes I had prepared.

As I continued, I scanned the room and saw Mom, Dad and Grandma in one of the back rows. I noticed that they were seated with their heads high, looking proud as I kept on talking. I looked directly in front of me and saw Pat's continuous smile of approval. I threw in some light-hearted thoughts. For example, I talked about the time I took the PACE bus with a load of grandmothers. Instead of feeling sorry for myself during that ride, I wondered how I could be fixed up with a good-looking granddaughter. That drew laughs. *How encouraging!* I summed up what I was currently doing and explained my theory about exercise. I also explained the reason for the facial paralysis, talked about the initial nerve implantation and the upcoming facial surgery on June 9, then held up my cheek. I ended with, "I will get back to work at Merrill Lynch. The cancer is out of here. Thank you!" Everyone applauded then gave me a standing ovation. *Wow! I guess I did it!* People came up, shook my hand and made encouraging, supportive comments. *What a great experience. I'll do it again, again, again!*

June 9, 1992. Surgery again: second phase of the left facial reconstruction. The surgery was conducted at Evanston Hospital and performed by a team of two doctors: Dr. Pensler, the main surgeon, and Dr. Casas to assist with the muscle excavation and transplantation.

At the end of the 10-hour surgery, Dr. Pensler implanted two sutures to keep the newly transplanted muscle anchored in the correct place in my left cheek so it wouldn't droop during recovery. Shortly after surgery when I was in the ICU room, I accidentally pulled out the sutures. I was hallucinating from the painkillers that were prescribed and I thought I was in the washroom looking at my facial reflection in the mirror. I noticed two large lumps slightly to the left of my nostril. I knew these lumps weren't normal so I tugged and pulled and tugged and pulled until I successfully removed the irregularities. Dr. Pensler entered my ICU room later that afternoon to see how I was doing. He glanced down at me with a stunned look, his right hand stroking his chin. In a curious voice, he said, "You pulled out the sutures! How did you do that?" He was dumbfounded as he slowly glanced from side to side. According to Dad, he was visibly upset that I had done such a thing. *Oh man, you did it again! You created a real mess! Oh, great, you idiot! So much for wanting to leave the hospital as quickly as possible!* I was so disgusted and angry with myself I couldn't believe that I had done such a dumb thing.

I was brought again to the surgical room to try to replace the muscle in the correct place, and three new sutures were used to keep it snug. This time during the recovery phase, I had my hands restrained for two days, so I couldn't be fidgety again.

Throughout the night, the nurse injected painkillers so I could sleep soundly. When I awoke I was really hallucinating. I was frightened out of my wits because I thought all the medical assistants and nurses were out to get me. For example, I remember very clearly that a nurse, wearing a purple exercise outfit, tried unsuccessfully to insert an IV. *She is no nurse! Aaah, get me out of here! She has no idea what she is doing!* I rolled over on my right side and hallucinated that I was in the back corner of the hospital basement, left totally alone. *There is someone after me under my bed!* I looked to the left. *Ah hah!* I caught Dr. Pensler red-handed. He was running an underground business down there. *Hey! What's going on?* Now the doctor had a large group of migrant workers from Mexico preparing large quantities of food for distribution to local Mexican restaurants. *What? No way!* According to my father, the nursing staff was very concerned, so they called him to come to the hospital and bring me back to reality.

I was finally released the afternoon of June 14. When I returned home, I immediately, but slowly and cautiously, walked to the half-bathroom to see how handsome I looked. *Ha, ha, ha! I look like I am chewing a big wad of tobacco! I look stupid! Why did I do this again?* The swelling in my face had just about dissipated before the surgery; I had started to look normal! But, I didn't want to say, "What if?" when I was 40 years old. That's why I did it again.

July 10, 1992 I received an unfavorable report from the Secretary of State/Medical Review Unit. The unit felt I was medically unable to operate a motor vehicle. *I need more practice than just on the weekends with Dad!* I knew how I could do it; I called Adams Driving School. I wanted to practice without having to go through drivers' rehab at Marianjoy again, which was 30 minutes away, and I did not want to bother Mom and Dad. I thought I had a great idea. I was anxious to get the show on the road—to "Rock N Roll." But when I called the school to request their service, my "high-ness" was shot down. I explained my predicament. *What?* The woman said that under the circumstances, I needed a note from my doctor and an okay from the Secretary of State/Medical Review Unit specifying that I could drive safely.

July 28, 1992. Guest Celebrity for "Making Strides."

What a surprise! I was asked if I would like to be the celebrity spokesman for the ACS's annual three-mile walk-a-thon, "Making Strides." My heart thumped. Wow! *I am an actual celebrity!* I couldn't believe it, but I ate it up. As the "celebrity," I had the great opportunity to promote the event to the northeastern tier of Lake County.

I was interviewed, along with Carol, a tall, confident social worker at a nearby hospital, by a local radio station and the local newspaper: The Chicago Tribune, "Lake County Tempo" section.

During the interviews, Carol focused on the walk-a-thon itself, pointing out that it was a chance for cancer survivors to be recognized by the general public. Then I followed up, sharing my attitude about defeating cancer.

Wow! I had better come through! I tried to think of a strategic way to collect a number of sponsors for the walk-a-thon. Then it came to me. *Mmm! I know a good marketing ploy! Who can say no, with a young child pleading your case?* On a Sunday afternoon, I asked Courtney, my neighbor's third-grade daughter, if she would like to take part in a fun activity and visit all the neighbors with me. She agreed. As Courtney and I began to make the rounds, two, four then six grade-school kids joined us. I felt like the "Pied Piper" as I led the pack, carrying my cane from house to house. I couldn't make it up the two-foot step to the front porch without losing my balance, so I asked my little friends to ring the doorbell. When the homeowners opened their doors, the first things they saw were innocent little grins. That immediately put them into a good mood. Then I loudly and energetically introduced myself as a local resident and a cancer survivor. My "staff" and I collected $1,000 in donations as we visited 30 homes, or six blocks, in two weeks. All were very gracious.

The event was held at the Old School Forest Preserve, just 20 minutes from my house. *Wow, look at this. In all the years I have lived in this area, I have never been to this preserve,* as we drove through the speed-bumped winding road to the first overhang, where the walk-a-thon started. I scanned the area. About 100 people had shown up. Some of the friends I had called were scattered among the crowd at 7:30 a.m. on that sunny Saturday morning. *Great!* That provided even more motivation for me.

We were all gathered in front of the main shelter (the starting and ending point of the walk). I was nervous, and that was good. Whenever I am nervous, my energy is heightened, so the right thoughts come to mind. I was handed a microphone by Pat Rodbro. Standing on uneven, rocky terrain, I lost my balance, even with the cane in hand, and I didn't bother getting up again. I shared my story, adding motivational thoughts about overcoming cancer, while sitting on my rump.

"You are here. Cancer is here. You have to meet it head-on and beat it! Thank you for your help in trying to fight the dreaded disease. The American Cancer Society is very, very important. Your donations go to a great cause—to much-needed cancer research. In addition, the ACS provides transportation services to cancer patients who are unable to drive to doctor appointments or chemotherapy treatments. It provides educational programs to local grade schools and high schools. The ACS keeps in direct contact with local legislatures regarding laws to limit cancer-causing agents, like tobacco and certain chemicals. Only a very small percentage of all donations goes toward administrative costs. The ACS relies heavily on volunteers. Through all of you, the ACS has touched me in a big way, and I am only one minuscule cancer survivor out of millions. If I had not gotten cancer, I never would have met the wonderful people involved with the ACS. I wouldn't have had the opportunity to speak in front of terrific groups like you. I see many more opportunities down the road."

Everyone cheered as Mrs. Rodbro pulled me up to my feet. Mom and Dad (Brenda was at work that morning) were in the foreground, giving me the thumbs-up sign.

The three-mile fund-raising event began with a 30-minute warm-up led by an aerobics instructor. I sat and stretched, then started to walk without a cane down the car path that twisted, turned, and sloped, while Mom and Dad followed behind with the wheelchair, the cane hooked to the back in case my legs tired. My momentum began to increase. *Hey, I can do it, all three miles.* I kept up the pace, a quarter of a mile. A photographer ran five feet in front of me on several occasions. He would turn towards me, stoop down in a baseball catcher's crouch, and take a picture. *All right!* As the team, Mom, Dad, and I kept up the trot, a reporter from the Chicago Tribune walked along with me as I dodged to the left, then right. She held a micro-tape recorder and interviewed me, but it was difficult to walk and talk at the same time.

I wanted to show off and place an accent on my determination. I was lapped by many, and twice by my friend, Craig, from Indiana, who sported a big grin as he paraded around in a circle. He tried to spur my temper. He knew I was excitable. *Dang it!* By the second mile, my legs felt as though they had scrambled up. First Mom, then Dad, asked if I needed to rest or wanted the wheelchair or cane. *Gosh, no!* "I have to keep going." I swayed in all directions with little or no control. *Dang it! Come on! Eventually, it will come back! I have to keep walking on my own to build the endurance.* I finally gave in and slowly limped along the trail with the cane. When I made it around the bend for the straightaway, I eyed the finish line, 50 yards away. I picked up the tempo—so badly did I want to finish—but I had little control. I zigzagged across the finish line, with Mom and Dad following behind with the wheelchair. Six friends and two volunteers clapped and cheered. I came in last. That didn't matter. It was my personal race and I won! **Keep Going!**

August 16 1992, I had a check-up with Dr. Vick following another clear MRI scan, *yeah God!* I explained my driving situation to him. "How could the Medical Review Unit deny my case without knowing who I am? Each member of the unit hasn't personally examined me." Dr. Vick strongly agreed. "The next time you come in here," he said, "I want to see you drive yourself." *Yeah! I have a powerful person on my side!* Dad and I continued to practice.

That week I appealed. I enclosed a letter from Dr. Vick along with the report from Marianjoy's Occupational Therapy Driving program that stated I was medically and physically able to drive. I followed up by calling the Medical Review Unit every week; I knew the number by heart. Each time, a middle-aged man or woman answered the phone in a disinterested-sounding, monotone voice. "Hello, this is the Medical Review Unit." I repeated in a stern voice: "Hello, this is Darryl Didier!" I gave my driver's license number, and inquired about my case. "What's going on?!" "The Medical Review Unit is still deciding." *How could they make a decision without meeting me face to face?* I shared my aggravation with mom and she suggested I contact the State Representative to intercede.

On October 5, Mrs. Rodbro and I went to Stevenson High School to represent the ACS during the Lake County Health Fair in the gym. We pulled into the main parking lot that morning: *Wow! The school is huge!* The enrollment at Stevenson was roughly 3200. The size of the core building had doubled since I had seen it only one year before. Mrs. Rodbro parked the car at the last available spot in the last row at the end. With a large bag filled with cancer education pamphlets, she and I (with my cane) went to the gym.

The walls were painted light green and yellow, the school's colors; conference championship banners, with lettering the same color, representing different sports—football, basketball, softball, baseball and swimming—lined the walls. The entire basketball court was filled, on the out-of-bound edges, with booths representing many different kinds of local health care providers, from local hospitals, chiropractors, podiatrists, health food stores, to local police and fire departments. The booths' folding banquet tables were piled high with educational handouts for the students. The Vernon Hills Fire and Police Department booths had photographs on vertical boards that grossly showed the results of drinking and driving. Mrs. Rodbro unloaded the bag of pamphlets and stacked them in an orderly fashion. Our booth had been partially set up before we arrived. *Whew!* I felt that the ACS had the best representation of what smoking does to the human lungs. *Ah, I have the best booth!*

The "Smoking Lung," as it was called, was a large wooden, whitewashed, five-foot-long, three-foot-wide crate. The crate depicted, vertically on the front, a normal lung, an emphysema lung, and a cancer lung. The box was powered by an A/C outlet and once turned on, it looked very realistic. While illuminated, the lungs were life-sized and they pulsated as if they were inhaling and exhaling. The rate of motion diminished dramatically with the heightened discoloration between the lungs. The normal lung was clean and clear. The emphysema lung was purple with black spots; the cancer lung was beige in color and heavily bloated with cancer lesions. *Gross!*

I felt confident. I wore jeans and a green shirt with small blue figures of a fly-fisherman. I brought along my Spanish book so I could recite Spanish phrases out loud to exercise my tongue between class times. I wanted to be fluent when I spoke to the students. My speech was a concern, especially when I was among high school students. I didn't want to just sit and become complacent, so I planned to stand all day while I manned the booth, eight periods, with a lunch break in-between.

Wow! Do they look different; more radical dress. What? They wore hats inside the school. If they weren't wearing hats, they had funky hairstyles. They wanted to be recognized; they wanted to stand out among the large student population, which was multi-cultural. Just 10 years before, the students had been primarily of American and European descent, but now, many different ethnic groups were represented. Gosh, I felt old when the freshman class came to the table; they looked so young. All the students were engrossed with the "Smoking Lung." Occasionally, a student glanced away. Could that be a sign that he or she was a smoker? Many students asked if they could take the pamphlets home to show their parents, sisters, brothers, or neighbors. At times, a curious student would ask what had happened to me. I briefly explained then proudly said, "I am on the way back," standing with cane in hand.

During the lunch break, I ate my fruit-filled lunch at the booth. I then meandered off to see the sights. I walked around the gym to loosen up my leg and meet people. I literally ran into Mike Rodbro as we stomach-butted (the manly way to greet). It was a real booster. He sounded off praise about my physical improvement since the last time we had seen each other, two weeks before. I said, "You have to keep going! Charge ahead!" I went on to say that I had been on my feet for a long time, so my legs were loose. Mike responded, "Yeah, yeah! Right on!"

Four more periods…The scene was the same, just not as crowded. By 4:00 p.m., it was done, over; the school let out. I stayed at the booth until a bulky assistant football coach and a health teacher said they would take care of the rest. Mike entered the gym again and said he would drive me home. After slashing and dashing in and out of a large crowd of boisterous students bolting for the exits, Mike and I went up to the second floor to the weight room. Mike wanted to visit with the weight-training coach, Deno ("Bubba") Sampura. A large, dark-skinned, dark-haired man, with a weight-belt around his waist, the coach smiled when he saw Mike. Then he grinned from ear to ear as the two shared pleasantries. He looked at me, and I at him. "Hey,

Bubba; what's going on?" I asked him. I recalled pumping weights, periodically, in that weight room with Chris.

"Darryl, how are things going?"

"Great!" I tried to stand firmly with the cane in hand. "You heard what happened, right?"

"Yes, I did!"

"I work out all the time now and I attribute my overall comeback to that!"

Bubba said, "You can come here and train any time." *Yeah, he remembers me and I am respected.*

During the second week in October, Pat Rodbro, who has taught breast self-examination classes to the girls at Stevenson High School for many years, called me. She asked if I would like to go with her to Stevenson on two alternate days, the morning of October 19th, and the afternoon of the 21st. My job would be to share my story with eight boys' health classes that were being taught testicular self-exam along with the hazards of smokiung and chewing tobacco. Pat said I would be good for the students because of the relative closeness in age.

"They will be able to relate to you more."

"Great, I will do it!"

Wow! This will be good! I will get a chance to tell it like it is! What life is all about, its challenges. The high school students are the target popula-tion where I could have a great influence: they are making decisions about where to go in life.

On the night before the talk, Mom, Dad, and I were seated around the table, enjoying one of Mom's stupendous meals. I shared my ner-vous anticipation with them. "What should I say?" Dad suggested that I tell the same story I had told at the ACS's annual meeting. Mom said I had better not talk above them. "Yeah, sometimes I tend to do that." After dinner, I bolted upstairs to my computer and printed out a copy of the May 20 outline of the speech I gave at the ACS's annual dinner. I practiced and practiced to Dad and to Jelly Bean, who hissed, and ran away.

October 19. I awoke at the usual time without an alarm, 5:30 a.m., and exercised on the stationary bike to energetic Hip-Hop music. I wanted to be at peak performance. After the 20-minute ride, I felt as though I'd had two cups of coffee. I was wide-awake. "Hey, Mom and Dad, good morning." After my shower: I sat at the kitchen table, ate breakfast and drank a cup of coffee while I recited Spanish phrases over and over. "El chocolate es muy favorita de los españoles." I wanted to energize my tongue.

Mrs. Rodbro called ahead as planned and I immediately rushed to the great outdoors. It was windy and chilly that day as I walked back and forth on the driveway. *You have to keep going!* She picked me up on time. *Wow! She was dressed to the "T,"*

When we pulled up to the front entrance of the school, Mrs. Rodbro, who was carrying a shopping bag filled with ACS pamphlets and three videos, opened the doors for me. *Hey, I should be holding the door for her, not her for me. I'm a man. Men open doors for women!*

I waited in the corridor between the inside and outside doors. A stout, middle-aged custodian, wearing a dark green uniform, noticed my imbalance and offered me a folding chair. I politely declined. *I do not want to succumb!* As the students entered, I peered out to the bustling parking lot, holding my head high, wanting to give the impression that I was important. That was how I combated direct glances. I knew I looked different.

Mrs. Rodbro appeared with her nice smile. "Let's go, hon." We walked through the corridor to a set of stairs up to the second level. "Can you handle this?" "Yep, no problem." I held onto the railing and scaled both flights of six steps, each.

I made it. I heard the scrambling feet of students rushing off to their morning homerooms before the bell sounded. *Ah!* I received a vote of confidence as three girls walked by and offered welcoming smiles. *Hey, maybe I don't look too bad.* I often wondered what the people saw when they looked at me.

We entered the classroom—high school wonders of mixed genders, 20 juniors. There was a large amount of socializing going on while the class was settling in. "Hello, Pat," the health teacher said as he dashed between the aisles, handing out results of a quiz. Mrs. Rodbro returned the greeting as we walked to the front of the room. I wobbled and waggled. *Uh-oh, they are all staring!* Pat unloaded the bag of pamphlets on a table next to the teacher's desk. I stood in front of the class, trying to seem cool and controlled. But wouldn't you know it? My legs jumped; I bounded to the left and then to the right. The room became silent and I was embarrassed. *Come on, hurry up! Think of something!* "I am trying a new tap-dance routine. Ha, Ha!" They laughed. Again, one way to ease the tension was to make fun of myself.

I sat in the front row next to a girl. *Geesh! I hope I don't make her freak out!* I had approached the seat like a sly cat, not wanting to make a fuss. The brunette glanced and offered a warm smile. *Whew!* The teacher concluded his business, taking attendance and reminding the kids to take gum out of mouths and hats off. *Oh, boy. Now I feel guilty.* I was chewing gum myself. I tried to keep my jaws motionless.

The teacher introduced Mrs. Rodbro and me and explained our purpose for being there.

When the bell sounded to begin class, the teacher told the students to split up into two groups—male and female. The girls were to go into the next room with Mrs. Rodbro and the boys stayed. I introduced myself. Not a peep was uttered when I said I had had a brain tumor and now, two years later, it was gone. "I work out every day."

The teacher, who was also assistant coach of the varsity football team, caught one of the boys secretly chewing gum, he instructed him to do 20 push-ups while reciting that he would never chew gum again in class. I was impressed; Catholic school discipline upheld in public school. Once the class calmed down, the teacher announced that they were going to see a film on testicular self-examination. Some smirks emitted. The teacher interjected, as he passed out pamphlets about the self-exam, "These are for men, not boys who snicker."

I was getting restless from sitting so much; I wanted to get to my part. The video took a total of 20 minutes. The anti-chewing-tobacco video was very graphic, depicting a man in his mid-twenties who had chewed since he was 15, and developed lip cancer. The next photo showed him after the removal of his jaw. The narrator said the boy died two months after the surgery. That video hit home; exclamations of shock filled the room. Chewing tobacco was a common practice among teenage boys in my area, seeming like a "cool" thing to do. I had done it, myself, for a short time back in high school and a few years in college. *I'm sure glad I quit when I did!!!*

Finally, it was my turn to talk, and my heart rate picked up. The teacher provided a resounding introduction, focusing on the fact that I was a local product who had participated in football and baseball at Carmel High, just a 20-minute drive to the north. He said I was a good athlete and had been healthy and lively, just like them. I bounded to the front of the room, cane in hand.

> "Yes, I was just like you when I was your age. I thought I was inde-structible. When I saw something about a discussion on cancer on my schedule, I would think, 'Hey, more time to relax! Big deal; nothing is going to happen to me!' Two years out of college, I told myself that I would grab life and not let go! I worked for the top financial institution in the world. A hot red sports car. The girl-friend of my dreams. Then bam, I got it. I got cancer!"

I went on with the rest of my story, emphasizing self-motivation, and a positive attitude, developing goals with added self-disci-pline—responsibility.

> "I would not be here today if I hadn't decided to take self-responsi-bility and exercise every single day! I don't take any medication, only natural nutrients. Life threw me a curve ball, but I stepped up to the plate, waited for the ball to curve, and now I am hitting a home run. You have to take on challenges. Do not shy away! Meet whatever comes along head-on! Do the best you can in everything

you do, or don't do it. Seize the day. Live every day like it's your last day. I asked my doctor what caused the cancer. Do you know what he said? He had no idea! What? I drank a little recreationally in college, but I did not abuse it. I did not smoke."

I went on to talk about the car accident that occurred in 1988, when I was at Indiana State University. I explained the determination it took to get back on my feet again and graduate. I shared my theory that the accident had had a big influence on the tumor growth.

"The doctors could not substantiate the cause. They could not prove, nor disprove, that there was any correlation between the accident and the tumor, but I believe there was a correlation. On the other hand, we all know what causes lung cancer. What do you think?" [Ninety-nine percent of the class raised their hands.] "Smoking. We all know, right? Well then, why do people do it? I know of people who smoked and got lung cancer. The cancer metastasized, or spread to become a brain tumor. When I see somebody smoking, I want to run over to them, take the cigarette out of their mouth and yell, 'What are you doing!?' I know it isn't socially correct, so I don't do it. But why do they do it? There are more cancer-causing agents—carcinogens—in our environment than there were twenty years ago. We don't have to add to it!

"As I look back on my own case history, there were early signs that I ignored. Days before I had the severe headache, I threw up at work twice. I rationalized. I thought I had drunk too much coffee in the morning, or that it was from stress on the job. Wrong! It was an early sign. Days before, as I drove to work, I had trouble with my vision. I rationalized again; I told myself I was just getting older; twenty-four at the time. If I had gone to the ophthalmologist to have my eyes checked, he would have noticed my optic nerve swelling, due to the tumor. If I hadn't rationalized, like we all do, the doctors would have caught the tumor growth at an earlier stage, and I wouldn't have experienced that horrendous headache—and that close call on my life.

"Early detection is the key. Know your body and know it well. If there is an unusual growth, or it something unusual occurs, get it checked out by a doctor. Don't be a wimp like I was and ignore it!

I don't want you to turn into a bunch of hypochondriacs, but know what is normal and what is abnormal. That's it. Any questions?"

Of course, no one raised his hand. "Gosh, I didn't know I was that thorough. I must be getting good at this. I'll even do my tap dance routine again," I said, as the nerves in my legs jumped. The students became more comfortable and opened up. They asked questions about my current medical status: my vision, hearing, and upcoming surgeries to repair my left cheek, MRIs, and so forth. "Great questions!" I exclaimed. The teacher prompted the class to congratulate me, and as they did, they all stood and applauded. "Thanks!" The bell sounded. *Wow! What timing!* A group of students came forward, looking very curious, and offered encouraging remarks. They said that I had a lot of courage and had given them more self-determination. After the handshaking, four of the students stayed and talked further. One was distraught over his grandfather, who had passed away from a brain tumor. The other three asked if they could take an "anti-smoking" pamphlet home to a family member or friend. *Hey, I did it! Great! What a booster!* I felt the power and spirit in me, as though I were on a mission. I was doing what I was supposed to be doing, thanks to the ACS. *All right! Three more classes to go!*

The reactions were the same—all clapped vigorously, and they taught me a valuable lesson: Everybody is touched by cancer in some way. Students came forward and shared that people close to them—grandfather, grandmother, aunt, uncle, friend, friend of a friend—currently had, or recently died from lung cancer, prostate cancer, colon cancer, breast cancer. I felt like a shining light of hope. *Yes, you can overcome!* I was very impressed with the students and the instructors. Their awareness was much greater than cancer awareness had been when I was in high school, eight years before.

It's done, at least for that day. There were four more classes to talk to on Wednesday afternoon, two days later. I was flying high after receiving all those affirmations. Mrs. Rodbro opened the car door for me.

"There you go, hon." We pulled out of the parking lot, I talked about how lucky I was to be able to speak to the students. "I love it." **Keep Going**!

Wednesday, October 21. Afternoons were usually difficult for me. That was the time of day when I wasn't heightened with energy. My body tended to be drained of the morning's vigor. It was difficult to walk straight, talk right and recite from the top of my head. *Come on, Didier, no excuses.* As we had done the first time, I met with the whole class and then they split up into a boys' group and a girls' group.

This time around, I was more at ease. "Hey, guys!" I wanted to say. "I am normal!" I was immediately introduced by the young female health teacher as the guest speaker, representing ACS. She left the rest up to me. That was a mistake; I like to talk! I used up most of the time sharing my story. Only 15 minutes was allotted, so there was no time for questions. I imitated what the other teacher had said: "These are for men only!" then handed the testicular self-exam packets to a nearby student, to take one and pass the rest along.

As the bell sounded and the students left the room, I thought to myself, *I hope I left a message!*

Ah! I sighed, three more to go! I waited in the multi-media room. *Come on, Didier, pick it up!* I searched desperately for a stick of gum, but couldn't find one. Then my left eye became irritated; it dried out. I searched my pockets, in which I normally stocked several vials of eye droppers. I found three, but they were already used up from the earlier need. *Ah! The emergency supply!* I felt around in my sock, left ankle. *Whew!*

"Hi, guys. Who is on the football team?"…etc. As I shared my story three more times, I peered into each student's eyes. Some looked down; others stared right back at me. One could tell by their attentiveness if they had goals to achieve or not, like furthering their education—if they were doing the best they could do or not smoking and\or chewing.

At the end of each class, the question that was usually directed at me was:

"Were you ever down?"
"Generally, no! Why be down? It takes too much energy. Sometimes on Friday nights or on the weekends, I felt lonely. I wanted to go out with friends, but I had priorities. I had work to get done, so the feeling quickly faded.

"With the human spirit in mind, anyone would make it back! People like you helped me incredibly just by listening and by being encouraging. People are so important. So whenever you come across someone with a challenge, somebody in a wheelchair, a walker or a cane,offer encouragement."

3:30 p.m. It was over; I felt a let-down. *Now what do I have to look forward to?* I was led by the teacher back to the main health room on the second floor. The two teachers helped load the paper bag with the leftover pamphlets. As Mrs. Rodbro and I departed, the teachers said, "See ya in the spring." *They will see us in the spring?! They will see us again! Did I hear correctly: Us? All right! They liked what I had to say.* We made our way through the maze of students and out to the parking lot. "Okay, Hon," said Mrs. Rodbro as she opened the passenger door. She told me she had heard from the health teacher that I had done a fine job. We were off! *Yea! We did it.*

On January 26, 1993: *That's it, I need to do something.* I went back, with Dad, to Marianjoy Drivers' Rehab to re-start the process of achieving my driver's license with a clean slate, another $400 the family incurred. I knew what to expect this time, I felt confident. *They better not have that same light blue Cutlass that swayed in all directions!*

The same vision, simulator and road tests were administered by an attractive, vivacious occupational therapist, Ms. Koerber and that kept me focused. Once the tests were concluded she reported I had minimal impaired coordination of right leg for quick responses but scored significantly better than the last evaluation and recommended I would be a good driving candidate without adaptive equipment.

I still could not drive on my own, however. I had to re-submit the report to the State of Illinois Medical Review and you know how mundane they are. *Come on!*

February, 1993: Crusade Campaign Organization. Here we go again. I said yes to every request. Besides helping other people, I helped myself. It would be good rehab—to call, call, call and organize the towns. *Great, it will be good for my speech and exercise my left cheek.*

What was the Crusade Campaign anyway?: A fund-raiser for the ACS that ran all through the month of May. The charity event, which was organized in various suburbs in the northeastern section of Lake County, was structured towards volunteers (the "Crusaders") who canvassed the street on which they lived. It was my job to recruit people to be "Crusaders" on every single street in Lincolnshire, Deerfield, and Riverwoods. The ACS was quick on its feet by starting the planning early. They knew it would be a tough task.

Dorothy Small, an ACS field representative, mailed three packets to me, one for each town. Each packet contained a multitude of forms, which represented various sections of the town. A section of town consisted of two, four, or six blocks. Each section had a captain to guide and oversee the "Crusaders." In the packet was an address and telephone list of all the potential "Crusaders" who lived in that particular town. So, if the individuals who had "Crusaded" before didn't want to participate, I had to cold-call a neighbor on the street.

I put it off until March. I was not too excited about cold-calling residents to volunteer to go door-to-door. But then I thought, *hey, the potential "Crusader" will be representing the ACS. That will be exciting!*

I put together a spiel and made it personal. "Good evening, Ms. Wasucko! My name is Darryl Didier. I am a neighbor of yours. I live here in Lincolnshire. Ms. Wasucko, I represent the American Cancer Society and am calling about the Crusade Campaign. I am trying to find a lovely neighbor who will represent part of Kisock Street, on the odd side, numbers 3 to 15. Wouldn't you like the job?" The majority said, "No way!" Some hung up; a lot of people said they did not have time to do it. "No! no! no!" I was beat. I used all my energy with every calling, exuding enthusiasm. Ten calls later, Mr. Lapke, who lived in the last house on the block, heard my excited plea. "I'll do it!" Mr. Lapke replied energetically. "What? You will do it?" "Yes!" "Great! Thank you so much!!" *Ah, he fed off my excitement, like when I cold-called companies at MerrillLynch.* That really gave me the impetus to go on and make another 10 recruiting calls on two different blocks. Lincolnshire was organized by the end of March. Out of 3200 residents, 150 had volunteered.

Deerfield, with its 17,000 residents, is much like Lincolnshire from a socioeconomic standpoint, but the houses are closer together and it is a closer-knit community. Deerfield had the same response rate as Lincolnshire. I tried to make the cold calling personable, stating that I was their neighbor in Lincolnshire (which butts up against Deerfield to the west). It was done! The town was organized by March—220 volunteers.

Riverwoods, which is adjacent to Lincolnshire, just to the southeast, was a different story. The homes are mansions hidden in multi-acres of pine trees, maples and oaks. It is not a close-knit community that has block parties. Many of the residents travel a great deal, so the contacts were limited. Some of the people I actually talked to sounded like I was crazy to think they might canvass the neighborhood. Some happened to be doctors, and we didn't talk about the "Crusade;" we discussed my case history. Anyway, I kept going. I tried and tried and tried. A third of the Riverwoods residents were contacted and about 10 percent very graciously accepted. It was done! I recruited eager volunteers from Riverwoods, which I never thought I would be able to do.

The three towns were organized for the campaign by mid-April. *Yea, I did it!* What had seemed like an impossible goal was completed. With the power of enthusiasm, any formidable task can be conquered. *There is nothing like coming through on your promises!* Keep Going!

March 12 and 14, 1993. I excitedly went back to Stevenson High School with Pat Rodbro to conduct cancer education classes. It was the same schedule of events as the previous time—four classes in the morning on the 12th, and four in the afternoon on the 14th. The boys' health classes ranged from freshmen to seniors. Towards the end of the classes, I always felt more at ease. I was fulfilling my goal—to spread the word. Keep Going!

April 16, 1993. I had the honor again: I was asked to be the guest speaker at the "Crusade Kickoff Luncheon," held at Baxter Health Care, in Deerfield. Mrs. Rodbro thought it would be good for the "Crusaders" to get feedback from the grassroots.

The Crusade luncheon was called for 11:30 a.m. *Shoot, I will not get a chance to exercise at the health club. I will have to exercise early in the morning on the stationary bike.*

Mrs. Rodbro picked me up at 11:00 to go to Baxter, a multi-billion-dollar health care company with headquarters in Deerfield, is located 10 minutes from my home. It is a large campus with 2,000 employees, situated on beautifully groomed grounds. We parked in the four-story garage and marched to the main entrance across the way. *Wow, my balance is pretty good!*

Lunch was number one on the agenda and during the luncheon, Pat spoke at the podium about the conviction of the volunteers, and about the difficulties of canvassing door-to-door in this day and age, because people really don't know their neighbors like they used to. Pat very graciously introduced me as the one who organized all of Lincolnshire, Riverwoods, and Deerfield. My heart pounded again. *Good! The more worried I get, the better I talk.* Pat said that I was a cancer survivor, looking toward me with that ingratiating smile. She called me up to the podium, and I mauled my way to the front, knocking over two empty chairs at the table to my right. I tried to keep my balance steady. MMM! I finally realized that it was not good to exercise my legs early in the morning, then sit for a long time. My legs tightened up while the nerves twitched uncontrollably. I had to say something goofy to show that it didn't bother me.

"Believe me, my balance is getting better. Next year, I will crusade on roller blades! *Ha, ha, ha.*"

I summarized my story, with emphasis on the great assistance of the ACS, and talked about the experiences I'd had when I made the calls to organize the Crusade. I concluded by saying, "You all have helped me and many other cancer survivors by being involved in this great event." Everyone clapped, energy circulated through my body. As the meeting ended, people formed small groups and talked among themselves. I saw the chance to dash to the dessert tray and secretly slipped two palm-sized oatmeal raisin cookies into my pocket. They are my favorite.

16

There Is Never Too Much Spirit!

May 12, 1993. I was in-between the two counter tops, working on my balance control. *Come on! Dang!* I flopped to the right. The telephone rang just in time—or else! I was frantic! "Hello?" Mrs. Rodbro was at the other end. She told me that the ACS Board of Directors requested that I return as the guest speaker for their annual dinner meeting. *Wow!* I was very, very honored. Pat said no one had ever been invited back two years in a row. I felt unique, special. I put pressure on myself again. *I had better come through!* I prepared notes to stay on track, and read and read them aloud, for weeks.

That evening, May 20, I had the opportunity to be chauffeured by Dr. and Mrs. Rodbro. When they escorted me into the large dining room, the majority of the members knew my first name:

"Hi, Darryl, Darryl, Darryl...etc."

Wow! I was embarrassed. I couldn't reciprocate; I was bad at names. The annual meeting soon began everyone scrambled to the convention-sized dinner tables and the president gave the financial reports for each department. Dinner was served as the meeting continued. Mrs. Rodbro stepped up to the podium and offered another vibrant introduction. I sighed. I wasn't as nervous the second time around. The entire crowd were my friends; they were in my corner. The members clapped when I walked to the podium without the cane. I stood straight, tall and proud. The most important message: **Keep Going**. I still maintained the "Go get 'em" attitude, even though some days were harder than others.

> "I have had three M.R.I. scans over the last year and they were all clear! The cancer will not dare try to recur! However, there is a slim chance it could. But no way. There is too much spirit!"

I summarized my experiences as I gave back to the community. I loved it. I went on to explain why my left cheek was grossly enlarged compared to the previous year, as a result of the plastic surgery last June. Again, everyone clapped as many of the members told me to: **Keep Going!**

June 5: A letter from the office of the Secretary of State arrived. I ripped it open. *Yes!* They finally agreed. My driving privileges had been medically approved but were restricted to daytime driving only. *So what? I can work at Merrill Lynch during the normal business hours. But there is more surgery on my face coming up; I better not be too hasty.*

For a whole day, I studied the Rules of the Road book. It seemed too easy. Everything came back. I practiced driving with Mom a few times in the afternoon, since it was her summer vacation time. In mid-June, I went for the test, with Mom. At 4:00 p.m., we arrived at the Secretary of State's office in Libertyville.

I sat in a designated waiting line and Mom sat in the visitors' section on the opposite side. Two middle-aged men were trying to obtain their motorcycle licenses. Two women with heavy European accents applied. A class of teenagers eagerly awaited their first driving exam. They were wide-eyed and excited, like little puppies jumping up and down at a pet store. I was anxious, too—a nervous wreck. But as I witnessed other people's anxiety, I calmed down; I wasn't the only one. Twenty minutes later, my number was called. I presented the legal document giving me the medical O.K. I also showed three forms of identification proving that I was really me! Then I slid to the right of the counter, where I took the simple eye exam with the patch on. I passed then took the written exam. I aced it! Everything was going in my favor. Next on the agenda was the road test. A grumpy woman examiner and I went to my car in the parking lot. She witnessed my challenge as I weaved to the car with the cane. We went out to the main drag, a four-lane road, at 5:00 p.m. The sun was setting as I drove due west, directly into the rays. Traffic had built up due to the rush hour, even though we were in the country. At 100 yards, as I approached an intersection, the instructor ordered me to turn left. After strategically downshifting into second, I flashed my signal and entered the left-turn lane. I had to squint at the traffic light to see if the arrow was green, yellow or red. As I approached, I differentiated the colors through the harsh sunlight. The arrow changed to yellow. All was clear. I jammed the gear shift into third and went. In a scolding voice, the tester said I had turned left on yellow. *Dang! I had better not flub up now!* I continued down the street, a quarter of a mile. Then I was instructed to turn left onto a two-lane residential street. I zipped along. She called out: "Do you realize that you are going forty-two in a thirty-mile-per-hour zone?" *Dang, it's over! I blew it!* We came back to the office parking lot and I parked the car in the designated area for those waiting for their results. Two teenage girls were waiting, too. They passed and gleefully took part in the photo session. I was jealous as I watched. I was denied; I didn't make it. The opportunity I had worked for during the past two years faded. Two middle-aged male instructors urged me to return the next day to retake the road test. *They want me to pass. They're not as mean as I thought;* bad timing. The very next day I was going on vacation for two weeks with Mom and Dad to see Grandma in San Diego. *Dang! I shouldn't go!* But, I did go because I missed Grandma, I wanted to be with my family, and I wanted to rub shoulders with those beautiful California girls. *Wishful thinking!*

July 8, 1993. I was back from vacation. Mrs. Rodbro called. She wanted to know how the trip was and if I could fill in to help promote the "Making Strides" campaign on a local radio station and cable TV channel. "Yes!" *Wow!* I was honored to be selected to help promote the great event again.

"Mrs. Rodbro, I will drop everything to help out the ACS in some way." The intended "Guest Celebrity"—a cancer survivor, who had touched the lives of people in the Lake County community—Beth Green, would not be available on the pre-scheduled date because of an unexpected business meeting. Beth is the charming mother of two daughters and is a professional businesswoman.

WKRS-AM is a local radio station in Waukegan. Its frequency reaches from Vernon Hills, Illinois, as far north as Green Bay, Wisconsin. The taping was to take place at one p.m.

On that hazy, sunny day—the second sunny day following four consecutive days of heavy rain—Mom drove me to the station. Sandbags surrounded the quaint one-story building. As I hurried out of the car, I saw the debris from the receding flood waters, and the air smelled like a swamp. Carol Working, Chairwoman for "Making Strides," who was a social worker at Lake Forest Hospital, came in her black luxury sedan. We greeted each other in the parking lot.

We entered the building and walked through the corridor. It was a mess, filled with dark leaves. I felt like I was walking along a river bed. We were greeted by a large, congenial man sporting sunglasses, Bill Lackover. With his booming tenor voice, he sounded off a hello and led us to the studio.

Three…two…one…We were pre-recorded because the tape would be played during different intervals at night and the early morning for three days until the walk-a-thon. Carol provided information about the "Making Strides" campaign, and I did the motivational bit.

"One has to keep going!"

On the way out, we faced the heap of sandbags again. Mom and Carol glided over. Ah, I stepped over! *Yes!* My momentum carried me 10 yards beyond, and I cleared the lot. *I will not be hindered!* Keep Going!

That same evening at 7:00 p.m., Carol and I promoted the campaign on the US Cable local news program. I felt as though I were a star. Once again, Mom provided a ride to the cable station, which was situated in a strip-mall on the southwest corner of Green Bay Road and Grand Avenue, in Waukegan. The cable company served the northeastern section of Lake County, 45,000 households. I looked forward to it because Carol and I were to be interviewed on the sports cable channel. *It fits perfectly.* "Making Strides" was a sporting event—running and walking—to beat cancer. I was doubly excited because I took on the challenge of cancer as a competition to win.

Winston Ramsey, a twenty-eight -year-old ex-football player from Illinois State, was the host. We all sipped sodas and conversed. Winston put Carol and me at ease with his hearty laugh.

The stage was designed to give the feeling that we were lounging in someone's living room, with the coffee table and all. Carol and I sat on-stage left. Winston sat across, on-stage right, towards the center. *Excellent, my better side is facing the camera* (my right side). The program started. Carol was asked questions about the upcoming fundraiser. After 20 minutes of taping, the first half concluded. There was a 10-minute break; then it was my turn to add the exclamation point! Winston forwarded questions that focused on how my previous involvement in sports had helped me with the current battle.

> "Being involved in sports has taught me the value of competition, hard work and goal setting. It has helped me tremendously. 'Making Strides' is a sporting event that is a celebration over cancer and it educates the public. You know what makes me feel disgusted? Sometimes when I say the word, 'cancer!' to someone, the person freaks out. I am proud that I overcame cancer. What is their problem?"

Ten minutes later, the taping ended. Chuck Small, the director of the show, a short man with blonde hair, offered a very enthusiastic hello and said he enjoyed the taping. Mom told me that I was funny, and I said, "It was because of the great host." Chuck went on to relate that he had seen me a few days before at the health club, working out hard.

"Yep, that is the only way to come back." Keep Going!

July 10, I wanted to practice driving then go back to the same Secretary of State facility. I did not want to lose the edge. On August 3, Tuesday morning, at 8:30, I worked-out with Paul at the health club for two hours. As we drove back in his truck, I told him about my predicament: I wanted to go back to Libertyville to retake the driver's test in the afternoon when there was light traffic, but I had no way to get there. My entire family worked during the day and so did Paul, as a limousine driver. *Dang!* "I need more independence," I told Paul. At 11:00 a.m., Paul dropped me off at home. I took a shower, dressed then meandered downstairs where I munched a bowl of Raisin Bran. The phone rang; it was the cheery voice of Mrs. Mozeck, Paul's mom. "I will take you to get your license." *All right! Paul had shared my plea!* My heart began to thump. Mrs. Mozeck asked what car we should take. *Mmmm!* My car was easier to handle because of the tight steering. "What do you have?" I asked. "A '92 Buick Le Sabre." "Is it automatic?" Mrs. Mozeck responded yes and that it handled well. *Maybe it will be easier and less complicated with her car.* I quickly walked two blocks to the Moczeck house and asked Mrs. Mozeck if I could drive the two-door maroon car to the Secretary of State's office to become more familiar with it. She had guts! She let me drive. She was right—the car did handle well.

The facility was very quiet, due to the time of the day: 12:30 p.m. (There weren't any restaurants around in the area so the lunch traffic was limited.) This time, I was calm and focused. I was less jittery even though I had downed a cup of coffee to be more alert. *The rules of the road book states that one should drive at the height of energy.* The instructor was an older, laid-back type of guy, with a belly. We drove along the same route as the time before, but without the setting sun. I performed well and passed. I sighed in great relief. *I did it!* Another goal achieved.

Mrs. Mozeck was sitting in a chair by the front door, engrossed in a book. I whispered: "I passed." She gave me a big smile. *There is nothing like friends!* Coincidentally, Mrs. Mozeck drove back as I stared at my laminated license. (In my photo, I looked like a war criminal. But who cared???)

July 12, 1993. After a year of periodic follow-ups with Dr. Pensler, Plastic Reconstructive Surgeon at Children's Memorial Hospital, I needed surgery again to readjust my transplanted muscle up in my left cheek, like a face-lift. My cheek still drooped because of the damage I had caused after surgery the year before when I pulled out the sutures. The surgery would take place on July 22 at Evanston Hospital, only a 30-minute drive. *Here we go again; this is like a yearly tradition.* I couldn't believe it! Summer was just beginning. I felt great and looked halfway decent. My balance had improved greatly because all the continuous work at the health club and taking frequent walks. *Surgery again! Leave me alone!* I was nervous, much more so than the time before. A week before the surgery, I was in an all-male Catholic retreat group at Holy Cross Parish, which included 10 professional men, ranging in age from 40 to 60. Our group was being prepared to lead a new retreat group in September, so we met at the church every Tuesday night. I was furnished a ride with a fellow retreat member. To start the meeting, we listened to each person share their past week's experiences, from a human and spiritual standpoint. When it was my turn, I expressed my concern about the upcoming surgery. I said I was worried because I had made a personal pact with God back in April of '91, the night before I met with Dr. Vick at Evanston Hospital, to decide whether or not I would have chemotherapy. *Please keep the cancer away so I will not need chemo. I don't care if the cheek ever comes back. Just keep the cancer away!* I was very concerned about that pact because I was going to break it when I had my surgery. I said, "God has been faithful to his end of the deal. Something drastic could happen." The members all told me that I was wrong to think that way. Pat Burke, an outgoing man who ran a medium-sized chocolate company and had five kids, said, "God does not make pacts with people. He loves everybody." I sighed with relief and the priest said, "God helps those who help themselves."

On the morning of the surgery, I got up early and exercised in the basement for 20 minutes on a recently bought Stair Master, listening to uplifting, energizing music. *Aaahhh, let's go! I am not going to lose!* I took a shower and put on a sweat suit. Because of the surgery, I couldn't eat anything or even drink water. While Mom, Dad and I drove to Evanston Hospital, I sat in front, "jamming" with the sounds of the motivational Hip-Hop music. I was wearing a Walkman. *Let's get 'em!*

Once in the hospital, I thought of myself as a prizefighter in my stylish exercise suit, walking, without my cane, through the halls, being escorted by my two promoters, Mom and Dad. We approached the front desk to check in before the match (surgery). After I was admitted, we were led to a hospital room, where I changed into a hospital gown. I lay partway up on the hospital bed and was asked the usual questions by the anesthesiologist. Mom, Dad and I watched TV for an hour; than a male nurse brought me down to a pre-surgery room, which seemed like a holding pen—10 people waiting in hospital beds for surgery. I was given an anesthetic and was out.

I was released, four days later with no complications. I was swollen to the gills again, but only on one side, the left. I looked like Dr. Jeckle and Mr. Hyde! It was hard to deal with. Everybody, I mean everybody looked at me as if I'd forgotten to take off my Halloween mask. I would talk to Dad about it: "People really tick me off!" Dad would calm me down and point out that all people are curious. "But why must they be so disrespectful?" I wanted to know. In some situations, people can be the nastiest critics through non-verbal communication, and then be the nicest, most supportive friends by offering encouragement with a simple smile of recognition. Oh well, I had to deal with it; things would improve in time. **Keep Going!**

August, 93 the swelling in my left cheek had subsided. I went back to volunteer at Condell Memorial Hospital with the history display, but this time I drove myself. I felt great inside when the nurses, staff members, and hospital engineers recognized me and said, "Hello, where have you been?" After that great experience of volunteering, I drove home on my own, and just as I entered the house at 2:00 p.m., the phone rang! Pat Lellon, ACS Field Representative, warmly asked if I would be the guest speaker on August 28, at the Allstate Insurance Golf Tournament to be held at the Ivanhoe Country Club in Mundelein. I happily accepted and the Rodbros graciously offered to drive me there.

"Wow." It was so serene. I rode in the back seat of the Rodbros' car, going up and down the hilly terrain, lined with oak trees. The glorious sunset poked through the historic landmarks. "I can't believe this is Mundelein. It seems like we are traveling in the rural areas of Wisconsin," I bellowed to the Rodbros.

Dr. Rodbro dropped Mrs. Rodbro and me off at the front entrance of the club; *beautiful* ten-foot-high, five-inch-thick, five-foot-wide wooden oak doors, which had a stained-glass window grooved in the center, shaped like an elongated egg. The design was sprinkled with green and blue, as if symbolizing a fairway surrounded by water.

Inside the front lobby, the wooden floor gleamed from what seemed to be a new polish job. The receptionist at the front desk greeted Mrs. Rodbro with great fanfare. Well, that was to be expected. The Rodbros were long-time active members of the club. We went through the sports shop and opened the sliding glass doors. Boom, there I was! Mrs. Rodbro and I stood on the deck, overlooking the front nine holes of the golf course. The deck was enclosed by a five-foot wooden railing so that no one would accidentally take a tumble. One hundred and fifty people—Allstate executives, insurance agents, claim adjusters, administrators, etc.—were feasting on their meal as an announcer standing next to me read off winning raffle tickets. One elated guest leaped off the bench, and egg salad splattered all over his navy-blue shirt. Shortly after, a tall, middle-aged gentleman, wearing a white Allstate baseball cap, climbed up to greet me. He introduced himself as Al Bordi, insurance executive, and Chairman of the Planning Committee. As we talked, I used my diaphragm and spoke in a very deep voice, which I normally don't do. *Wow, he understood every word I said. Maybe I should speak this way all the time!* Al made an announcement to the group and introduced me as the spokesperson for the ACS.

I stood with the microphone in front of me, looking out at the crowd. I saw oceans of men and women wearing white baseball caps that were turned towards me. Again, I knew I looked different, but I also knew that I had a good message to relay. I continued speaking from my diaphragm while I shared my story, emphasizing how thankful I was to the ACS for their active support.

I mingled with the crowd as they were walking up to the clubhouse, and I heard my name being spoken in an eastern accent.

"Hi, Mr. Vane! Wow, it is great to see you."

Vinny Vane was a retired Allstate Insurance agent. He and his wife had raised three girls and three boys just down the street from my house. Their youngest son, Chris, four years my senior, was an all-area basketball player (on the Lake County All-Star Team) and a baseball player at Carmel High School. He always smiled, laughed, and brought cheer to a scene. He had been a mentor to me during the latter part of grade school and my freshman year in high school. We always played ball together—basketball, baseball, football, or whatever.

I did it! Feeling proud and relieved, I turned and walked up the four steps to the second deck to meet Dr. Rodbro. As I glanced out over the front nine again and noticed the beautiful rays of sun setting over the rolling landscape, I thought, *thank you, God, for being on my side.* Dr. Rodbro then led me through the clubhouse to the exit and we greeted Mrs. Rodbro. I remarked, "That was fun. What a great group of people." We walked to the parking lot, got into the car and zoomed away.

September 1, 1993: I was back from a workout at the health club, ready to head for the shower. The phone rang in the kitchen. *A phone call!* "Hello!" "Hi, Hon, this is Pat. The health teacher at Lake Forest High School requested someone to speak to the boys when they learn about testicular cancer on September 6. Is that all right, Darryl? Can you do it?" "Yes!" I said, and jumped for joy! I was fired up, ready to go! I wanted to send a clear message to the economically advantaged kids not to take things for granted. Sharing my story, I felt, would emphasize that point. Even though I was from an upper-middle class neighborhood, I see myself as a "blue collar" kind of guy. I always worked hard, never expecting anything to be handed to me on a silver platter. I love to work.

On September 6, I drove myself to Lake Forest High School. It felt great being an ACS representative as I pulled a large shopping bag filled with pamphlets and two videos out of the back seat. I steadied my balance with the cane in my left hand while I held the shopping bag with my right. *Hey, this is just like doing a one-armed curl with a 40-pound barbell*, as I dodged the school buses that were driving up to the posh high school.

I met with the health teacher at the front entrance. A tall, middle-aged man with a deep voice, he offered a vise-like grip when he shook my hand. *Wow, what respect!* I walked with him down the side corridor to the gym, passing through a group of giggly freshman girls. When we made it to the gym and were going down a flight of stairs, the teacher asked if I would rather take the elevator.

"I'll take the stairs; I like the challenge." As long as there were railings, I could handle it.

We made it to the wrestling room where the eight classes were to be held. There were wall-to-wall wrestling mats in the school's colors, royal blue and gold. A TV and video player had already been set up. An aluminum folding table was next to the TV so I could spread out the pamphlets. The teacher left the wrestling room to bring in the class. A bunch of wide-eyed freshmen entered without the teacher. I felt compelled to do something "goofy."

"Good morning! My name is Darryl Didier! I am a volunteer with the American Cancer Society. We are here this morning to watch a video about testicular cancer and learn how to conduct a self-exam.

Today, we have a very unique opportunity. Ida, a nurse from Russia, who is six-feet-two and weighs 220 pounds, flew in this morning. After the video, we will go to the locker room and Ida will show each and every one of us how to do a self-exam. It hurts a little, but it's not that bad."

This was where my facial paralysis came in handy; I didn't flinch. The room was completely silent. Twenty bug-eyes turned to each other as the students sat on the mats. The teacher strolled in at just the right time. He looked around, confused.

"Ha, ha, ha, I am just kidding."

All gave a sigh of relief! Then laughter echoed off the walls of the large gym. The videos were shown and the reactions were the same. The giggles and groans. I shared my story with gusto, adding a different twist. I talked about having my driver's license reinstated and what I had to go through to reclaim the privilege.

It seemed as though I reached the students when I joshed. How did I know? They asked more questions, sensing that I wouldn't be offended.

"Can you see out of that eye?"

"Yes, but I can't blink it."

"Can you hear? Can you feel on that side of your face?"

"Yes."

"Can you remember new things?"

"Yes! I am taking a course in Advanced Marketing Research, at Barat College. (Barat is a small private college in Lake Forest.) I had a test last week and I aced it." (By the way, I aced the class.)

Half-time. I had lunch in the teachers' lounge. After that, 4 more classes to go, and this time around, I was to face juniors and seniors. I felt very confident because of the respect shown to me by the staff members.

Back in the wrestling room the health teacher left to gather the class, and I sat at the table with stacks of pamphlets, reading aloud from my Spanish book. The kids filtered in after 10 minutes elapsed, but I had

to go the washroom. I walked along the mats to the locker room/wash-
room behind me. *Wow, I walk steady on the mats.* My feet gripped at
every step. Five minutes later, when I stepped out of the locker room, I
heard the teacher explaining the reason for the meeting. Then, as he
began to speak about the testicular self-exam video, I moved slowly
with a limp. I hunched over and moaned while I covered my crotch.
The teacher smiled and got into the act.

"How was the self-exam by Ida?" he asked.

"It hurt a little, but it wasn't that bad."

The 15 junior boys were stunned. I smirked, "Just kidding." Again,
relieved laughter filled the room. I beamed inside because the teacher
had taken the cue. This time, after the videos, two female teachers
entered the wrestling room through a door in the back. *Word's getting
around!* As I witnessed their interest, my waning energy picked up
steam. But I was nervous. *I had better come through.* I think I did, as I
faced three additional classes, which several different teachers or
administrators attended.

3:30 p.m. The health teacher walked with me to my gray two-door
Honda Accord that I was so proud to show off. It symbolized success.
We shook hands as he offered his gratitude. *Yeah, I did it!*

Through November until mid-December, I stuck to my word. I
kept going and going through exercise, motivating people and doing
volunteer work at Condell Medical Center. Then, on December 22,
my family and I headed for Kiawa Island, South Carolina, on the
shores of the Atlantic Ocean.

My Aunt Betty and Uncle Dick had rented an exquisite three-story
house for the winter months on the island, so they could escape the
frigid winters in Maine. There would be nine of us: Mom, Dad,
Brenda, and me, Uncle Dick, Aunt Betty, their daughter, Maureen,
their son-in-law, Staff, and their 14-year old granddaughter, Summer,
who had a bushel of red hair. I still didn't like vacations because of the
vacillating effect that depleted my will power. I had to keep going. But
this one I was looking forward to. Besides being together with loved

ones, Uncle Dick said there were miles and miles of beachfront, so I could walk, walk, and walk.

On the day of New Year's Eve, Dad and I went for a two-mile walk on the beach. It was in the mid-50's and cloudy with no wind; a nice day compared to the freezing arctic air of Chicago that time of year. As we started out on our journey, I took notice of the splendid flora all around us. Northern pine trees—hardwoods decorated by Spanish moss—along with the tropical plants and palmettos. As Dad and I walked down the road to a pathway that led us to the beach, we had to cross a footbridge over a lagoon that reminded me of pictures I had seen of southern Florida. The 500-foot sturdy footbridge was enclosed by tall railings so no one could take a dive into the lagoon. There were herons sneaking up on their prey and a sign that said: "Beware of Alligators." *Wow!* Then, as we crossed to the other side, we came to the oceanic flora and fauna.

Dad and I approached the sand dunes that provided a view overlooking the miles and miles of beach, with a few scatterings of vacationers out for a walk, bike riding, or playing a fun game of catch. Some were in their bent-over stance, looking for sea shells where the ocean waves caressed the sandy edges. We walked down the boardwalk "zigzagging" and headed towards the sand. The tide was out so there were many morsels for the multitude of seagulls to munch on.

I felt as though I were in heaven with the low clouds, light fog, and the foam left over by the creeping ocean waters. Gentle ocean tunes brushed up against the shore. People in the distance were walking and laughing happily. I noticed many other things as well: little children playing in the sand; a friendly dog racing along the shore. Seagulls flew in unison as if in a choreographed ballet; sandpipers teased the ocean; porpoises swam and jumped as I continued walking. I was in awe. What peace! I soaked in God's radiance.

Later that night, the family gathered together and rang in the New Year, 1994, by clinking our champagne glasses together. We each revealed our New Year's resolutions. As we were taking turns, Brenda shared a very profound and motivating vision. She said she had ridden her bike over the boardwalk to the sand dunes and looked out over the beach. At that moment, she had seen the exact scene she had envisioned when she visited me in SICU during the critical period following surgery—when I was full of tubes, and wires were entangled around me to sustain my life. She now looked up at me with watery eyes and said, "I saw you walking with no tubes, no walker, no cane. You were free as a bird. You have to write that book."

July, 1995: My MRI report came in as clear as a bell again. The cancer is still out of here, in remission, after five years. As they say, it is a cure! The hard-work attitude that God has instilled in me through my parents' example has borne fruit. I will share what my sister wrote on a card to mark the day of celebration.

> *Dear Darryl,*
> *The time has finally come for your cure. I always knew you had it in you to fight this battle. From the first night at Lake Forest Hospital, I saw the inner strength and fire in your eyes to overcome this—and you did—I am more proud of you than you will ever know...*
> *Love, Brenda*

0-595-22688-4